EXCEL MODELING IN THE FUNDAMENTALS OF INVESTMENTS
Second Edition

CRAIG W. HOLDEN
Max Barney Faculty Fellow and Associate Professor
Kelley School of Business
Indiana University

To Kathryn, Diana, and Jimmy.

VP/Editorial Director: Jeff Shelstad
Acquisitions Editor: Jackie Aaron
Associate Editor: Francesca Calogero
Manager, Print Production: Christy Mahon
Production Editor & Buyer: Carol O'Rourke
Cover Printer: Phoenix Color Corporation
Printer/Binder: VonHoffman Graphics, Inc., MD

PEARSON
Prentice Hall

10 9 8 7 6 5 4 3 2 1
ISBN 0-13-142413-0

CONTENTS

Contents on CD

Readme.txt

All Chapters – Bodie Version

- Excel Mod Fund Inv 2e Bodie.pdf

Chap 2 3 4 14 – Alt Notations

- Chap 2 3 4 14 - Corrado Ver.pdf
- Chap 2 3 4 14 - Reilly Ver.pdf
- Chap 2 3 4 14 - Sharpe Ver.pdf

Databases

- US Yield Cur Dyn - Database.xls
- US Yield Cur Dyn - Dyn Chart.xls
  (Annual updates available at www.excelmodeling.com)

Preface

For more than 20 years, since the emergence of PCs, Lotus 1-2-3, and Microsoft Excel in the 1980's, spreadsheet models have been the dominant vehicles for finance professionals in the business world to implement their financial knowledge. Yet even today, most Fundamentals of Investments textbooks rely on calculators as the primary tool and have little (if any) coverage of how to build Excel models. This book fills that gap. It teaches students how to build financial models in Excel. It provides step-by-step instructions so that students can build models themselves (active learning), rather than handing students canned "templates" (passive learning). It progresses from simple examples to practical, real-world applications. It spans nearly all quantitative models in the fundamentals of investments.

Why I Wrote This Book

My goal is simply to *change finance education from being calculator based to being Excel modeling based.* This change will better prepare students for the 21st century business world. This change will increase student satisfaction in the classroom by allowing more practical, real-world applications and by enabling a more hands-on, active learning approach.

There are many features which distinguish this book from anything else on the market:

- **Teach By Example.** I believe that the best way to learn Excel modeling is by working through examples and completing a lot of problems. This book fully develops this hands-on, active learning approach. Active learning is a well-established way to increase student learning and student satisfaction with the course / instructor. When students build financial models themselves, they really "get it."

- **Supplement For All Popular Fundamentals of Investments Textbooks.** This book is a supplement to be combined with a primary textbook. This means that you can keep using whatever textbook you like best. You don't have to switch. It also means that you can take an incremental approach to incorporating Excel modeling. You can start modestly and build up from there. Alternative notation versions of chapters 2, 3, 4, and 14 are available on the CD. These alternative versions match the notation of all popular fundamentals of investments textbooks.

- **Plain Vanilla Excel.** Other books on the market emphasize teaching students programming using Visual Basic for Applications (VBA) or using macros. By contrast, this book does everything in plain vanilla Excel. Although programming is liked by a minority of students, it is seriously disliked by the majority. Plain vanilla Excel has the advantage of being a very intuitive, user-friendly environment that is accessible to all. It is fully capable of handling a wide range of applications, including quite sophisticated ones.

Further, your students already know the basics of Excel and nothing more is assumed. Students are assumed to be able to enter formulas in a cell and to copy formulas from one cell to another. All other features of Excel (graphing, built-in functions, Solver, etc.) are explained as they are used.

- **Build From Simple Examples To Practical, Real-World Applications.** The general approach is to start with a simple example and build up to a practical, real-world application. In many chapters, the previous Excel model is carried forward to the next more complex model. For example, the chapter on binomial option pricing carries forward Excel models as follows: (a.) single-period model with replicating portfolio, (b.) eight-period model with replicating portfolio, (c.) eight-period model with risk-neutral probabilities, (d.) full-scale, fifty-period model with volatilities estimated from real returns data. Whenever possible, this book builds up to full-scale, practical applications using real data. Students are excited to learn practical applications that they can actually use in their future jobs. Employers are excited to hire students with Excel modeling skills, who can be more productive faster.

- **A Change In Content Too.** Excel modeling is not merely a new medium, but an opportunity to cover some unique content items which require computer support to be feasible. For example, the full-scale, real data Excel model in Portfolio Optimization has you collect historical stock prices for 20 companies from Yahoo! Finance and calculate the sample means, standard deviations, and correlations. These inputs are feed into the matrix functions of Excel to calculate the efficient frontier, the tangent line, and the weights of the tangent portfolio, and then graph everything. The Excel model in Life-Cycle Financial Planning includes a detailed treatment of federal and state tax schedules, social Security taxes and benefits, etc., which permit the realistic exploration savings, retirement, and investments choices over a lifetime. The Excel model in US Yield Curve Dynamics shows you 30 years of monthly US yield curve history in just a few minutes. Real call and put prices are feed into the Black Scholes Option Pricing model and Excel's Solver is used to back-solve for the implied volatilities. Then the "smile" pattern (or more like a "scowl" pattern) of implied volatilities is graphed. As a practical matter, all of these sophisticated applications require Excel modeling.

Second Edition Changes

My highest priority for the Second Edition is to create an extremely high quality product by eliminating all known typos and by polishing the book formatting. I've made the introduction to Bond Pricing easier by adding an initial Annual Payments model. I've made Lifetime Financial Planning more sophisticated by allowing consumption to be set as a percentage of total wealth (the sum of human capital and financial capital). I've updated the US Yield Curve Dynamics database to the present. Future updates to the database can be downloaded from www.excelmodeling.com. To keep all references timely, I've updated the tax rates and all calendar dates throughout the book.

Conventions Used In This Book

This book uses a number of conventions.

- **Time Goes Across The Columns And Variables Go Down The Rows.** When something happens over time, I let each column represent a period of time. For example in life-cycle financial planning, date 0 is in column B, date 1 is in column C, date 2 is in column D, etc. Each row represents a different variable, which is usually a labeled in column A. This manner of organizing Excel models is so common because it is how financial statements are organized.

- **Color Coding.** A standard color scheme is used to clarify the structure of the Excel models. The printed book uses: (1) light gray shading for input values, (2) no shading (i.e. white) for throughput formulas, and (3) dark gray shading for final results ("the bottom line"). The accompanying CD uses: (1) yellow shading for input values, (2) no shading (i.e. white) for throughput formulas, and (3) green shading for final results ("the bottom line"). A few Excel models include choice variables. Choice variables use medium gray shading in the printed book and blue shading in the electronic version.

- **The Time Line Technique.** The most natural technique for discounting cash flows in an Excel model is the time line technique, where each column corresponds to a period of time. As an example, see the section labeled Calculate Bond Price using the Cash Flows in the figure below.

	A	B	C	D	E	F	G	H	I	J
1	**BOND PRICING**	**Annual Payments**								
2										
3	**Inputs**									
4	Number of Periods to Maturity (T)	8								
5	Face Value (PAR)	$1,000								
6	Discount Rate / Period (r.)	9.0%								
7	Coupon Payment (PMT)	$25								
8										
9	**Calculate Bond Price using the Cash Flows**									
10	Period	0	1	2	3	4	5	6	7	8
11	Cash Flows		$25.00	$25.00	$25.00	$25.00	$25.00	$25.00	$25.00	$1,025.00
12	Present Value of Cash Flow		$22.94	$21.04	$19.30	$17.71	$16.25	$14.91	$13.68	$514.41
13	Bond Price	$640.24								
14										
15	**Calculate Bond Price using the Formula**									
16	Bond Price	$640.24								
17										
18	**Calculate Bond Price using the PV Function**									
19	Bond Price	$640.24								

- **Using As Many Different Techniques As Possible.** In the figure above, the bond price is calculated using as many different techniques as possible. Specifically, it is calculated three ways: (1) discounting each cash flow on a time line, (2) using the closed-form formula, and (3) using Excel's PV function. This approach makes the point that all three techniques are equivalent. This approach also develops skill at double-checking these calculations, which is a very important method for avoiding errors in practice.

- **Dynamic Charts.** Dynamic charts allow you to see such things as a "movie" of the Term Structure of Interest Rates moves over time or an "animated graph" of how increasing the volatility of an underlying stock increases the value of an option. Dynamic charts are a combination of an up/down arrow (a "spinner") to rapidly change an input and a chart to rapidly display the changing output. I invented dynamic charts back in 1995 and I have included many examples of this useful educational tool throughout this book.

Craig's Challenge

I challenge the readers of this book to dramatically improve your finance education by personally constructing all 38 Excel models in all 15 chapters of this book. This will take you about 19 to 38 hours depending on your current Excel modeling skills. Let me assure you that it will be an excellent investment. You will:

- gain a practical understanding of the core concepts of the Fundamentals of Investments,
- develop hands-on, Excel modeling skills, and
- build an entire suite of finance applications, which you fully understand.

When you complete this challenge, I invite you to send an e-mail to me at **cholden@indiana.edu** to share the good news. Please tell me your name, school, (prospective) graduation year, and which Excel modeling book you completed. I will add you to a web-based honor roll at:

http://www.excelmodeling.com/honor-roll.htm

We can celebrate together!

The Excel Modeling Series

This book is part a series on **Excel Modeling** by Craig W. Holden, published by Prentice Hall / Pearson Education. The series includes:

- **Excel Modeling in Corporate Finance**,
- **Excel Modeling in the Fundamentals of Corporate Finance**,
- **Excel Modeling in Investments**, and
- **Excel Modeling in the Fundamentals of Investments**.

Each book teaches value-added skills in constructing financial models in Excel. Complete information about the **Excel Modeling** series is available at my web site:

http://www.excelmodeling.com

The **Excel Modeling** books can be purchased any time at:

http://www.amazon.com

The Excel Modeling Community

You can access the worldwide Excel modeling community by clicking on **Community (Free Enhancements)** at my web site **http://www.excelmodeling.com**. You will find free additions, extensions, and problems that professors and practitioners from around the world have made available for you. I will post annual updates of the U.S. yield curve database and occasional new Excel models. If you would like to make available your own addition, extension, or problem to the worldwide finance community, just e-mail it to me at **cholden@indiana.edu** and I will post it on my web site. Your worldwide finance colleagues thank you.

If you have any suggestions or corrections, please e-mail them to me at **cholden@indiana.edu**. I will consider your suggestions and will implement any corrections in future editions.

Suggestions for Faculty Members

There is no single best way to use **Excel Modeling in the Fundamentals of Investments**. There are as many different techniques as there are different styles and philosophies of teaching. You need to discover what works best for you. Let me highlight several possibilities:

1. **Out-of-class individual projects with help.** This is a technique that I have used and it works well. I require completion of several short Excel modeling projects of every individual student in the class. To provide help, I schedule special "help lab" sessions in a computer lab during which time myself and my graduate assistant are available to answer questions while students do each assignment in about an hour. Typically about half the questions are Excel questions and half are finance questions. I have always graded such projects, but an alternative approach would be to treat them as ungraded homework.

2. **Out-of-class individual projects without help.** Another technique is to assign Excel modeling projects for individual students to do on their own out of class. One instructor assigns seven Excel modeling projects at the beginning of the semester and has individual students turn in all seven completed Excel models for grading at the end of the semester. At the end of each chapter are numerous "Skill-Building Problems" and more challenging "Skill-Enhancing Problems" that can be assigned with or without help. Faculty members can download the completed Excel models at **http://www.prenhall.com/holden**. See your local Prentice Hall (or Pearson Education) representative to gain access.

3. **Out-of-class group projects.** A technique that I have used for the last ten years is to require students to do big Excel modeling projects in groups. I have students write a report to a hypothetical boss, which intuitively explains their method of analysis, key assumptions, and key results.

4. **In-class reinforcement of key concepts.** This is the direction I have moved in recent years. The class session is scheduled in a computer lab or equivalently students are required to bring their (required) laptop computers to a technology classroom, which has a data jack and a power outlet at every student station. I explain a key concept in words and equations. Then I turn to a 10-15 minute segment in which I provide students with an Excel model that is partially complete (say, 80% complete) and have them finish the last few lines of the Excel model. This provides real-time, hands-on reinforcement of a key concept. This technique can be done often throughout the semester. At the end of each chapter are numerous "Live In-class Problems" that can be implemented this way. Faculty members can download the partially complete Excel models at **http://www.prenhall.com/holden**. See your local Prentice Hall (or Pearson Education) representative to gain access.

5. **In-class demonstration of Excel modeling.** The instructor can perform an in-class demonstration of how to build Excel models. Typically, only a small portion of the total Excel model would be demonstrated.

6. **In-class demonstration of key relationships using Dynamic Charts.** The instructor can dynamically illustrate comparative statics or dynamic properties over time using dynamic charts. For example, one dynamic chart illustrates 30 years of U.S. term structure dynamics. Another dynamic chart provides an "animated" illustration of the sensitivity of bond prices to changes in the coupon rate, yield-to-maturity, number of payments / year, and face value.

I'm sure I haven't exhausted the list of potential teaching techniques. Feel free to send an e-mail to **cholden@indiana.edu** to let me know novel ways in which you use this book.

Alternative Notation Versions on CD

One nice thing about Excel models is that you can use long descriptive labels to describe most variables and their corresponding formulas. However, some finance formulas are complex enough that they really require mathematical notation. This happens in chapters 2, 3, 4, and 14. For these four chapters, the printed book uses the mathematical notation of the Bodie-Kane-Marcus textbook. The CD provides PDF files with alternative notation versions of these four chapters. The PDF files are easy to print. There are PDF files to accompany all popular fundamentals of investments textbooks: (1) Corrado-Jordan, (2) Reilly-Norton, and (3) Alexander-Sharpe-Bailey. The symbol list below shows the mathematical symbols that are used in each of these alternative notation versions. I have selected the notation to fill in any gaps.

	A	B	C	D	E
1	**SYMBOL LIST**	**All Notation Versions**			
2		Bodie	Corrado	Reilly	Sharpe
3	**Bonds**				
4	Annual Coupon Rate	CR	CR	CR	CR
5	Yield To Maturity (Annualized)	y	YTM	i	y
6	Number of Payments / Period	NOP	NOP	NOP	NOP
7	Number of Periods to Maturity	T	T	T	T
8	Face Value	PAR	FV	P_p	FV
9	Discount Rate / Period	r.	DR	DR	RATE
10	Coupon Payment	PMT	C.	PMT	PMT
11	Bond Price	P	PV	P_m	P_0
12	Forward Rate from T-1 to T	$f_{T-1,T}$	$f_{T-1,1}$	${}_{t-1,}r_1$	$f_{T-1,T}$
13	Duration	D	D	D	D
14	Modified Duration	D*	D*	D*	D*
15					
16	**Black-Scholes Option Pricing**				
17	Stock Price	S_0	S	P_s	P_s
18	Exercise Price	X	K	X	E
19	Riskfree Rate	r	r	r	R
20	Volatility	σ	σ	σ	σ
21	Time To Maturity	T	T	t	T
22	d_1	d_1	d_1	d_1	d_1
23	d_2	d_2	d_2	d_2	d_2
24	$N(d_1)$	$N(d_1)$	$N(d_1)$	$N(d_1)$	$N(d_1)$
25	$N(d_2)$	$N(d_2)$	$N(d_2)$	$N(d_2)$	$N(d_2)$
26	Call Price	C_0	C	P_0	V_c
27	Put Price	P_0	P	P_p	P_p
28	Dividend Yield	d	y	d	d

Acknowledgements

I thank Jackie Aaron, P.J. Boardman, Mickey Cox, Maureen Riopelle, and Paul Donnelly of Pearson / Prentice Hall for their vision, innovativeness, and encouragement of **Excel Modeling in the Fundamentals of Investments**. I thank Lori Braumberger, Holly Brown, Debbie Clare, Cheryl Clayton, Kevin Hancock, Josh McClary, Bill Minic, Melanie Olsen, Beth Ann Romph, Erika Rusnak, Gladys Soto, and Lauren Tarino of Pearson / Prentice Hall for many useful contributions. I thank Professors Alan Bailey (University of Texas at San Antonio), Zvi Bodie (Boston University), Jack Francis (Baruch College), David Griswold (Boston University), Carl Hudson (Auburn University), Robert Kleiman (Oakland University), Mindy Nitkin (Simmons College), Steve Rich (Baylor University), Tim Smaby (Penn State University), Charles Trzcinka (Indiana University), Sorin Tuluca (Fairleigh Dickinson University), Marilyn Wiley (Florida Atlantic University), and Chad Zutter (University of Pittsburgh) for many thoughtful comments. I thank my graduate students Ryan Brewer,

Ruslan Goyenko, Wendy Liu, and Wannie Park for careful error-checking. I thank Jim Finnegan and many other students for providing helpful comments. I thank my family, Kathryn, Diana, and Jimmy, for their love and support.

About The Author

CRAIG W. HOLDEN

Craig Holden is the Max Barney Faculty Fellow and Associate Professor of Finance at the Kelley School of Business at Indiana University. His M.B.A. and Ph.D. are from the Anderson School at UCLA. He is the winner of multiple schoolwide teaching awards and multiple schoolwide research awards. His research on security trading and market making ("market microstructure") has been published in leading academic journals. He has written several books on **Excel Modeling** in finance, which are published by Pearson / Prentice Hall. He has chaired twelve dissertations, served on the program committee of the *Western Finance Association* for five years, and served as an associate editor of the *Journal of Financial Markets* for seven years. He has chaired a department committee for ten years and chaired various schoolwide committees for seven years. He has lead several major curriculum innovations in the finance department. More information is available at Craig's home page: **www.kelley.iu.edu/cholden**.

PART 1 BONDS / FIXED INCOME SECURITIES

Chapter 1 Reading Bond Listings

1.1 Basics

Problem. Given bond prices and yields as published by the financial press or other information sources, obtain the U.S. Treasury Yield Curve.

Solution Strategy. Collect information about Treasury Bills and Treasury Strips for a variety of different maturity dates. Graph the yield to maturity of these bonds against their time to maturity. See the figure below.

FIGURE 1.1 Excel Model of Reading Bond Listings - Basics.

	A	B	C	D
1	READING BOND LISTINGS			Basics
2		Maturity	Time To	Yield To
3	**Inputs**	Date	Maturity	Maturity
4	Today	9/18/2003		
5	One month Treas Bill	10/16/2003	0.08	0.87%
6	Three month Treas Bill	12/18/2003	0.25	0.93%
7	Six month Treas Bill	3/18/2004	0.50	1.01%
8	One year Treas Strip	8/15/2004	0.91	1.08%
9	Two year Treas Strip	8/15/2005	1.91	1.45%
10	Three year Treas Strip	8/15/2006	2.91	2.02%
11	Four year Treas Strip	8/15/2007	3.91	2.60%
12	Five year Treas Strip	8/15/2008	4.91	3.02%
13	Ten year Treas Strip	8/15/2013	9.91	4.59%
14	Fifteen year Treas Bond	8/15/2018	14.91	4.81%
15	Twenty year Treas Bond	8/15/2023	19.91	5.14%
16	Twenty five year Treas E	8/15/2028	24.91	5.21%
17	Thirty year Treas Bond	2/15/2031	27.41	5.09%
18				

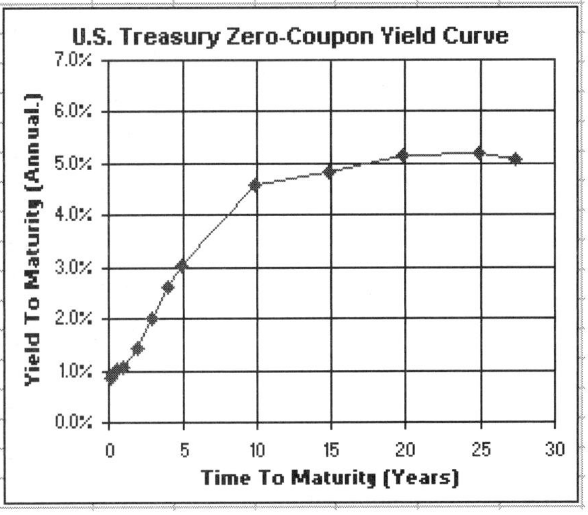

How To Build This Excel Model.

1. **Inputs.** Enter the today's date in cell **B4**.We wish to graph the *zero-coupon* yield curve, so we will use zero coupon bonds (i.e., bonds that make a single payment on the maturity date and nothing before then) when they are available. We will use U.S. Treasury Bills for maturities of less than one year, U.S. Treasury Strips for maturities of one to ten years, and U.S. Treasury Bonds for longer maturities. In the financial press, identify 1, 3, and 6 month Treasury Bills, 1, 2, 3, 4, 5, and 10 year Treasury Strips, and 15, 20, 25, and 30 year Treasury Bonds. We use more frequent maturities at the short end (1, 3, and 6 month), because often there is more curvature in the yield curve for short maturities. For each Treasury Bill, Strip, or Bond enter the

maturity date in the range **B5:B17** and yield to maturity (the "ask yield" column in the *Wall Street Journal*) in the range **D5:D17** . When entering the maturity date, be sure to use four-digit years ("2030"), rather than two-digit years ("30"). Excel assumes that two-digit years in the range 00 to 29 are really 2000 to 2029, but that years in the range 30 to 99 are really 1930 to 1999! This distinction doesn't matter for most applications, but it does matter for long-term bonds maturing in 2030 and beyond!

2. **Time To Maturity.** For a given bond, Time To Maturity = Maturity Date - Today's Date. We can calculate the fraction of a year between two calendar dates using Excel's Analysis ToolPak Add-In **YEARFRAC** function. Excel's Analysis ToolPak Add-In contains several advanced date functions that are useful in finance.

    - Click on **Tools**, **Add-Ins**, check the **Analysis ToolPak** checkbox on the **Add-Ins** dialog box (see the figure below), and click on **OK**.

    FIGURE 1.2 The Add-Ins dialog box.

    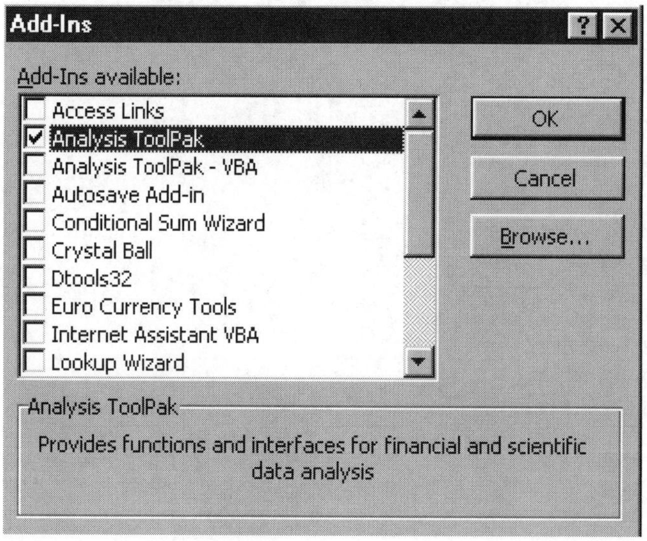

    - The date function we will use is **YEARFRAC(Today's Date, Maturity Date)**. Enter **=YEARFRAC($B$4,B5)** in cell **C5**. The two **$** in **$B$4** lock in the row and column when the cell formula is copied. Copy cell **C5** to the range **C6:C17**.

3. **Graph the Yield Curve.** Highlight the range **C5:D17** and then choose **Insert Chart** from the main menu. Select an **XY(Scatter)** chart type and make other selections to complete the Chart Wizard.

This yield curve demonstrates some frequently-observed properties of the yield curve. Often, there is a sharp rise at the short-end, a gentle rise after that, and a small dip at the long-end.

Problems

Live In-class Problems.

1. Given the partial Reading Bond Listings file **ReadbasZ.xls**, do step **2 Time To Maturity**.

Chapter 2 Bond Pricing

2.1 Annual Payments

Problem. An annual bond has a face value of $1,000, makes an annual coupon payment of $25 per year, has a discount rate per year of 9.0%, and has 8 years to maturity. What is price of this bond?

Solution Strategy. We will calculate the bond price in three equivalent ways. First, we will calculate the bond price as the present value of the bond's cash flows. Second, we use a formula for the bond price. Third, we use Excel's PV function for a bond price.

FIGURE 2.1 Excel Model of Bond Pricing – Annual Payments.

	A	B	C	D	E	F	G	H	I	J
1	BOND PRICING	Annual Payments								
2										
3	**Inputs**									
4	Number of Periods to Maturity (T)	8								
5	Face Value (PAR)	$1,000								
6	Discount Rate / Period (r.)	9.0%								
7	Coupon Payment (PMT)	$25								
8										
9	**Calculate Bond Price using the Cash Flows**									
10	Period	0	1	2	3	4	5	6	7	8
11	Cash Flows		$25.00	$25.00	$25.00	$25.00	$25.00	$25.00	$25.00	$1,025.00
12	Present Value of Cash Flow		$22.94	$21.04	$19.30	$17.71	$16.25	$14.91	$13.68	$514.41
13	Bond Price	$640.24								
14										
15	**Calculate Bond Price using the Formula**									
16	Bond Price	$640.24								
17										
18	**Calculate Bond Price using the PV Function**									
19	Bond Price	$640.24								

How To Build This Excel Model

1. **Enter The Inputs and Name Them.** Enter the inputs into the range **B4:B7** and then name each one. Put the cursor on cell **B4**, click on **Insert**, **Name**, **Define**, enter **T** in the **Names in Workbook** box, and click on **OK**. Put the cursor on cell **B5** and repeat the process to name it **PAR**. Repeat the process to give the cells **B6** and **B7** the names **r.** and **PMT**, respectively.

2. **Calculate Bond Price using the Cash Flows.** Calculate the bond price as the present value of the bond's cash flows. This bond has a single cash flow per year for eight years (periods). Enter the period numbers **0, 1, 2, …, 8** in the range **B10:J10**. Complete the bond price calculation as follows:

   - Cash Flows in Periods 1-7 = Coupon Payment. Enter **=PMT** in cell **C11** and copy this cell to the range **D11:J11**.

- Cash Flow in Period 8 = Coupon Payment + Face Value. Add **+PAR** to the formula in cell **J11**, so that it reads **=PMT+PAR**.

- Present Value of Cash Flow =(Cash Flow)/((1+Discount Rate/Period)^ Period) = Cash Flow / ((1+ r.)^Period). Enter **=C11/((1+r.)^C10)** in cell **C12** and copy this cell to the range **D12:J12**.

- Present Value of the Bond = Sum of all the Present Value of Cash Flows (row 19). Enter **=SUM(C12:J12)** in cell **B13**.

3. **Calculate Bond Price using the Formula.** The present value of the bond's cash flows can be simplified down to an equivalent formula. The bond price formula is

$$P = \frac{PMT \cdot \left(1 - \left((1+r.)^{-T}\right)\right)}{r.} + \frac{PAR}{(1+r.)^{T}},$$

where the first term is the present value of an annuity for the string of coupon payments and the second term is the present value of the face value payment at the end. Enter **=PMT*(1-((1+r.)^(-T)))/r.+PAR/((1+r.)^T)** in cell **B16**.

4. **Calculate Bond Price using the PV Function.** Excel has a function to calculate the price of a bond. The format is =-PV(Discount Rate / Period, Number of Periods to Maturity, Coupon Payment, Face Value). Enter **=-PV(r.,T,PMT,PAR)** in cell **B19**.

The resulting annual bond price is $640.24. Notice you get the same answer all four ways: using the cash flows, using the formula, using the PV function, or using the PRICE function!

2.2 APR and EAR

Problem. A semi-annual bond has a face value of $1,000, an annual coupon rate of 5.0%, a yield to maturity of 9.0%, makes 2 (semi-annual) coupon payments per year, and 8 periods to maturity (or 4 years to maturity). What is price of this bond based on the Annual Percentage Rate (APR) convention? What is price of this bond based on the Effective Annual Rate (EAR) convention?

Solution Strategy. We will create a switch that can be used to select either the EAR or APR rate convention. The choice of rate convention will determine the discount rate / period. For a given discount rate / period, we will calculate the bond price in four equivalent ways. First, we will calculate the bond price as the present value of the bond's cash flows. Second, we use a formula for the bond price. Third, we use Excel's PV function for a bond price. Fourth, we use Excel's Analysis ToolPak Add-In PRICE function, which only works under the APR convention.

FIGURE 2.2 Excel Model of Bond Pricing – APR and EAR.

	A	B	C	D	E	F	G	H	I	J
1	BOND PRICING	APR and EAR			Annual Percentage Rate					
2										
3	**Inputs**									
4	Rate Convention: 1 = EAR, 0 = APR	0								
5	Annual Coupon Rate (CR)	5.0%								
6	Yield to Maturity (Annualized) (y)	9.0%								
7	Number of Payments / Year (NOP)	2								
8	Number of Periods to Maturity (T)	8								
9	Face Value (PAR)	$1,000								
10										
11	**Outputs**									
12	Discount Rate / Period (r.)	4.5%								
13	Coupon Payment (PMT)	$25								
14										
15	**Calculate Bond Price using the Cash Flows**									
16	Period	0	1	2	3	4	5	6	7	8
17	Time (Years)	0.0	0.5	1.0	1.5	2.0	2.5	3.0	3.5	4.0
18	Cash Flows		$25.00	$25.00	$25.00	$25.00	$25.00	$25.00	$25.00	$1,025.00
19	Present Value of Cash Flow		$23.92	$22.89	$21.91	$20.96	$20.06	$19.20	$18.37	$720.76
20	Bond Price	$868.08								
21										
22	**Calculate Bond Price using the Formula**									
23	Bond Price	$868.08								
24										
25	**Calculate Bond Price using the PV Function**									
26	Bond Price	$868.08								
27										
28	**Calculate Bond Price using the PRICE Function (under APR)**									
29	Bond Price	$868.08								

How To Build This Excel Model

1. **Start with the Annual Payments Excel Model and Insert Rows.** Open the Excel model that you created for Bond Pricing – Annual Payments and immediately save the Excel model under a new name using the **File Save As** command. Insert four rows by selecting the range **A4:A7** and clicking on **Insert**, **Rows**. Insert two more rows by selecting the range **A10:A11** and clicking on **Insert**, **Rows**. Insert one more row by selecting the cell **A17** and clicking on **Insert**, **Rows**.

2. **Enter New Inputs and Name Them.** Enter **0** in cell **B4**. This will serve as a switch between the APR and the EAR rate conventions. To highlight which rate convention is in use, enter **=IF($B$4=1,"Effective Annual Rate","Annual Percentage Rate")** in cell **E1**. Enter the other new inputs into the range **B5:B7** and then name each one. Put the cursor on cell **B5**, click on **Insert**, **Name**, **Define**, enter **CR** in the **Names in Workbook** box, and click on **OK**. Repeat the process to give the cells **B6** and **B7** the names **y** and **NOP**, respectively.

3. **Calculate the Discount Rate / Period.** The Discount Rate / Period depends on the rate convention being used as follows:

$$\text{Discount Rate / Period} = \begin{cases} (1+\text{Yield To Maturity})^\wedge(1/(\text{Number of Payments / Year}))-1 & \text{under EAR} \\ (\text{Yield To Maturity})/(\text{Number of Payments / Year}) & \text{under APR} \end{cases}.$$

Enter **=IF($B$4=1,((1+y)^(1/NOP))-1,y/NOP)** in cell **B12** and use the process above to give the cell **B12** the name **r.**.

4. **Calculate the Coupon Payment.** The formula is Coupon Payment = Coupon Rate * Face Value / (Number of Payments / Year). Enter **=CR*PAR/NOP** in cell **B13** and use the process above to give the cell **B13** the name **PMT**.

5. **Add Time.** Clarify the timeline by adding calendar time below the periods. Time (years) = (Period) / (Number of Payments / Year) = Period / NOP. Enter **=B16/NOP** in cell **B17** and copy this cell to the range **C17:J17**.

6. **Calculate Bond Price using the PRICE Function (under APR).** Excel's Analysis ToolPak Add-In contains several advanced bond functions, including a Bond Price function assuming the APR convention is being used.

   - Click on **Tools**, **Add-Ins**, check the **Analysis ToolPak** checkbox on the **Add-Ins** dialog box (see the figure below), and click on **OK**.

FIGURE 2.3 The Add-Ins dialog box.

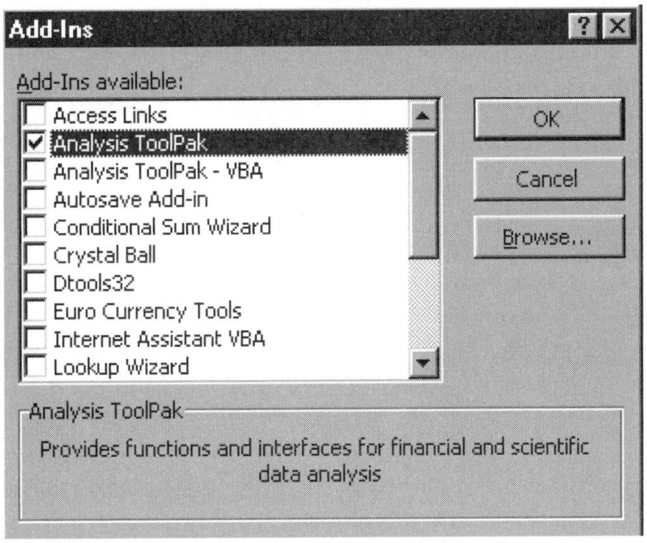

   - The bond price function is =PRICE(Settlement Date, Maturity Date, Annual Coupon Rate, Yield To Maturity, Redemption Value, Number of Payments). The Settlement Date is the date when you exchange money to purchase the bond. Specifying the exact day of settlement and maturity allows a very precise calculation. For our purpose, we simple want the difference between the two dates to equal the (8 Periods To Maturity) / (2 Payments / Year) = 4 Years To Maturity. This is easily accomplished by the use of the DATE function. The DATE Function has the format =DATE(Year, Month, Day). We will enter an arbitrary starting date of

1/1/2000 for the Settlement Date and then specify a formula for 1/1/2000 plus T / NOP for the Maturity Date. We need to add an IF statement to test for the rate convention being used. The bond function is only valid with APR. Enter **=IF($B$4=1,"",PRICE(DATE(2000,1,1), DATE(2000+T/NOP,1,1),CR,y,100,NOP)*PAR/100)** in cell **B29**. This uses a conventional Redemption Value of $100.00 and scales the resulting price by the ratio of (Par Value) / $100.00.

The resulting semi-annual bond price is $868.08. Notice you get the same answer all four ways: using the cash flows, using the formula, using the PV function, or using the PRICE function!

2.3 By Yield To Maturity

What is the relationship between bond price and yield to maturity? We can construct a graph to find out.

FIGURE 2.4 Excel Model of Bond Pricing - By Yield To Maturity.

	A	B	C	D	E	F	G	H	I	J
1	BOND PRICING	By Yield To Maturity				Annual Percentage Rate				
2										
3	**Inputs**									
4	Rate Convention: 1 = EAR, 0 = APR	0								
5	Annual Coupon Rate (CR)	5.0%								
6	Yield to Maturity (Annualized) (y)	9.0%								
7	Number of Payments / Year (NOP)	2								
8	Number of Periods to Maturity (T)	8								
9	Face Value (PAR)	$1,000								
10										
11	**Outputs**									
12	Discount Rate / Period (r)	4.5%								
13	Coupon Payment (PMT)	$25								
14										
15	**Chart Outputs**									
16	Yield to Maturity (Annualized)	1.0%	2.0%	3.0%	4.0%	5.0%	6.0%	7.0%	8.0%	9.0%
17	Discount Rate / Period	0.5%	1.0%	1.5%	2.0%	2.5%	3.0%	3.5%	4.0%	4.5%
18	Bond Price	$1,156	$1,115	$1,075	$1,037	$1,000	$965	$931	$899	$868

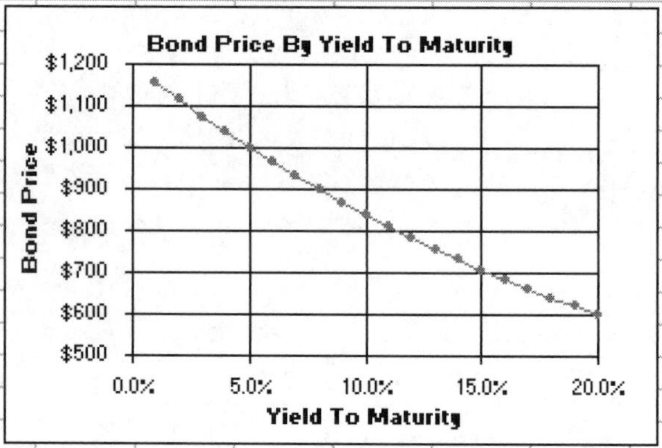

How To Build This Excel Model

1. **Start with the APR and EAR Excel Model and Delete Rows.** Open the Excel model that you created for Bond Pricing – APR and EAR and immediately save the Excel model under a new name using the **File | Save As** command. Delete rows **15** through **29** by selecting the range **A15:A29**, clicking on **Edit | Delete**, selecting the **Entire Row** radio button on the **Delete** dialog box, and clicking on **OK**.

2. **Enter Yield To Maturity (Annualized).** Enter Yield To Maturity values **1.0%, 2.0%, 3.0%, 4.0%, …, 20%** in the range **B16:U16**.

3. **Calculate Discount Rate / Period.** Copy the Discount Rate / Period formula from cell **B12** to the cell **B17**. In cell **B17**, change the variable **y** to **B16**, so that the formula reads **=IF($B$4=1,((1+B16)^(1/NOP))-1,B16/NOP)** and copy the cell **B17** to the range **C17:U17**.

4. **Calculate Bond Price.** Calculate the bond price using **PV** function and the inputs **T**, **PMT**, **PAR**, and the Discount Rate / Period in cell **B17**. Enter **=-PV(B17,T,PMT,PAR)** in cell **B18** and copy the cell to the range **C18:U18**.

5. **Graph the Bond Price By Yield To Maturity.** Highlight the range **B16:U16** and then while holding down the **Ctrl** button highlight the ranges **B18:U18**. Next choose **Insert Chart** from the main menu. Select an **XY(Scatter)** chart type and make other selections to complete the Chart Wizard. Place the graph in the range **C2:J15**.

This graph shows the inverse relationship between bond price and yield to maturity. In other word, a higher discount rate (yield to maturity) lowers the present value of the bond's cash flows (price). The graph also shows that the relationship is curved (nonlinear) rather than being a straight line (linear).

2.4 System of Five Bond Variables

There is a system of five bond variables: (1) Number of Periods to Maturity (T), (2) Face Value (PAR), (3) Discount Rate / Period (r.), (4) Coupon Payments (PMT), and (5) Bond Price (P). Given any four of these variables, the fifth variable can be found by using Excel functions (and in some cases by formulas).

FIGURE 2.5 Excel Model of Bond Pricing - System of Five Bond Variables.

	A	B	C	D	E	F	G	H	I
1	**BOND PRICING**	System of Five Bond Variables			Annual Percentage Rate				
2									
3	**Inputs**								
4	Rate Convention: 1 = EAR, 0 = APR	0							
5	Annual Coupon Rate (CR)	5.0%							
6	Yield to Maturity (Annualized) (y)	9.0%							
7	Number of Payments / Year (NOP)	2							
8	**(1) Number of Periods to Maturity (T)**	8							
9	**(2) Face Value (PAR)**	$1,000							
10	**(3) Discount Rate / Period (r.)**	4.5%							
11	**(4) Coupon Payment (PMT)**	$25							
12	**(5) Bond Price (P)**	$868.08							
13									
14	**(1) Number of Periods to Maturity (T)**								
15	Number of Periods to Maturity using the NPER Function	8							
16									
17	**(2) Face Value (PAR)**								
18	Face Value using the FV Function	$1,000.00							
19	Face Value using the Formula	$1,000.00							
20									
21	**(3) Find Discount Rate / Period (r.)**								
22	Discount Rate / Period using the RATE Function	4.5%							
23									
24	**(4) Coupon Payment (PMT)**								
25	Coupon Payment using the PMT Function	$25.00							
26	Coupon Payment using the Formula	$25.00							
27									
28	**(5) Bond Price (PV)**								
29	Bond Price using the PV Function	$868.08							
30	Bond Price using the Formula	$868.08							

How To Build This Excel Model

1. **Start with the Basics Excel Model and Delete Rows.** Open the Excel model that you created for Bond Pricing – APR and EAR and immediately save the Excel model under a new name using the **File Save As** command. Delete rows **27** through **29** by selecting the range **A27:A29**, clicking on **Edit**, **Delete**, selecting the **Entire Row** radio button on the **Delete** dialog box, and clicking on **OK**. Then repeat this procedure to delete rows **14** through **25** and repeat this procedure again to delete rows **10** through **11**. This places the five bond variables in rows **8** through **12**, highlighted with **purple labels** above.

2. **Calculate Number of Periods to Maturity (T).** NPER is the Excel function to calculate the number of periods to maturity. The format is =NPER(Discount Rate / Period, Coupon Payment, -Bond Price, Par Value). Enter **=NPER(r.,PMT,-P,PAR)** in cell **B15**.

3. **Calculate Face Value (PAR).** There are two ways to calculate the face value of the bond.

- Use the Excel Function FV. The format is =FV(Discount Rate / Period, Number of Periods to Maturity, Coupon Payment, -Bond Price). Enter **=FV(r.,T,PMT,-P)** in cell **B18**.

- Use the face value formula

$$PAR = P \cdot (1+r.)^T - \frac{PMT \cdot \left(\left((1+r.)^T\right)-1\right)}{r.},$$

where the first term is the future value of the bond price and the second term is the future values of the string of coupon payments. Enter **=P*((1+r.)^T)-PMT*(((1+r.)^T)-1)/r.** in cell **B19**.

4. **Calculate Discount Rate / Period (r.).** RATE is the Excel function to calculate the discount rate per period. The format is =RATE(Number of Periods to Maturity, Coupon Payment, -Bond Price, Par Value). Enter **=RATE(T,PMT,-P,PAR)** in cell **B22**.

5. **Calculate Coupon Payment (PMT).** There are two ways to calculate the coupon payment of the bond.

- Use the Excel Function PMT. The format is =PMT(Discount Rate / Period, Number of Periods to Maturity, -Bond Price, Par Value). Enter **=PMT(r.,T,-P,PAR)** in cell **B25**.

- Use the coupon payment formula

$$PMT = \frac{P - {PAR}/{(1+r.)^T}}{{\left(1-\left((1+r.)^{-T}\right)\right)}/{r.}},$$

where the numerator is the bond price minus the present value of the par value and the denominator is the present value of a \$1 coupon payment. Enter **=(P-PAR/((1+r.)^T))/((1-((1+r.)^(-T)))/r.)** in cell **B26**.

6. **Calculate Bond Price (P).** There are two ways to calculate the price of the bond.

- Use the Excel Function PV. The format is =PV(Discount Rate / Period, Number of Periods to Maturity, Coupon Payment, Par Value). Enter **=-PV(r.,T,PMT,PAR)** in cell **B29**.

- Use the bond price formula

$$P = \frac{PMT \cdot \left(1-\left((1+r.)^{-T}\right)\right)}{r.} + \frac{PAR}{(1+r.)^T},$$

where the first term is the present value of the string of coupon payments and the second term is the present value of the par value. Enter **=PMT*(1-((1+r.)^(-T)))/r.+PAR/((1+r.)^T)** in cell **B30**.

We see that the system of five bond variables is internally consistent. The five outputs in rows 15 through 30 (T=8, PAR=1000, r.=4.5%, PMT=$25, P=$868.08) are identical to the five inputs in rows 8 through 12. Thus, any of the five bond variables can be calculated from the other four in a fully consistent manner.

2.5 Dynamic Chart

If you increased the coupon rate of a bond, what would happen to its price? If you increased the yield to maturity of a bond, what would happen to its price? You can answer these questions and more by creating a *Dynamic Chart* using "spinners." Spinners are up-arrow / down-arrow buttons that allow you to easily change the inputs to the model with the click of a mouse. Then Excel recalculates the model and instantly redraws the model outputs on the graph.

FIGURE 2.6 Excel Model of Bond Pricing – Dynamic Chart.

	A	B	C	D	E	F	G	H	I	J
1	BOND PRICING	Dynamic Chart			Annual Percentage Rate					
2										
3	**Inputs**									
4	Rate Convention: 1 = EAR, 0 = APR	0		0						
5	Annual Coupon Rate (CR)	5.0%		10						
6	Yield to Maturity (Annualized) (y)	9.0%		18						
7	Number of Payments / Year (NOP)	2		2						
8	Face Value (PAR)	$1,000		20						
9										
10	**Outputs**									
11	Discount Rate / Period (r.)	4.5%								
12	Coupon Payment (PMT)	$25								
13										
14	**Dynamic Chart Outputs**									
15	Time to Maturity (Years)	1	2	3	4	5	6	7	8	9
16	Number of Periods to Maturity	2	4	6	8	10	12	14	16	18
17	Bond Price of Coupon Bond	$963	$928	$897	$868	$842	$818	$796	$775	$757
18	Bond Price of Par Bond	$1,000	$1,000	$1,000	$1,000	$1,000	$1,000	$1,000	$1,000	$1,000

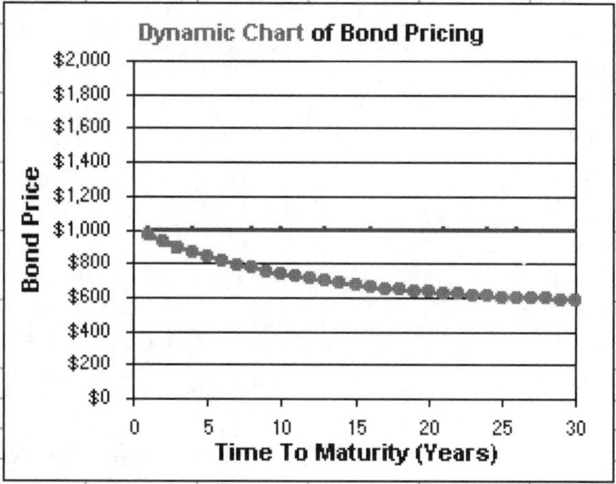

How To Build This Excel Model.

1. **Start with the Basics Excel Model and Delete Rows.** Open the Excel model that you created for Bond Pricing – APR and EAR and immediately save the file under a new name using the **File Save As** command. Delete

rows **15** through **29** by selecting the range **A15:A29**, clicking on **Edit**, **Delete**, selecting the **Entire Row** radio button on the **Delete** dialog box, and clicking on **OK**. Repeat this procedure to delete row **8**.

2. **Increase Row Height for the Spinners.** Select the range **A4:A8**. Then click on **Format Row Height** from the main menu. Enter a height of **30** and click on **OK**.

3. **Display the Forms Toolbar.** Click on **View**, **Toolbars**, **Forms** from the main menu.

4. **Create the Spinners.** Look for the up-arrow / down-arrow button on the **Forms** toolbar (which will display the word "**Spinner**" if you hover the cursor over it) and click on it. Then draw the box for a spinner from the upper left corner of cell **C4** down to the lower right corner of the cell. Then a spinner appears in the cell **C4**. Right click on the spinner (press the right mouse button while the cursor is above the spinner) and a small menu pops up. Click on **Copy**. Then select the cell **C5** and click on **Paste**. This creates an identical spinner in the cell **C5**. Repeat the process three times more. Select cell **C6** and click on **Paste**. Then select cell **C7** and click on **Paste**. Then select cell **C8** and click on **Paste**. You now have five spinners down column **C**.

5. **Create The Cell Links.** Right click on the first spinner in the cell **C4** and a small menu pops up. Click on **Format Control** and a dialog box pops up. Click on the **Control** tab, then enter the cell link **D4** in the **Cell link** edit box and click on **OK**. Repeat this procedure for the other four spinners. Link the spinner in cell **C5** to cell **D5**. Link the spinner in cell **C6** to cell **D6**. Link the spinner in cell **C7** to cell **D7**. Link the spinner in cell **C8** to cell **D8** and also on the **Control tab**, set the **Minimum value** equal to **1**. Test your spinners by clicking on the up-arrows and down-arrows of the spinners to see how they change the values in the linked cells.

6. **Create Scaled Inputs.** The values in the linked cells are always integers, but they can be scaled appropriately to the problem at hand. Restrict the value in cell **B4** to be either 1 or 0 by entering **=IF(D4>1,1,D4)**. In cell **B5**, enter **=D5/200**. In cell **B6**, enter **=D6/200**. In cell **B7**, enter **=D7**. In cell **B8**, enter **=D8*50**.

7. **Enter Time To Maturity.** Enter Time To Maturity values **1, 2, 3, 4, …, 30** in the range **B15:AE15**.

8. **Calculate Number of Periods to Maturity.** The Number of Periods to Maturity = (Time to Maturity) * (Number of Periods / Year). In cell **B16**, enter **=B15*NOP** and copy the cell **B16** to the range **C16:AE16**.

9. **Calculate Bond Price of a Coupon Bond.** Calculate the duration of a coupon bond using the **PV** bond duration function and the scaled inputs in cells **r.**, **PMT**, **PAR** and the Time to Maturity in cell **B16**. Specifically, enter **=-PV(r.,B$16,PMT,PAR)** in cell **B17**. Be sure that **B$16** has a **$** in the middle to lock in the row, but not the column.

10. **Calculate Bond Price of a Par Bond.** A par bond is a bond with a coupon rate equal to the yield to maturity. As a benchmark for comparison, calculate the bond price of a par bond using the same inputs for everything else. Copy the formula in cell **B17** to cell **B18**. Then change the coupon payment from **PMT** to **r.*PAR** so that the formula reads **=-PV(r.,B$16,r.*PAR,PAR)**. Copy the range **B17:B18** to the range **C17:AE18**.

11. **Graph the Bond Price of a Coupon Bond and Par Bond.** Highlight the range **B15:AE15** and then while holding down the **Ctrl** button highlight the range **B17:AE18**. Next choose **Insert Chart** from the main menu. Select an **XY(Scatter)** chart type and make other selections to complete the Chart Wizard. Place the graph in the range **E3:J12**.

Your *Dynamic Chart* allows you to change the Bond Price inputs and instantly see the impact on a graph of the price of a coupon bond and par bond by time to maturity. This allows you to perform instant experiments on Bond Price. Below is a list of experiments that you might want to perform:

- What happens when the annual coupon rate is increased?
- What happens when the yield to maturity is increased?
- What happens when the number of payments / year is increased?
- What happens when the face value is increased?
- What is the relationship between the price of a par bond and time to maturity?
- What happens when the annual coupon rate is increased to the point that it equals the yield to maturity?
- What happens when it is increased further?

Problems

Skill-Building Problems.

1. An annual bond has a face value of $1,000, makes an annual coupon payment of $12 per year, has a discount rate per year of 4.3%, and has 8 years to maturity. What is price of this bond?

2. A semi-annual bond has a face value of $1,000, an annual coupon rate of 4.60%, an yield to maturity of 8.1%, makes 2 (semi-annual) coupon payments per year, and 10 periods to maturity (or 5 years to maturity). Determine the price of this bond based on the Annual Percentage Rate (APR) convention and the price of this bond based on the Effective Annual Rate (EAR) convention.

3. Determine the relationship between bond price and yield to maturity by constructing a graph of the relationship.

4. Given four of the bond variables, determine the fifth bond variable.

   a. Given Number of Periods to Maturity is 10, Face Value is $1,000, Discount Rate / Period is 3.2%, and Coupon Payment is $40, determine the Bond Price.

   b. Given Number of Periods to Maturity is 8, Face Value is $1,000, Discount Rate / Period is 4.5%, and the Bond Price is $880.00, determine the Coupon Payment.

   c. Given Number of Periods to Maturity is 6, Face Value is $1,000, Coupon Payment is $30, and the Bond Price is $865.00, determine Discount Rate / Period.

   d. Given Number of Periods to Maturity is 8, Discount Rate / Period is 3.8%, Coupon Payment is $45, and the Bond Price is $872.00, determine Face Value.

   e. Given Face Value is $1,000, Discount Rate / Period is 4.3%, Coupon Payment is $37, and the Bond Price is $887.00, determine the Number of Periods to Maturity.

5. Perform instant experiments on whether changing various inputs causes an increase or decrease in the Bond Price and by how much.

   a. What happens when the annual coupon rate is increased?

   b. What happens when the yield to maturity is increased?

   c. What happens when the number of payments / year is increased?

   d. What happens when the face value is increased?

   e. What is the relationship between the price of a par bond and time to maturity?

   f. What happens when the annual coupon rate is increased to the point that it equals the yield to maturity? What happens when it is increased further?

Live In-class Problems.

6. Given the partial Annual Payments file **BpricanZ.xls**, complete step **2 Calculate Bond Price using the Cash Flows**.

7. Given the partial APR and EAR file **BpricanZ.xls**, do steps **3 Calculate the Discount Rate / Period** and **4 Calculate the Coupon Payment**.

8. Given the partial By Yield To Maturity file **BpricyiZ.xls**, do steps **2 Enter Yield To Maturity (Annualized), 3 Calculate Discount Rate / Period,** and **4 Calculate Bond Price**.

9. Given the partial Dynamic Chart file **BpricdyZ.xls**, do steps **8 Calculate the Number of Periods to Maturity, 9 Calculate Bond Price of a Coupon Bond,** and **10 Calculate Bond Price of a Par Bond**.

10. Given the partial System of Five Bond Variables file **BpricsyZ.xls**, complete step **2 Calculate Number of Periods to Maturity** using the NPER function, complete **step 3 Calculate Face Value** using the FV function, complete step **4 Calculate Discount Rate / Period** using the RATE function, complete step **5 Calculate Coupon Payment** using the PMT function, and complete step **6 Calculate Bond Price** using the PV function.

Chapter 3 Bond Duration

3.1 Basics

Problem. A bond has a face value of $1,000, an annual coupon rate of 5.0%, a yield to maturity of 9.0%, makes 2 (semi-annual) coupon payments per year, and 8 periods to maturity (or 4 years to maturity). What is duration and modified duration of this bond based on the Annual Percentage Rate (APR) convention? What is duration and modified duration of this bond based on the Effective Annual Rate (EAR) convention? What is the intuitive interpretation of duration?

Solution Strategy. The choice of either the EAR or APR rate convention will determine the discount rate / period. For a given the discount rate / period, we will calculate duration and modified duration three equivalent ways. First, we will calculate duration as the weighted-average time to the bond's cash flows. This method illustrates the intuitive interpretation of duration. Second, we use a formula for duration. In both cases, modified duration is a simple adjustment of regular duration (also called Macaulay's Duration). Third, we use Excel's Analysis ToolPak Add-In **DURATION** and **MDURATION** functions, which only work under the APR convention.

FIGURE 3.1 Excel Model of Bond Duration - Basics.

	A	B	C	D	E	F	G	H	I	J	K
1	BOND DURATION	Basics			Annual Percentage Rate						
2											
3	**Inputs**										
4	Rate Convention: 1 = EAR, 0 = APR	0									
5	Annual Coupon Rate (CR)	5.0%									
6	Yield to Maturity (Annualized) (y)	9.0%									
7	Number of Payments / Year (NOP)	2									
8	Number of Periods to Maturity (T)	8									
9	Face Value (PAR)	$1,000									
10											
11	**Outputs**										
12	Discount Rate / Period (r.)	4.5%									
13	Coupon Payment (PMT)	$25									
14											
15	**Calculate Bond Duration using the Cash Flows**										
16	Period	0	1	2	3	4	5	6	7	8	
17	Time (Years)	0.0	0.5	1.0	1.5	2.0	2.5	3.0	3.5	4.0	Total
18	Cash Flows		$25.00	$25.00	$25.00	$25.00	$25.00	$25.00	$25.00	$1,025.00	
19	Present Value of Cash Flow		$23.92	$22.89	$21.91	$20.96	$20.06	$19.20	$18.37	$720.76	$868.08
20	Weight		2.8%	2.6%	2.5%	2.4%	2.3%	2.2%	2.1%	83.0%	100.0%
21	Weight * Time		0.01	0.03	0.04	0.05	0.06	0.07	0.07	3.32	3.65
22	Duration	3.65									
23	Modified Duration	3.49									
24											
25	**Calculate Bond Duration using the Formula**										
26	Duration	3.65									
27	Modified Duration	3.49									
28											
29	**Calculate Bond Duration using the Function (under APR)**										
30	Duration	3.65									
31	Modified Duration	3.49									

How To Build This Excel Model

1. **Enter The Inputs and Name Them.** Enter **0** in cell **B4**. This will serve as a switch between the APR and the EAR rate conventions. To highlight which rate convention is in use, enter **=IF($B$4=1,"Effective Annual Rate","Annual Percentage Rate")** in cell **E1**. Enter the other inputs into the range **B5:B9** and then name each one. Put the cursor on cell **B5**, click on **Insert**, **Name**, **Define**, enter **CR** in the **Names in Workbook** box, and click on **OK**. Put the cursor on cell **B6** and repeat the process to name it **y**. Repeat the process to give the cells **B7**, **B8**, and **B9** the names **NOP**, **T**, and **PAR**, respectively.

2. **Calculate the Discount Rate / Period.** The Discount Rate / Period depends on the rate convention being used as follows:

$$\text{Discount Rate / Period} = \begin{cases} (1+\text{Yield To Maturity})\wedge(1/(\text{Number of Payments / Year}))-1 & \text{under EAR} \\ (\text{Yield To Maturity})/(\text{Number of Payments / Year}) & \text{under APR} \end{cases}.$$

   Enter **=IF($B$4=1,((1+y)^(1/NOP))-1,y/NOP)** in cell **B12** and use the process above to give the cell **B12** the name **r.**.

3. **Calculate the Coupon Payment.** The formula is Coupon Payment = Coupon Rate * Face Value / (Number of Payments / Year). Enter **=CR*PAR/NOP** in cell **B13** and use the process above to give the cell **B13** the name **PMT**.

4. **Calculate Bond Duration using the Cash Flows.** Calculating duration as a weighted-average time to cash flows directly illustrates the key intuition for duration. This bond has two cash flows per year for four years or eight periods. Enter the period numbers **0, 1, 2, …, 8** in the range **B16:J16**. Complete the duration calculation as follows:

   - Time (years) = (Period) / (Number of Payments / Year) = Period / NOP. Enter **=B16/NOP** in cell **B17** and copy this cell to the range **C17:J17**.

   - Cash Flows in Periods 1-7 = Coupon Payment. Enter **=PMT** in cell **C18** and copy this cell to the range **D18:J18**.

   - Cash Flow in Period 8 = Same as above + Face Value. Add **+PAR** to the formula in cell **J18**, so that it reads **=PMT+PAR**.

   - Present Value of Cash Flow =(Cash Flow)/((1+(Discount Rate / Period))^ Period) = Cash Flow / ((1+ r.)^Period). Enter **=C18/((1+r.)^C16)** in cell **C19** and copy this cell to the range **D19:J19**.

   - Present Value of the Bond = Sum of all the Present Value of Cash Flows (row 19). Enter **=SUM(C19:J19)** in cell **K19**.

- Weight on date t = Present Value of Cash Flow on date t / Present Value of the Bond. Enter **=C19/$K$19** in cell **C20** and copy this cell to the range **D20:K20**.

- Weight * Time. Enter **=C20*C17** in cell **C21** and copy this cell to the range **D21:J21**.

- (Macaulay's) Duration = Sum of all the Weight * Time variables (row 21). Enter **=SUM(C21:J21)** in cell **B22**. Optionally for completeness, enter the same formula in cell **K21**.

- Modified Duration = Duration / (1+(Discount Rate / Period)) = Duration / (1 + r.). Enter **=B22/(1+r.)** in cell **B23**.

This method of calculation directly illustrates the key intuition that (Macaulay's) duration is the weighted-average of the time until cash flows are received. The weights are based on the ratio of the present value of each cash flow over the present value of the total bond.

5. **Calculate Bond Duration using the Formula.** The weighted-average time calculation can be simplified down to an equivalent formula for (Macaulay's) duration.

- The duration formula is

$$D = \frac{1+r.}{r.\cdot NOP} - \frac{1+r.+T\cdot\left(CR/NOP-r.\right)}{CR\cdot\left(\left(1+r.\right)^{T}-1\right)+r.\cdot NOP}$$

Enter **=(1+r.)/(r.*NOP)-(1+r.+T*(CR/NOP-r.)) /(CR*((1+r.)^T-1)+r.*NOP)** in cell **B26**.

- Modified Duration uses the same formula as above. Copy the formula in cell **B23** to cell **B27**.

6. **Calculate Bond Duration by Function.** Excel's Analysis ToolPak Add-In contains several advanced bond functions, including duration and modified duration.

- Click on **Tools**, **Add-Ins**, check the **Analysis ToolPak** checkbox on the **Add-Ins** dialog box (see the figure below), and click on **OK**.

FIGURE 3.2. The Add-Ins dialog box.

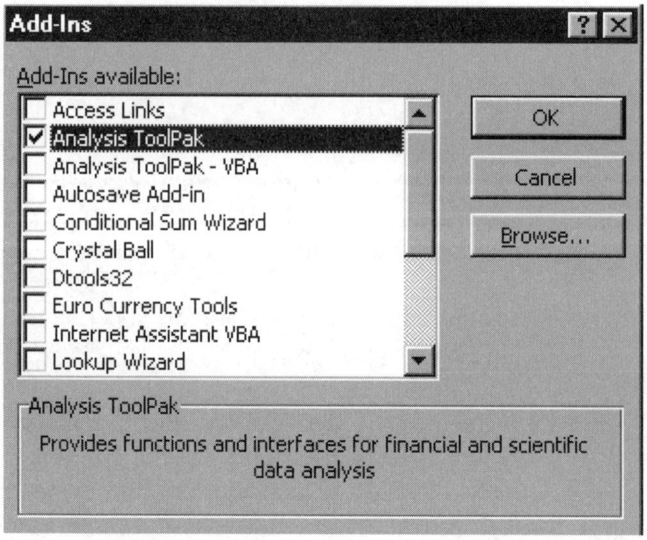

- The duration function is =DURATION(Settlement Date, Maturity Date, Annual Coupon Rate, Yield To Maturity, Number of Payments). The Settlement Date is the date when you exchange money to purchase the bond. Specifying the exact day of settlement and maturity allows a very precise calculation. For our purpose, we simple want the difference between the two dates to equal the (8 Periods To Maturity) / (2 Payments / Year) = 4 Years To Maturity. This is easily accomplished by the use of the DATE function. The DATE Function has the format =DATE(Year, Month, Day). We will enter an arbitrary starting date of 1/1/2000 for the Settlement Date and then specify a formula for 1/1/2000 plus T / NOP for the Maturity Date. We need to add an IF statement to test for the rate convention being used. The duration and modified duration functions are only valid with APR. Enter **=IF($B$4=1,"",DURATION(DATE(2000,1,1), DATE(2000+T/NOP,1,1),CR,y,NOP))** in cell **B30**.

- The modified duration function is =MDURATION(Settlement Date, Maturity Date, Annual Coupon Rate, Yield To Maturity, Number of Payments) and has identical arguments. Enter **=IF($B$4=1,"",MDURATION(DATE(2000,1,1), DATE(2000+T/NOP,1,1),CR,y,NOP))** in cell **B31**.

The duration is 3.65 years and the modified duration is 3.49 years. Notice you get the same answer all three ways: using the cash flows, using the formula, or using the Analysis ToolPak Add-In function!

3.2 Price Sensitivity using Duration

Bond duration is a measure of the price sensitivity of a bond to changes in interest rates. In other words, it is a measure of the bond's interest rate risk. Duration tells you approximately what percent change in bond price will result from a given change in yield to maturity. The duration approximation can be shown on a graph and compared to the actual percent change in the bond price.

FIGURE 3.3 Excel Model of Bond Duration – Price Sensitivity using Duration.

	A	B	C	D	E	F	G	H	I	J
1	BOND DURATION	Price Sensitivity Using Duration								
2		Annual Percentage Rate								
3	**Inputs**									
4	Rate Convention: 1 = EAR, 0 = APR	0								
5	Annual Coupon Rate (CR)	5.0%								
6	Yield to Maturity (Annualized) (y)	9.0%								
7	Number of Payments / Year (NOP)	2								
8	Number of Periods to Maturity (T)	8								
9	Face Value (PAR)	$1,000								
10										
11	**Outputs**									
12	Discount Rate / Period (r.)	4.5%								
13	Coupon Payment (PMT)	$25								
14										
15										
16										
17										
18										
19										
20	**Graph Outputs**									
21	Yield to Maturity (Annualized)	1.0%	2.0%	3.0%	4.0%	5.0%	6.0%	7.0%	8.0%	9.0%
22	Discount Rate / Period	0.5%	1.0%	1.5%	2.0%	2.5%	3.0%	3.5%	4.0%	4.5%
23	Change in Yield to Maturity	-8.0%	-7.0%	-6.0%	-5.0%	-4.0%	-3.0%	-2.0%	-1.0%	0.0%
24	Actual Bond Price	$1,156	$1,115	$1,075	$1,037	$1,000	$965	$931	$899	$868
25	Current Bond Price	$868	$868	$868	$868	$868	$868	$868	$868	$868
26	Actual Percent Change in Price	33.2%	28.4%	23.8%	19.4%	15.2%	11.2%	7.3%	3.6%	0.0%
27	Modified Duration	3.49	3.49	3.49	3.49	3.49	3.49	3.49	3.49	3.49
28	Duration Approximation	27.9%	24.4%	20.9%	17.4%	14.0%	10.5%	7.0%	3.5%	0.0%

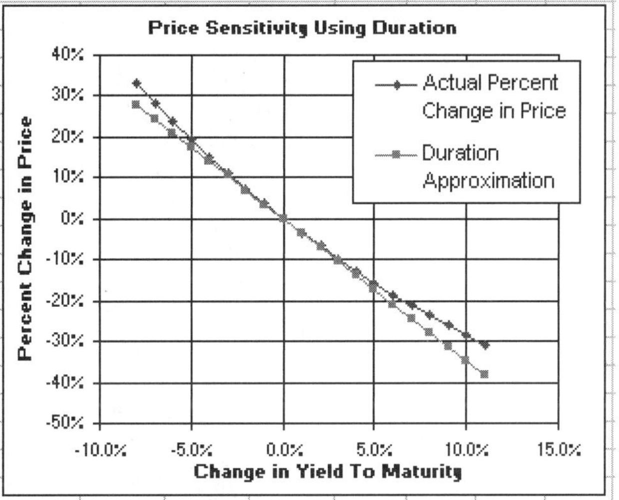

How To Build This Excel Model

1. **Start with the Basics Excel Model and Delete Rows.** Open the Excel model that you created for Bond Duration – Basics and immediately save the Excel model under a new name using the **File Save As** command. Delete rows **27** through **31** by selecting the range **A27:A31**, clicking on **Edit**, **Delete**, selecting the **Entire Row** radio button on the **Delete** dialog box, and clicking on **OK**. Repeat this procedure to delete rows **14** through **25**.

2. **Yield To Maturity (Annualized).** Enter Yield To Maturity values **1.0%**, **2.0%**, **3.0%**, **4.0%**, …, **20.0%** in the range **B21:U21**.

3. **Discount Rate / Period.** The Discount Rate / Period depends on the rate convention being used as follows:

$$\text{Discount Rate / Period} = \begin{cases} (1+\text{Yield To Maturity})\,\hat{}\,(1/(\text{Number of Payments / Year}))-1 & \text{under EAR} \\ (\text{Yield To Maturity})/(\text{Number of Payments / Year}) & \text{under APR} \end{cases}.$$

Enter **=IF($B$4=1,((1+B21)^(1/NOP))-1,B21/NOP)** in cell **B22** and copy the cell **B22** to the range **C22:U22**.

4. **Change in Yield To Maturity.** The Change in Yield To Maturity = New Yield To Maturity – Current Yield To Maturity (y). In cell **B23**, enter **=B21-y** and copy the cell **B23** to the range **C23:U23**.

5. **Actual Bond Price.** Calculate the bond price using the inputs **T**, **PMT**, **PAR**, and the Discount Rate / Period in cell **B22**. Specifically, enter **=-PV(B22,T,PMT,PAR)** in cell **B24** and copy the cell **B24** to the range **C24:U24**.

6. **Current Bond Price.** Calculate the bond price using the original inputs. Copy the formula in cell **B24** to cell **B25**. Then change the yield to maturity from **B23** to **r.** so that the formula reads **=-PV(r.,T,PMT,PAR)** and copy the cell **B25** to the range **C25:U25**.

7. **Actual Percent Change in Price.** The percent Actual Percent Change in Price = (Actual Bond Price -Current Bond Price) / Current Bond Price. In cell **B26**, enter **=(B24-B25)/B25** and copy the cell **B26** to the range **C26:U26**.

8. **Modified Duration.** Calculate modified duration in two steps. First, copy the duration formula in cell **B14** to cell **B27**. Then change the formula to modified duration by adding **(** at the beginning of the formula and adding **)/(1+r.)** at the end of the formula. Thus, the modified duration formula in cell **B27** will look like **=((1+r.)/(r.*NOP)-(1+r.+T*(CR/NOP-r.))/(CR*((1+r.)^T-1)+r.*NOP))/(1+r.)**. Then copy the cell **B27** to the range **C27:U27**. Delete the content of the range **A14:B14** by selecting the range and then pressing the **Delete** key.

9. **Duration Approximation.** The Duration Approximation of the Percent Change in Price = - Modified Duration * Change in Yield To Maturity. In cell **B28**, enter **=-B27*B23** and copy the cell **B28** to the range **C28:U28**.

10. **Graph the Actual Percent Change in Price and the Duration Approximation.** Highlight the range **A23:U23** and then while holding down the **Ctrl** button highlight the ranges **A26:U26** and **A28:U28**. Next choose **Insert Chart** from the main menu. Select an **XY(Scatter)** chart type and make other selections to complete the Chart Wizard. Place the graph in the range **C3:J20**.

It is clear from the graph that duration does a very good job of approximating the price sensitivity of a bond. That is, the percent change in bond price from the duration approximation is very close to the actual percent change. This is especially true for relatively small changes in yield to maturity (say, plus or minus 3%). For larger changes in yield to maturity, there is a gap between the duration approximation and the actual percent change. The gap comes from the fact that the actual percent change is curved, whereas the duration approximation is a straight line. One could do a better job of approximating the price sensitivity of a bond for larger changes in yield to maturity if one could account for the curvature. That is exactly what bond convexity does. To see what kind of improvement you can get by using convexity, check out Bond Convexity – Price Sensitivity using Duration and Convexity.

3.3 Dynamic Chart

If you increased the coupon rate of a bond, what would happen to its duration? If you increased the yield to maturity of a bond, what would happen to its duration? You can answer these questions and more by creating a *Dynamic Chart* using "spinners." Spinners are up-arrow / down-arrow buttons that allow you to easily change the inputs to the model with the click of a mouse. Then Excel recalculates the model and instantly redraws the model outputs on the graph.

FIGURE 3.4 Excel Model of Bond Duration – Dynamic Chart.

	A	B	C	D	E	F	G	H	I	J	K
1	BOND DURATION	Dynamic Chart				Annual Percentage Rate					
2											
3	**Inputs**										
4	Rate Convention: 1 = EAR, 0 = APR	0		0							
5	Annual Coupon Rate (CR)	5.0%		10							
6	Yield to Maturity (Annualized) (y)	9.0%		18							
7	Number of Payments / Year (NOP)	2		2							
8											
9	**Outputs**										
10	Discount Rate / Period (r.)	4.5%									
11											
12	**Dynamic Chart Outputs**										
13	Time to Maturity (Years)	1	2	3	4	5	6	7	8	9	10
14	Number of Periods to Maturity	2	4	6	8	10	12	14	16	18	20
15	Duration of Coupon Bond	0.99	1.92	2.81	3.65	4.43	5.16	5.84	6.47	7.06	7.59
16	Duration of Zero-Coupon Bond	1.00	2.00	3.00	4.00	5.00	6.00	7.00	8.00	9.00	10.00

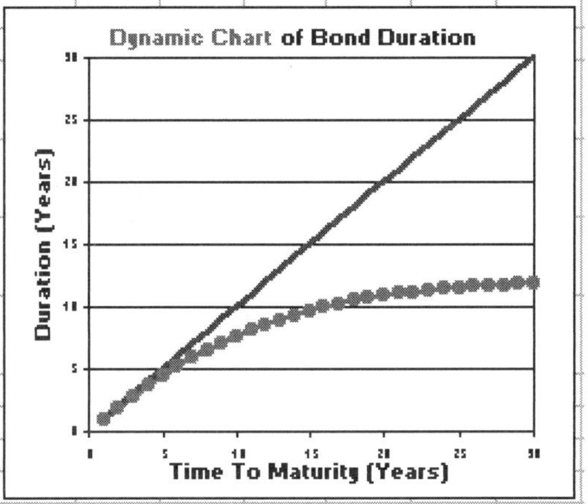

How To Build This Excel Model.

1. **Start with the Basics Excel Model and Delete Rows.** Open the Excel model that you created for Bond Duration – Basics and immediately save the file under a new name using the **File Save As** command. Delete rows 27 through 31 by selecting the range A27:A31, clicking on **Edit**, **Delete**, selecting the **Entire Row** radio button on the **Delete** dialog box, and clicking on **OK**. Repeat this procedure to delete rows 13 through 25.Repeat this procedure to delete rows 9 through 10.

2. **Increase Row Height for the Spinners.** Select the range A4:A7. Then click on **Format Row Height** from the main menu. Enter a height of **30** and click on **OK**.

3. **Display the Forms Toolbar.** Click on **View**, **Toolbars**, **Forms** from the main menu.

4. **Create the Spinners.** Look for the up-arrow / down-arrow button on the **Forms** toolbar (which will display the word "**Spinner**" if you hover the cursor over it) and click on it. Then draw the box for a spinner from the upper left corner of cell C4 down to the lower right corner of the cell. Then a spinner appears in the cell C4. Right click on the spinner (press the right mouse button while the cursor is above the spinner) and a small menu pops up. Click on **Copy**. Then select the cell C5 and click on **Paste**. This creates an identical spinner in the cell C5. Repeat the process twice more. Select cell C6 and click on **Paste**. Select cell C7 and click on **Paste**. You now have four spinners down column C.

5. **Create The Cell Links.** Right click on the first spinner in the cell C4 and a small menu pops up. Click on **Format Control** and a dialog box pops up. Click on the **Control** tab, then enter the cell link **D4** in the **Cell link** edit box and click on **OK**. Repeat this procedure for the other three spinners. Link the spinner in cell C5 to cell **D5**. Link the spinner in cell C6 to cell **D6**. Link the spinner in cell C7 to cell **D7** and also on the **Control tab**, set the **Minimum value** equal to **1**. Test your spinners by clicking on the up-arrows and down-arrows of the spinners to see how they change the values in the linked cells.

6. **Create Scaled Inputs.** The values in the linked cells are always integers, but they can be scaled appropriately to the problem at hand. Restrict the value in cell B4 to be either 1 or 0 by entering **=IF(D4>1,1,D4)**. In cell B5, enter **=D5/200**. In cell B6, enter **=D6/200**. In cell B7, enter **=D7**.

7. **Time To Maturity.** Enter Time To Maturity values **1, 2, 3, 4, …, 30** in the range B13:AE13.

8. **Number of Periods to Maturity.** The Number of Periods to Maturity = (Time to Maturity) * (Number of Periods / Year). In cell B14, enter **=B13*NOP** and copy the cell B14 to the range C14:AE14.

9. **Duration of a Coupon Bond.** Copy the duration formula from cell B11 to cell B15. Edit cell B15 to change the Number of Periods To Maturity from **T** to **B$14** so that the formula reads **=(1+r.)/(r.*NOP)-(1+r.+B$14*(CR/NOP-r.))/(CR*((1+r.)^B$14-1)+r.*NOP)**. Be sure that **B$14** has a **$** in the middle to lock in the row, but not the column. Then copy the cell B15 to the range C15:AE15.

10. **Duration of a Zero Coupon Bond.** A zero coupon bond is a bond with a coupon rate equal to 0.0%. As a benchmark for comparison, calculate the duration of a zero-coupon bond using the same inputs for everything else. Copy the formula in cell B15 to cell B16. Then change the coupon rate from **CR** to **0** so that the formula reads **=(1+r.)/(r.*NOP)-(1+r.+B$14*(0/NOP-r.))/(0*((1+r.)^B$14-1)+r.*NOP)**. Copy the cell B16 to the range C16:AE16.

11. **Clean Up.** Delete the contents of the range **A8:B8** by selecting the range and then pressing the **Delete** key. Similarly, delete the contents of the range **A11:B11** by selecting the range and then pressing the **Delete** key.

12. **Graph the Duration of a Coupon Bond and Zero Coupon Bond.** Highlight the range **B13:AE13** and then while holding down the **Ctrl** button highlight the range **B15:AE16**. Next choose **Insert Chart** from the main menu. Select an **XY(Scatter)** chart type and make other selections to complete the Chart Wizard. Place the graph in the range **E2:K11**.

Your *Dynamic Chart* allows you to change the Bond Duration inputs and instantly see the impact on a graph of the duration of a coupon bond and zero coupon bond by time to maturity. This allows you to perform instant experiments on Bond Duration. Below is a list of experiments that you might want to perform:

- What happens when the annual coupon rate is increased?
- What happens when the yield to maturity is increased?
- What happens when the number of payments / year is increased?
- What happens when the annual coupon rate is decreased to zero?
- What is the relationship between the duration of a zero coupon bond and time to maturity?
- Does an increase in the time to maturity *always* increase the duration of a coupon bond or is it possible for it to decrease duration at some point? Asked differently, does the red curve always go up or can it be hump shaped?

Problems

Skill-Building Problems.

1. A bond has a face value of $1,000, an annual coupon rate of 3.70%, an yield to maturity of 7.4%, makes 2 (semi-annual) coupon payments per year, and 6 periods to maturity (or 3 years to maturity). Determine the duration of this bond based on the Annual Percentage Rate (APR) convention and the duration of this bond based on the Effective Annual Rate (EAR) convention.

2. A bond has a face value of $1,000, an annual coupon rate of 6.50%, an yield to maturity of 9.2%, makes 2 (semi-annual) coupon payments per year, and 10 periods to maturity (or 5 years to maturity). Determine approximately what percent change in bond price will result from a given change in yield to maturity by comparing on a graph the duration approximation versus the actual percent change in the bond price.

3. Perform instant experiments on whether changing various inputs causes an increase or decrease in the Bond Duration and by how much.

a. What happens when the annual coupon rate is increased?

b. What happens when the yield to maturity is increased?

c. What happens when the number of payments / year is increased?

d. What happens when the annual coupon rate is decreased to zero?

e. What is the relationship between the duration of a zero coupon bond and time to maturity?

f. Does an increase in the time to maturity always increase the duration of a coupon bond or is it possible for it to decrease duration at some point? Asked differently, does the duration curve always go up or can it be hump shaped?

Live In-class Problems.

4. Given the partial Basics file **BdurbasZ.xls**, complete step **4 Calculate Bond Duration using the Cash Flows.**

5. Given the partial Price Sensitivity Using Duration file **BdursenZ.xls**, do steps **7 Actual Percent Change in Price** and **9 Duration Approximation**.

6. Given the partial Dynamic Chart file **BdurdynZ.xls**, do steps **9 Duration of a Coupon Bond** and **10 Duration of a Zero Coupon Bond**.

Chapter 4 Bond Convexity

4.1 Basics

Problem. A bond has a face value of $1,000, an annual coupon rate of 5.0%, an yield to maturity of 9.0%, makes 2 (semi-annual) coupon payments per year, and 8 periods to maturity (or 4 years to maturity). What is the convexity of this bond?

Solution Strategy. We will calculate convexity two equivalent ways. First, we will calculate convexity as the weighted-average (time-squared plus time) to the bond's cash flows. Second, we use a formula for convexity.

FIGURE 4.1 Excel Model of Bond Convexity - Basics.

	A	B	C	D	E	F	G	H	I	J	K
1	BOND CONVEXITY	Basics		Annual Percentage Rate							
2											
3	**Inputs**										
4	Rate Convention: 1 = EAR, 0 = APR	0									
5	Annual Coupon Rate (CR)	5.0%									
6	Yield to Maturity (Annualized) (y)	9.0%									
7	Number of Payments / Year (NOP)	2									
8	Number of Periods to Maturity (T)	8									
9	Face Value (PAR)	$1,000									
10											
11	**Outputs**										
12	Discount Rate / Period (r)	4.5%									
13	Coupon Payment (PMT)	$25									
14											
15	**Calculate Bond Convexity using the Cash Flows**										
16	Period	0	1	2	3	4	5	6	7	8	
17	Time (Years)	0.0	0.5	1.0	1.5	2.0	2.5	3.0	3.5	4.0	Total
18	Cash Flows		$25.00	$25.00	$25.00	$25.00	$25.00	$25.00	$25.00	$1,025.00	
19	Present Value of Cash Flow		$23.92	$22.89	$21.91	$20.96	$20.06	$19.20	$18.37	$720.76	$868.08
20	Weight		2.8%	2.6%	2.5%	2.4%	2.3%	2.2%	2.1%	83.0%	100.0%
21	Weight * (Time^2+Time)		0.02	0.05	0.09	0.14	0.20	0.27	0.33	16.61	17.72
22	Convexity	16.23									
23											
24	**Calculate Bond Convexity using the Formula**										
25	Convexity	16.23									

How To Build This Excel Model

1. **Enter The Inputs and Name Them.** Enter **0** in cell **B4**. This will serve as a switch between the APR and the EAR rate conventions. To highlight which rate convention is in use, enter **=IF($B$4=1,"Effective Annual Rate","Annual Percentage Rate")** in cell **D1**. Enter the other inputs into the range **B5:B9** and then name each one. Put the cursor on cell **B5**, click on **Insert**, **Name**, **Define**, enter **CR** in the **Names in Workbook** box, and click on **OK**. Put the cursor on cell **B6** and repeat the process to name it y. Repeat the process to give the cells **B7**, **B8**, and **B9** the names **NOP**, **T**, and **PAR**, respectively.

2. **Calculate the Discount Rate / Period.** The Discount Rate / Period depends on the rate convention being used as follows:

$$\text{Discount Rate / Period} = \begin{cases} (1+\text{Yield To Maturity})\,^\wedge\,(1/(\text{Number of Payments / Year}))-1 & \text{under EAR} \\ (\text{Yield To Maturity})/(\text{Number of Payments / Year}) & \text{under APR} \end{cases}.$$

Enter **=IF($B$4=1,((1+y)^(1/NOP))-1,y/NOP)** in cell **B12** and use the process above to give the cell **B12** the name **r.**.

3. **Calculate the Coupon Payment.** The formula is Coupon Payment = Coupon Rate * Face Value / (Number of Payments / Year). Enter **=CR*PAR/NOP** in cell **B13** and use the process above to give the cell **B13** the name **PMT**.

4. **Calculate Bond Convexity using the Cash Flows.** Calculating duration as a weighted-average time to cash flows directly illustrates the key intuition for duration. This bond has two cash flows per year for four years or eight periods. Enter the period numbers **0, 1, 2, …, 8** in the range **B16:J16**. Complete the duration calculation as follows:

   - Time (years) = (Period) / (Number of Payments / Year) = Period / NOP. Enter **=B16/NOP** in cell **B17** and copy this cell to the range **C17:J17**.

   - Cash Flows in Periods 1-7 = Coupon Payment. Enter **=PMT** in cell **C18** and copy this cell to the range **D18:J18**.

   - Cash Flow in Period 8 = Coupon Payment + Face Value. Add **+PAR** to the formula in cell **J18**, so that it reads **=PMT+PAR**.

   - Present Value of Cash Flow =(Cash Flow)/((1+Yield to Maturity/Number of Payments)^ Period) = Cash Flow / ((1+ y / NOP)^Period). Enter **=C18/((1+r.)^C16)** in cell **C19** and copy this cell to the range **D19:J19**.

   - Present Value of the Bond = Sum of all the Present Value of Cash Flows (row 14). Enter **=SUM(C19:J19)** in cell **K19**.

   - Weight on date t = Present Value of Cash Flow on date t / Present Value of the Bond. Enter **=C19/$K$19** in cell **C20** and copy this cell to the range **D20:K20**.

   - Weight * (Time^2 + Time). Enter **=C20*(C17^2+C17)** in cell **C21** and copy this cell to the range **D21:J21**.

   - Convexity = (Sum of: Weight * (Time^2 + Time)) / ((1+Yield to Maturity / Number of Pmts)^2). Enter **=SUM(C21:J21)/((1+y/NOP)^2)** in cell **B22**. Optionally for completeness, enter **=SUM(C21:J21)** in cell **K21**.

5. **Calculate Bond Convexity by Formula.** The calculation above can be simplified down to an equivalent formula solution for convexity. The convexity formula is

$$\frac{\begin{pmatrix} CR\cdot(1+r.)^{1+T}\cdot(r.\cdot(NOP+1)+2) \\ -CR\cdot(r.^2\cdot(NOP+T+1)\cdot(T+1)+r.\cdot(NOP+2\cdot T+3)+2)+r.^3\cdot NOP\cdot T\cdot(NOP+T) \end{pmatrix}}{r.^2\cdot NOP^2\cdot\left(CR\cdot(1+r.)^T-CR+r.\cdot NOP\right)}$$

$$\div\left((1+r.)^2\right)$$

Enter **=((CR*((1+r.)^(1+T))*(r.*(NOP+1)+2)**

-CR*(r.^2*(NOP+T+1)*(T+1)+r.*(NOP+2*T+3)+2)

+r.^3*NOP*T*(NOP+T))

/(r.^2*NOP^2*(CR*(1+r.)^T-CR+r.*NOP)))

/((1+r.)^2) in cell **B25**.

The value of bond convexity is 16.23. Notice you get the same answer both ways: using the cash flows or using the formula!

4.2 Price Sensitivity Including Convexity

Bond convexity complements bond duration in measuring of the price sensitivity of a bond to changes in interest rates. In other words, duration and convexity combined give you a measure of the bond's interest rate risk. Adding convexity gives you a better approximation of what percent change in bond price will result from a given change in yield to maturity than you can get from duration alone. To get the overall picture we will compare all three on a graph: the duration approximation, the duration and convexity approximation, and the actual percent change in the bond price.

FIGURE 4.2 Excel Model of Bond Convexity – Price Sensitivity Including Convexity.

	A	B	C	D	E	F	G	H	I	J
1	BOND CONVEXITY	Price Sensitivity Including Convexity								
2		Annual Percentage Rate								
3	**Inputs**									
4	Rate Convention: 1 = EAR, 0 = APR	0								
5	Annual Coupon Rate (CR)	5.0%								
6	Yield to Maturity (Annualized) (y)	9.0%								
7	Number of Payments / Year (NOP)	2								
8	Number of Periods to Maturity (T)	8								
9	Face Value (PAR)	$1,000								
10										
11	**Outputs**									
12	Discount Rate / Period (r.)	4.5%								
13	Coupon Payment (PMT)	$25								
14										
15										
16										
17										
18										
19										
20	**Chart Outputs**									
21	Yield to Maturity (Annualized)	1.0%	2.0%	3.0%	4.0%	5.0%	6.0%	7.0%	8.0%	9.0%
22	Discount Rate / Period	0.5%	1.0%	1.5%	2.0%	2.5%	3.0%	3.5%	4.0%	4.5%
23	Change in Yield to Maturity	-8.0%	-7.0%	-6.0%	-5.0%	-4.0%	-3.0%	-2.0%	-1.0%	0.0%
24	Actual Bond Price	$1,156	$1,115	$1,075	$1,037	$1,000	$965	$931	$899	$868
25	Current Bond Price	$868	$868	$868	$868	$868	$868	$868	$868	$868
26	Actual Percent Change in Price	33.2%	28.4%	23.8%	19.4%	15.2%	11.2%	7.3%	3.6%	0.0%
27	Modified Duration	3.49	3.49	3.49	3.49	3.49	3.49	3.49	3.49	3.49
28	Duration Approximation	27.9%	24.4%	20.9%	17.4%	14.0%	10.5%	7.0%	3.5%	0.0%
29	Convexity	16.23	16.23	16.23	16.23	16.23	16.23	16.23	16.23	16.23
30	Duration and Convexity Approx.	33.1%	28.4%	23.9%	19.5%	15.3%	11.2%	7.3%	3.6%	0.0%

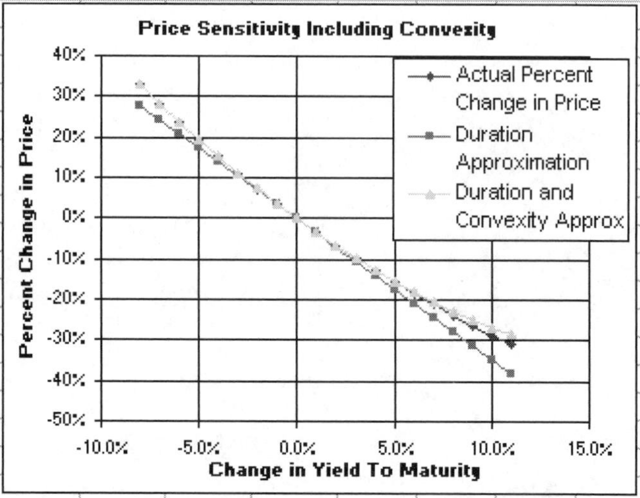

How To Build This Excel Model

1. **Start with the Basics Excel Model and Delete Rows.** Open the Excel model that you created for Bond Convexity – Basics and immediately save the Excel model under a new name using the **File Save As** command. Delete rows **14** through **24** by selecting the range **A14:A24**, clicking on **Edit**, **Delete**, selecting the **Entire Row** radio button on the **Delete** dialog box, and clicking on **OK**. **Do not delete row 25 at this time, since later we want to copy the convexity formula rather than reenter it!**

2. **Yield To Maturity (Annualized).** Enter Yield To Maturity values **1.0%**, **2.0%**, **3.0%**, **4.0%**, …, **20.0%** in the range **B21:U21**.

3. **Discount Rate / Period.** The Discount Rate / Period depends on the rate convention being used as follows:

$$\text{Discount Rate / Period} = \begin{cases} (1+\text{Yield To Maturity})\,\hat{}\,(1/(\text{Number of Payments / Year}))-1 & \text{under EAR} \\ (\text{Yield To Maturity})/(\text{Number of Payments / Year}) & \text{under APR} \end{cases}.$$

Enter **=IF($B$4=1,((1+B21)^(1/NOP))-1,B21/NOP)** in cell **B22** and copy the cell **B22** to the range **C22:U22**.

4. **Change in Yield To Maturity.** The Change in Yield To Maturity = New Yield To Maturity – Current Yield To Maturity (y). In cell **B23**, enter **=B21-y** and copy the cell **B23** to the range **C23:U23**.

5. **Actual Bond Price.** Calculate the bond price using the inputs **T**, **PMT**, **PAR**, and the Discount Rate / Period in cell **B22**. Specifically, enter **=-PV(B22,T,PMT,PAR)** in cell **B24** and copy the cell **B24** to the range **C24:U24**.

6. **Current Bond Price.** Calculate the bond price using the original inputs. Copy the formula in cell **B24** to cell **B25**. Then change the yield to maturity from **B23** to **r.** so that the formula reads **=-PV(r.,T,PMT,PAR)** and copy the cell **B25** to the range **C25:U25**.

7. **Actual Percent Change in Price.** The percent Actual Percent Change in Price = (Actual Bond Price -Current Bond Price) / Current Bond Price. In cell **B26**, enter **=(B24-B25)/B25** and copy the cell **B26** to the range **C26:U26**.

8. **Modified Duration.** Enter the modified duration formula **=((1+r.)/(r.*NOP)-(1+r.+T*(CR/NOP-r.))/(CR*((1+r.)^T-1)+r.*NOP))/(1+r.)** in cell **B27** to the range **C27:U27**.

9. **Duration Approximation.** The Duration Approximation of the Percent Change in Price = - Modified Duration * Change in Yield To Maturity. In cell **B28**, enter **=-B27*B23** and copy the cell **B28** to the range **C28:U28**.

10. **Convexity.** Copy the convexity formula in cell **B14** to cell **B29** and copy the cell **B29** to the range **C29:U29**. For appearances, delete the range **A14:B14**.

11. **Duration and Convexity Approx.** The Duration and Convexity Approximation = Duration Approximation + (1/2) * Convexity * (Change in Yield To Maturity)^2. In cell **B30**, enter **=B28+(1/2)*B29*B23^2** and copy the cell **B30** to the range **C30:U30**.

12. **Graph the Actual Percent Change in Price and the Duration Approximation.** Highlight the range **A23:U23** and then while holding down the **Ctrl** button highlight the ranges **A26:U26**, **A28:U28**, and **A30:U30**. Next choose **Insert Chart** from the main menu. Select an **XY(Scatter)** chart type and make other selections to complete the Chart Wizard. Place the graph in the range **C3:J20**.

The graph illustrates that duration and convexity approximation of the price sensitivity of a bond is better than the duration approximation alone. That is, the percent change in bond price from the duration and convexity approximation is very close to the actual percent change over a wide range of changes in yield to maturity (say, plus or minus 9%). Only for a very large change in yield to maturity is there any gap between the duration and convexity approximation and the actual percent change and the gap is pretty small. In approximating the actual percent change, duration alone does a good job of approximating the slope. Then convexity does a good job of adding the curvature. Together they do a great job of approximating the price sensitivity (i.e., interest rate risk) of a bond over a wide range of changes in yields.

4.3 Dynamic Chart

If you increased the coupon rate of a bond, what would happen to its convexity? If you increased the yield to maturity of a bond, what would happen to its convexity? You can answer these questions and more by creating a *Dynamic Chart* using "spinners." Spinners are up-arrow / down-arrow buttons that allow you to easily change the inputs to the model with the click of a mouse. Then Excel recalculates the model and instantly redraws the model outputs on the graph.

FIGURE 4.3 Excel Model of Bond Convexity – Dynamic Chart.

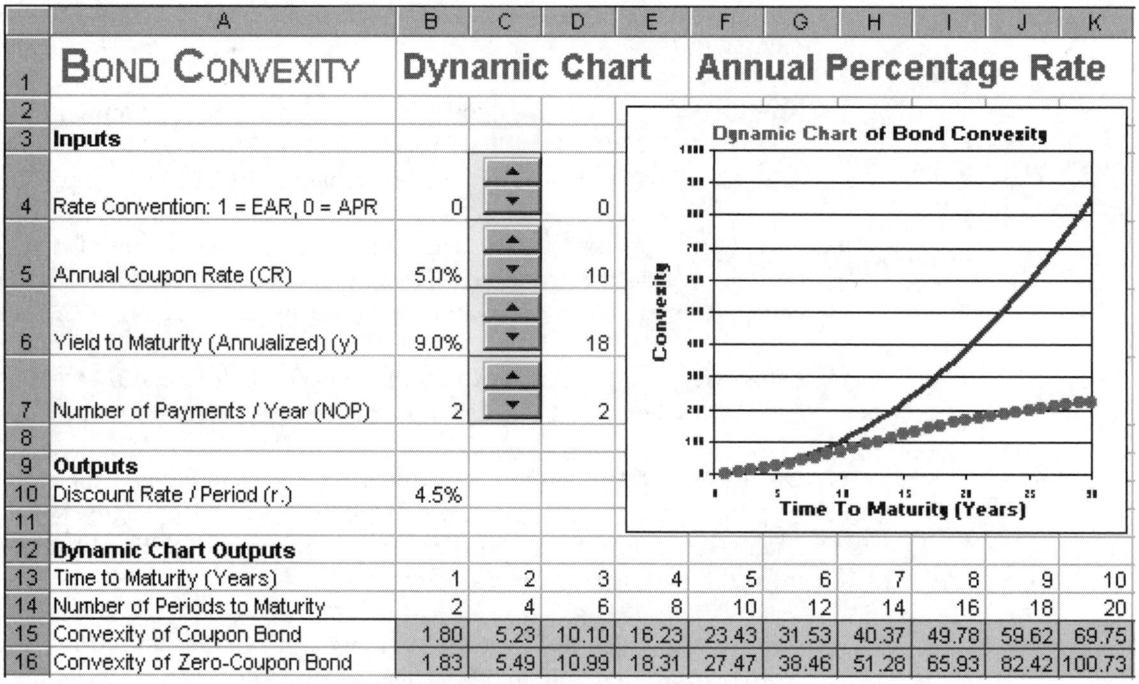

	A	B	C	D	E	F	G	H	I	J	K
1	BOND CONVEXITY	Dynamic Chart				Annual Percentage Rate					
2											
3	**Inputs**										
4	Rate Convention: 1 = EAR, 0 = APR	0		0							
5	Annual Coupon Rate (CR)	5.0%		10							
6	Yield to Maturity (Annualized) (y)	9.0%		18							
7	Number of Payments / Year (NOP)	2		2							
8											
9	**Outputs**										
10	Discount Rate / Period (r.)	4.5%									
11											
12	**Dynamic Chart Outputs**										
13	Time to Maturity (Years)	1	2	3	4	5	6	7	8	9	10
14	Number of Periods to Maturity	2	4	6	8	10	12	14	16	18	20
15	Convexity of Coupon Bond	1.80	5.23	10.10	16.23	23.43	31.53	40.37	49.78	59.62	69.75
16	Convexity of Zero-Coupon Bond	1.83	5.49	10.99	18.31	27.47	38.46	51.28	65.93	82.42	100.73

How To Build This Excel Model

1. **Start with the Basics Excel Model and Delete Rows.** Open the Excel model that you created for Bond Convexity – Basics and immediately save the Excel model under a new name using the **File Save As** command. Delete rows **13** through **24** by selecting the range **A13:A24**, clicking on **Edit**, **Delete**, selecting the **Entire Row** radio button on the **Delete** dialog box, and clicking on **OK**. Repeat this procedure to delete rows **9** through **10**.

2. **Increase Row Height for the Spinners.** Select the range **A4:A7**. Then click on **Format Row Height** from the main menu. Enter a height of **30** and click on **OK**.

3. **Display the Forms Toolbar.** Click on **View**, **Toolbars**, **Forms** from the main menu.

4. **Create the Spinners.** Look for the up-arrow / down-arrow button on the **Forms** toolbar (which will display the word "**Spinner**" if you hover the cursor over it) and click on it. Then draw the box for a spinner from the upper left corner of cell **C4** down to the lower right corner of the cell. Then a spinner appears in the cell **C4**. Right click on the spinner (press the right mouse button while the cursor is above the spinner) and a small menu pops up. Click on **Copy**. Then select the cell **C5** and click on **Paste**. This creates an identical spinner in the cell **C5**. Repeat the process twice more. Select cell **C6** and click on **Paste**. Select cell **C6** and click on **Paste**. You now have four spinners down column **C**.

5. **Create The Cell Links.** Right click on the first spinner in the cell **C4** and a small menu pops up. Click on **Format Control** and a dialog box pops up. Click on the **Control** tab, then enter the cell link **D4** in the **Cell link** edit box and click on **OK**. Repeat this procedure for the other three spinners. Link the spinner in cell **C5** to cell **D5**. Link the spinner in cell **C6** to cell **D6**. Link the spinner in cell **C7** to cell **D7** and also on the **Control tab**, set the **Minimum value** equal to **1**. Test your spinners by clicking on the up-arrows and down-arrows of the spinners to see how they change the values in the linked cells.

6. **Create Scaled Inputs.** The values in the linked cells are always integers, but they can be scaled appropriately to the problem at hand. Restrict the value in cell **B4** to be either 1 or 0 by entering **=IF(D4>1,1,D4)**. In cell **B5**, enter **=D5/200**. In cell **B6**, enter **=D6/200**. In cell **B7**, enter **=D7**.

7. **Time To Maturity.** Enter Time To Maturity values **1**, **2**, **3**, **4**, …, **30** in the range **B13:AE13**.

8. **Number of Periods to Maturity.** The Number of Periods to Maturity = (Time to Maturity) * (Number of Periods / Year). In cell **B14**, enter **=B13*NOP** and copy the cell **B14** to the range **C14:AE14**.

9. **Convexity of a Coupon Bond.** Copy the convexity formula in cell **B11** to cell **B15**. Then edit the formula in cell **B15** so as to change every occurrence of the variable **T** to **B$14** (with a **$** in the middle to lock in the row, but not the column). You will find 7 occurrences of the variable **T** to change. Copy the cell **B15** to the range **C15:AE15**. For appearances, delete the range **A11:B11**.

10. **Convexity of a Zero Coupon Bond.** A zero coupon bond is a bond with a coupon rate equal to 0.0%. As a benchmark for comparison, calculate the duration of a zero-coupon bond using the same inputs for everything else. Copy the formula in cell **B15** to cell **B16**. Then edit the formula in cell **B16** so as to change every occurrence of the variable **CR** to **0**. You will find 4

occurrences of the variable **CR** to change. Copy the cell **B16** to the range **C16:AE16**.

11. **Graph the Convexity of a Coupon Bond and Zero Coupon Bond.** Highlight the range **B13:AE13** and then while holding down the **Ctrl** button highlight the range **B15:AE16**. Next choose **Insert Chart** from the main menu. Select an **XY(Scatter)** chart type and make other selections to complete the Chart Wizard. Place the graph in the range **E2:K11**.

Your *Dynamic Chart* allows you to change the Bond Convexity inputs and instantly see the impact on a graph of the convexity of a coupon bond and zero coupon bond by time to maturity. This allows you to perform instant experiments on Bond Convexity. Below is a list of experiments that you might want to perform:

- What happens when the annual coupon rate is increased?
- What happens when the yield to maturity is increased?
- What happens when the number of payments / year is increased?
- What happens when the annual coupon rate is decreased to zero?
- Does an increase in the time to maturity *always* increase the convexity of a coupon bond or is it possible for it to decrease convexity at some point? Asked differently, does the red curve always go up or can it be hump shaped?

Problems

Skill-Building Problems.

1. A bond has a face value of $1,000, an annual coupon rate of 2.30%, an yield to maturity of 8.9%, makes 2 (semi-annual) coupon payments per year, and 10 periods to maturity (or 5 years to maturity). Determine the convexity of this bond based on the Annual Percentage Rate (APR) convention and the convexity of this bond based on the Effective Annual Rate (EAR) convention.

2. A bond has a face value of $1,000, an annual coupon rate of 4.70%, an yield to maturity of 7.8%, makes 2 (semi-annual) coupon payments per year, and 8 periods to maturity (or 4 years to maturity). Determine approximately what percent change in bond price will result from a given change in yield to maturity by comparing on a graph the duration approximation, the duration and convexity approximation, and the actual percent change in the bond price.

3. Perform instant experiments on whether changing various inputs causes an increase or decrease in the Bond Convexity and by how much.

a. What happens when the annual coupon rate is increased?

b. What happens when the yield to maturity is increased?

c. What happens when the number of payments / year is increased?

d. What happens when the annual coupon rate is decreased to zero?

e. Does an increase in the time to maturity always increase the convexity of a coupon bond or is it possible for it to decrease convexity at some point? Asked differently, does the convexity curve always go up or can it be hump shaped?

Live In-class Problems.

4. Given the partial Basics file **BconbasZ.xls**, complete step **4 Calculate Bond Convexity using the Cash Flows**.

5. Given the partial Price Sensitivity Including Convexity file **BconsenZ.xls**, do steps **7 Actual Percent Change in Price, 9 Duration Approximation,** and **11 Duration and Convexity Approx.**

6. Given the partial Dynamic Chart file **BcondynZ.xls**, do steps **9 Convexity of a Coupon Bond** and **10 Convexity of a Zero Coupon Bond**.

Chapter 5 US Yield Curve Dynamics

5.1 Dynamic Chart

How does the US yield curve change over time? What determines the volatility of changes in the yield curve? Are there differences in the volatility of short rates, medium rates, long rates, etc.? You can answer these questions and more using a *Dynamic Chart* of the yield curve, which is based on more than 33 years of monthly US zero-coupon, yield curve data.

I have made a major exception for this Excel model and provided the model already built. From the CD, open the Excel model **US Yield Cur Dyn - Dyn Chart.xls**. I will update this Excel model each year with the latest yield curve data and make it available for free in the "Free Samples" section of www.excelmodeling.com.

The step-by-step instructions below explain how it you can build this model. The dynamic chart uses “spinners,” which are up-arrow / down-arrow buttons that allow you to advance the yield curve graph from month to month. This allows you to see a dynamic "movie" or animation of the yield curve over time. Thus, you can directly observe the volatility of the yield curve and other dynamic properties. For details of what to look for, see the discussion below on "using the Excel model."

FIGURE 5.1 Excel Model of US Yield Curve Dynamics – Dynamic Chart.

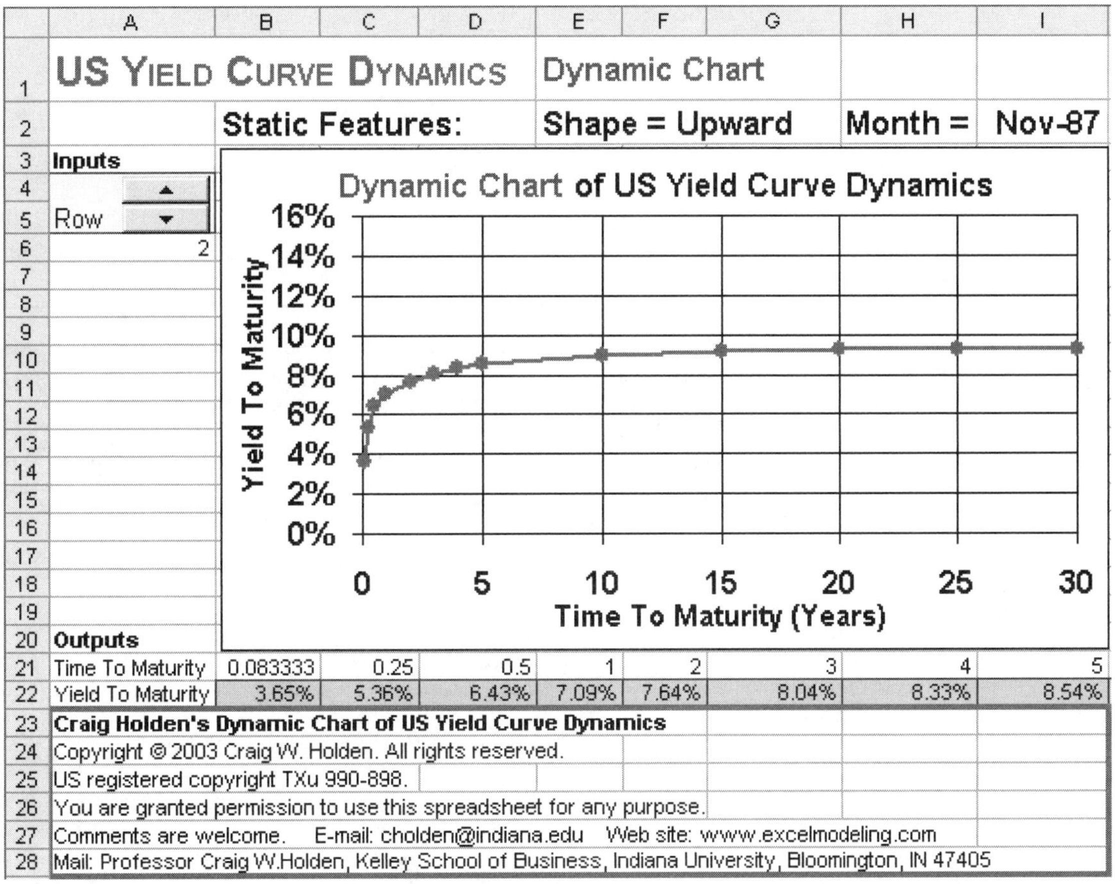

How To Build This Excel Model.

1. **Start with the Excel Model of the Yield Curve Database.** From the CD, open the Excel model **US Yield Cur Dyn - Database.xls**, which contains the yield curve database (see the figure below). Columns **Q**, **R**, and **S** contain three sets of titles for the dataset. Columns **T**, **U**, and **V** contain yield data for bond maturities of one month, three months, and six months (0.0833, 0.25, and 0.5 years, respectively). Columns **W** through **AG** contain yield data for bond maturities of 1, 2, 3, 4, 5, 7, 10, 15, 20, 25, and 30 years. Rows **2** through **9** contain examples of static features yield curve that can be observed from actual data in a particular month. For example, the yield curve is sometimes upward sloping (as it was in Nov 87) or downward sloping (in Nov 80) or flat (in Jan 70) or hump shaped (in Dec 78). Rows **10** through **413** contain monthly US zero-coupon, yield curve data from January 1970 through July 2003. For the period from January 1970 through December 1991, the database is based on the Bliss (1992) monthly estimates of the zero-coupon, yield curve.[1] For the period from January 1992 to July 2001,

[1] Bliss fits a parsimonious, nonlinear function that is capable of matching all of the empirically observed shapes of the zero-coupon, yield curve. For more details

the yield curve is directly observed from Treasury Bills and Strips in the *Wall Street Journal*. For the period from August 2001 to July 2003, the data is from the St Louis Fed's free online economic database FRED II at research.stlouisfed.org/fred2.

FIGURE 5.2 Excel Model of the Yield Curve Database.

	Q	R	S	T	U	V	W	X	Y
1				Time To Maturity	Time To Maturity	Time To Maturity	Time To Maturity	Time To Maturity	Time To Maturity
2	Title 1	Title 2	Title 3	0.0833	0.25	0.5	1	2	3
3	Static Features:	Shape = Upward	11/30/87	3.65%	5.36%	6.43%	7.09%	7.64%	8.04%
4	Static Features:	Shape = Downward	11/28/80	14.83%	14.60%	14.64%	14.17%	13.22%	12.75%
5	Static Features:	Shape = Flat	01/30/70	7.73%	8.00%	8.03%	7.98%	7.95%	7.94%
6	Static Features:	Shape = Hump	12/29/78	8.82%	9.48%	9.99%	10.18%	9.76%	9.40%
7	Static Features:	Level = Low	12/31/70	4.62%	4.91%	4.95%	5.02%	5.40%	5.69%
8	Static Features:	Level = High	10/30/81	12.65%	13.13%	13.53%	13.85%	14.01%	14.06%
9	Static Features:	Curvature = Little	12/29/72	4.93%	5.24%	5.44%	5.62%	5.86%	6.01%
10	Static Features:	Curvature = Lot	09/30/82	6.67%	7.87%	9.05%	10.29%	11.16%	11.43%
11	Monthly Dynamics:		01/30/70	7.73%	8.00%	8.03%	7.98%	7.95%	7.94%
12	Monthly Dynamics:		02/27/70	6.23%	6.99%	6.97%	6.96%	7.02%	7.04%
13	Monthly Dynamics:		03/31/70	6.33%	6.44%	6.53%	6.67%	6.85%	6.95%
14	Monthly Dynamics:		04/30/70	6.48%	7.03%	7.35%	7.50%	7.60%	7.67%
15	Monthly Dynamics:		05/29/70	6.22%	7.03%	7.28%	7.45%	7.58%	7.63%
16	Monthly Dynamics:		06/30/70	6.14%	6.47%	6.81%	7.17%	7.43%	7.53%
17	Monthly Dynamics:		07/31/70	6.32%	6.38%	6.55%	6.87%	7.19%	7.31%
18	Monthly Dynamics:		08/31/70	6.22%	6.38%	6.57%	6.83%	7.07%	7.18%
19	Monthly Dynamics:		09/30/70	5.32%	6.04%	6.49%	6.63%	6.64%	6.77%
20	Monthly Dynamics:		10/30/70	5.23%	5.91%	6.23%	6.33%	6.50%	6.69%
21	Monthly Dynamics:		11/30/70	4.86%	5.05%	5.11%	5.10%	5.29%	5.59%
22	Monthly Dynamics:		12/31/70	4.62%	4.91%	4.95%	5.02%	5.40%	5.69%
23	Monthly Dynamics:		01/29/71	4.04%	4.20%	4.23%	4.25%	4.68%	5.18%
24	Monthly Dynamics:		02/26/71	3.24%	3.45%	3.60%	3.77%	4.24%	4.75%
25	Monthly Dynamics:		03/31/71	3.45%	3.58%	3.69%	3.80%	4.11%	4.49%
26	Monthly Dynamics:		04/30/71	3.74%	4.02%	4.27%	4.63%	5.22%	5.61%
27	Monthly Dynamics:		05/28/71	4.28%	4.33%	4.51%	4.88%	5.41%	5.74%
28	Monthly Dynamics:		06/30/71	4.99%	5.09%	5.43%	5.98%	6.45%	6.61%
29	Monthly Dynamics:		07/30/71	5.07%	5.39%	5.70%	6.07%	6.45%	6.65%
30	Monthly Dynamics:		08/31/71	4.53%	4.39%	4.80%	5.22%	5.52%	5.69%
31	Monthly Dynamics:		09/30/71	4.31%	4.67%	4.98%	5.26%	5.50%	5.67%
32	Monthly Dynamics:		10/29/71	4.02%	4.37%	4.50%	4.59%	4.93%	5.25%
33	Monthly Dynamics:		11/30/71	4.14%	4.33%	4.51%	4.72%	5.01%	5.29%
34	Monthly Dynamics:		12/31/71	3.34%	3.72%	4.04%	4.33%	4.69%	5.03%

2. **Create a Spinner.** Click on **View | Toolbars | Forms** from the main menu. Look for the up-arrow / down-arrow button on the **Forms** toolbar (which will display the word "**Spinner**" if you hover the cursor over it) and click on it. Then draw the box for a spinner in the range **A4:A5**.

---

see Bliss, R., 1992, "Testing Term Structure Estimation Methods," Indiana University Discussion Paper #519.

3. **Create The Cell Link.** Right click on the spinner and a small menu pops up. Click on **Format Control** and a dialog box pops up. Click on the **Control** tab, then enter the cell link **A6** in the **Cell link** edit box, set the **Minimum value** equal to **2**, and click on **OK**. Test your spinner by clicking on the up-arrows and down-arrows of the spinner to see how it changes the value in the linked cell.

4. **Time To Maturity.** Reference the Database's Time To Maturity values in the range **T2:AG2**, by entering **=T2** in cell **B21** and copy it to the range **C21:O21**.

5. **Yield To Maturity.** Reference the Database's Yield To Maturity values using the Excel **HLOOKUP** function. The format is =HLOOKUP(Lookup value, Database, Row). The Lookup value is the corresponding Time To Maturity, the database is the range **Q2:AG600**, which has already been given the range name "**Database**," and the Row is the linked cell **A6**. Alternatively, if the lookup cell is blank, display the Excel's null value **NA**. Enter **=IF(HLOOKUP(B21,Database,$A$6)<0.0001,NA(), HLOOKUP(B21,Database,$A$6))** in cell **B22** and copy it across.

6. **Graph the Yield To Maturity by Time To Maturity.** Highlight the range **B21:O22**. Next choose **Insert | Chart** from the main menu. Select an **XY(Scatter)** chart type and make other selections to complete the Chart Wizard.

7. **Three Titles.** Reference the Database's three columns of Title values using the Excel **HLOOKUP** function. The format is same as above, except that the Lookup value will be the column headings ("Title 1", etc.) that we wish to reference. Enter **=HLOOKUP("Title 1",Database,$A$6)** in cell **B2**, **=HLOOKUP("Title 2",Database,$A$6)** in cell **E2**, and **=HLOOKUP("Title 3",Database,$A$6)** in cell **I2**. To format the date title, select cell **I2**, click on **Format | Cells,** click on **Date** in the Category list box, click on **Mar-98** format in the Type list box, and click on **OK**.

Using The Excel Model.

To run the Dynamic Chart, click on the up arrow of the spinner. The movie / animation begins with some background on the yield curve's static features. In the 33 year database we observe:

- four different **shapes**: upward-sloping, downward-sloping, flat, and hump-shaped,
- the overall **level** of the yield curve ranges from low to high, and
- the amount of **curvature** at the short end ranges from a little to a lot.

Keep clicking on the spinner and you will get to the section of the Dynamic Chart covering 33 years of the US yield curve history. This section shows the yield curve on a month by month basis. For example, the figure below shows the US yield curve in November 1970.

FIGURE 5.3 Excel Model of Month By Month History – Dynamic Chart.

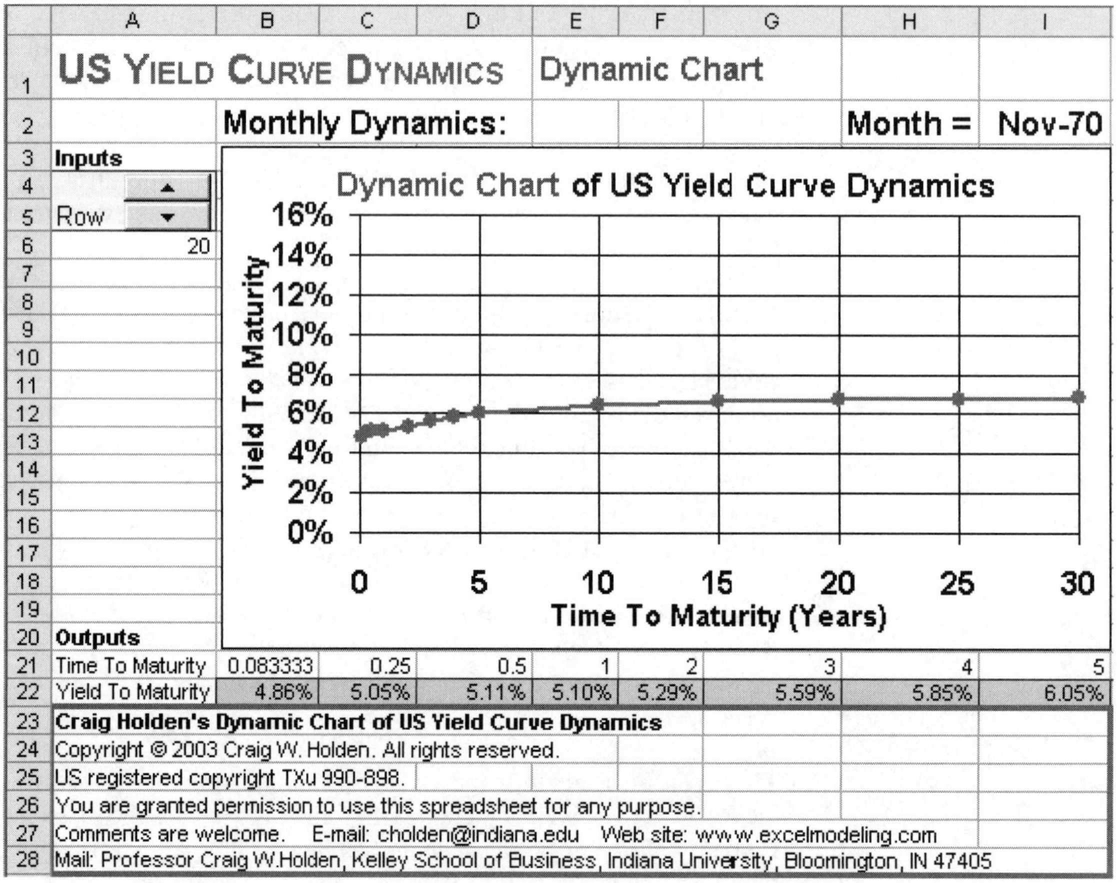

Keep clicking on the spinner and you will see the yield curve move around over time. By observing this movie / animation, you should be able to recognize the following key **dynamic** properties of the yield curve:

- short rates (the 0 to 5 year piece of the yield curve) are more volatile than long rates (the 15 to 30 year piece),
- the overall volatility of the yield curve is higher when the level is higher (especially in the early 80's), and
- sometimes there are sharp reactions to government intervention.

As an example of the later, consider what happened in 1980. The figure below shows the yield curve in January 1980.

FIGURE 5.4 Excel Model Showing The Yield Curve in January 1980.

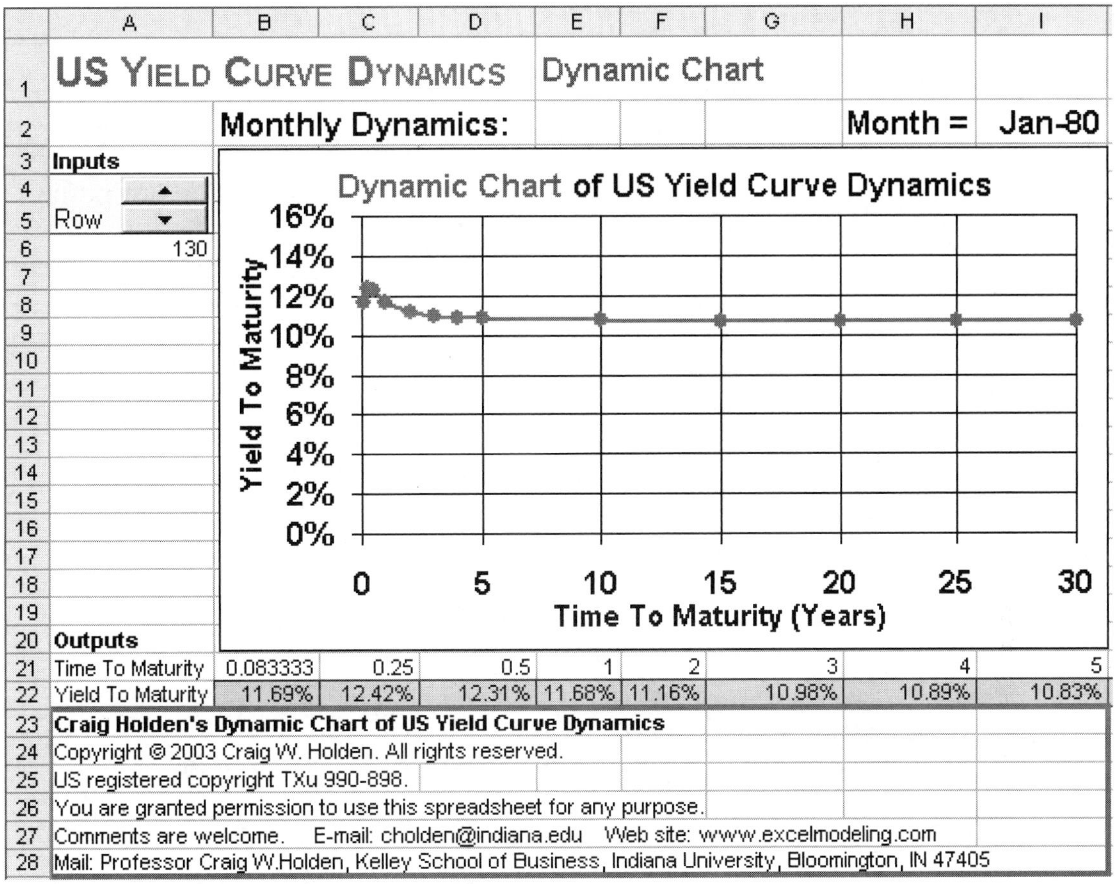

Short rates were around 12% and long rates were at 10.7%. President Jimmy Carter was running for re-election. He wished to manipulate the election year economy to make it better for his re-election bid. His strategy for doing this was to impose credit controls on the banking system. Click on the spinner to see what the reaction of the financial market was.

FIGURE 5.5 Excel Model Showing The Yield Curve in March 1980.

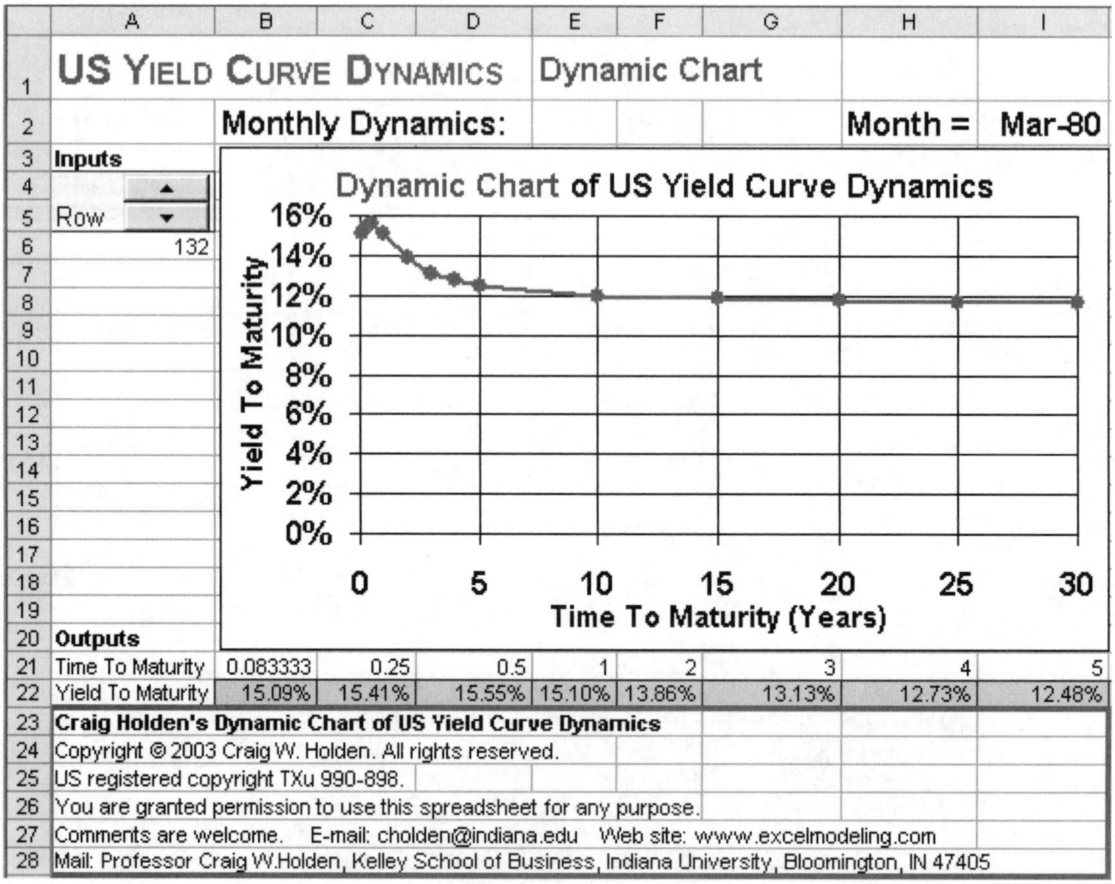

In two months time, the short rate when up to 15.5%, an increase of 3.5%! What a disaster! This was the opposite of the reaction the Carter had intended. Notice that long rates when up to 11.7%, an increase of only 1%. Apparently, the market expected that this intervention would only be a short-lived phenomenon. Carter quickly realized what a big political mistake he had made and announced that the credit controls were being dropped. Click on the spinner to see what the reaction of the financial market was.

FIGURE 5.6 Excel Model Showing The Yield Curve in April 1980.

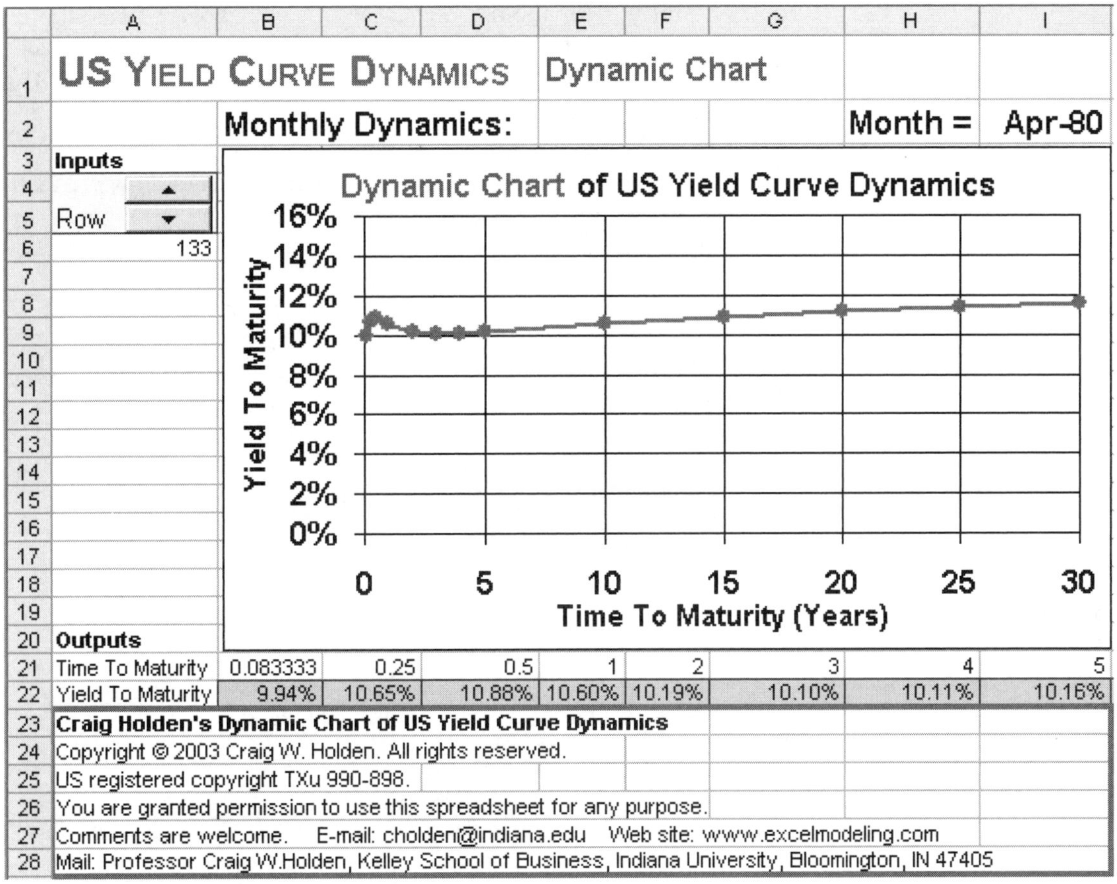

Short rates dropped to 10.9%! A drop of 4.6% in one month! The high interest rates went away, but the political damage was done. This is the single biggest change in the yield curve in 33 years.

Problems

Skill-Building Problems.

1. How volatile are short rates versus medium rates versus long rates?

   (a.) Get a visual sense of the answer to this question by clicking on the spinner (up/down arrow) to run through all of the years of US Yield Curve history in the database.

   (b.) Calculate the variance of the time series of: (i) one-month yields, (ii) five-year yields, (iii) fifteen-year yields, and (iv) thirty year yields. Use Excel's VAR function to calculate the variance of the yields in columns S, Z, AB, and AE in the file **US Yield Cur Dyn - Dyn Chart.xls**.

2. Determine the relationship between the volatility of the yield curve and the level of the yield curve. Specifically, for each five year time period (70-74,

75-79, 80-84, etc.) calculate the variance and the average level of the time series of: (i) one-month yields, (ii) five-year yields, (iii) fifteen-year yields, and (iv) thirty year yields. Use Excel's VAR and AVERAGE functions to calculate the variance and the average of five-year ranges of the yields in columns **T**, **AA**, **AC**, and **AG** in the file **US Yield Cur Dyn - Dyn Chart.xls**. For example:

- The 70-74 time series of one-month yields is in the range **T11-T70**.
- The 75-79 time series of one-month yields is in the range **T71-T130**.
- The 80-84 time series of one-month yields is in the range **T131-T190**.
- And so on.

Summarize what you have learned from this analysis.

Live In-class Problems.

3. Given the partial Dynamic Chart file **YcdyndyZ.xls**, complete steps **4 Time To Maturity** and **5 Yield To Maturity**.

PART 2 STOCKS / SECURITY ANALYSIS

Chapter 6 Portfolio Optimization

6.1 Two Assets

Problem. The riskless rate is 6.0%. Risky Asset 1 has a mean return of 14.0% and a standard deviation of 20.0%. Risky Asset 2 has a mean return of 8.0% and a standard deviation of 15.0%. The correlation between Risky Asset 1 and 2 is 0.0%. Graph the Efficient Trade-Off Line and the Risky Asset Trade-Off Curve.

Solution Strategy. Determine the Risky Asset Trade-Off Curve for two-asset portfolios by varying the proportion in the first asset and calculating the resulting portfolio's standard deviation and expected return. Then, determine the Optimal Combination of Risky Assets by calculating the optimal proportion in the first asset and calculating the corresponding standard deviation and expected return. Finally, determine the Efficient Trade-Off Line by varying the amount in the Optimal Combination and calculating the corresponding standard deviation and expected return. Then graph everything.

FIGURE 6.1 Excel Model of Portfolio Optimization - Two Assets

	A	B	C	D	E
1	PORTFOLIO OPTIMIZATION				Two Assets
2				Exp Ret	
3	Inputs	Expected	Standard	- Riskless	
4		Return	Deviation	[E(r) - r$_f$]	
5	Riskless Rate (r)	6.0%	0.0%	0.0%	
6	Risky Asset 1	14.0%	20.0%	8.0%	
7	Risky Asset 2	8.0%	15.0%	2.0%	
8	Correlation (ρ)		0.0%		

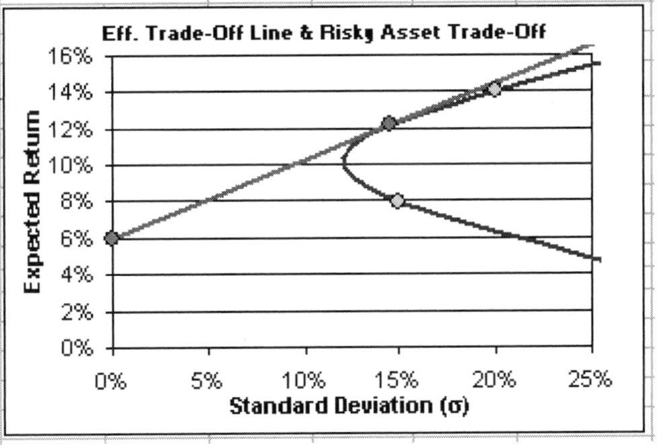

How To Build This Excel Model.

1. **Inputs.** Enter the inputs described above into the ranges **B5:B7** and **C6:C8**.

2. **Expected Return – Riskless Rate.** Calculate the Expected Return minus the Riskless Rate by entering **=B5-$B$5** in cell **D5** and copying that cell to the range **D6:D7**.

FIGURE 6.2 Excel Model Details of Portfolio Optimization - Two Assets

	A	B	C	D	E
18	**Outputs**			Risk - Ret	Efficient
19		Proportion		Trade-off	Trade-off
20		in Risky	(x-axis)	Curve	Line
21		Asset 1 or	Standard	Expected	Expected
22		Opt Comb	Deviation	Return	Return
23	Trade-off Curve	-60.0%	26.8%	4.4%	
24	Trade-off Curve	-50.0%	24.6%	5.0%	
25	Trade-off Curve	-40.0%	22.5%	5.6%	
26	Trade-off Curve	-30.0%	20.4%	6.2%	
27	Trade-off Curve	-20.0%	18.4%	6.8%	
28	Trade-off Curve	-10.0%	16.6%	7.4%	
29	Trade-off Curve	0.0%	15.0%	8.0%	
30	Trade-off Curve	10.0%	13.6%	8.6%	
31	Trade-off Curve	20.0%	12.6%	9.2%	
32	Trade-off Curve	30.0%	12.1%	9.8%	
33	Trade-off Curve	40.0%	12.0%	10.4%	
34	Trade-off Curve	50.0%	12.5%	11.0%	
35	Trade-off Curve	60.0%	13.4%	11.6%	
36	Trade-off Curve	70.0%	14.7%	12.2%	
37	Trade-off Curve	80.0%	16.3%	12.8%	
38	Trade-off Curve	90.0%	18.1%	13.4%	
39	Trade-off Curve	100.0%	20.0%	14.0%	
40	Trade-off Curve	110.0%	22.1%	14.6%	
41	Trade-off Curve	120.0%	24.2%	15.2%	
42	Trade-off Curve	130.0%	26.4%	15.8%	
43	Trade-off Curve	140.0%	28.6%	16.4%	
44	Optimal Comb.	69.2%	14.6%		12.2%
45	Eff Trade-off Lin	0.0%	0.0%		6.0%
46	Eff Trade-off Lin	100.0%	14.6%		12.2%
47	Eff Trade-off Lin	200.0%	29.2%		18.3%

3. **Proportion in Risky Asset 1.** In order graph the Risky Asset Trade-off Curve, we need to evaluate a wide range of values (-60.0% to 140%) for the Proportion in Risky Asset 1. Enter **–60.0%** in cell **B23**, **–50.0%** in cell **B24**, and highlight the range **B23:B24**. Then hover the cursor over the lower right corner and it turns to a "fill handle" (which looks like a "+" sign). Drag the fill handle down to **B43**.

4. **Standard Deviation.** The x-axis of our graph is the portfolio's standard deviation, which is calculated by the formula

   $$\sigma = \sqrt{w^2\sigma_1^2 + (1-w)^2\sigma_2^2 + 2w(1-w)\rho\sigma_1\sigma_2}\,.$$

   Enter **=SQRT(B23^2*$C$6^2+(1-B23)^2*$C$7^2 +2*B23*(1-B23)*$C$8*$C$6*$C$7)** in cell **C23** and copy the cell to the range **C24:C43**.

5. **Expected Return.** The formula for a portfolio's expected return is $E(r) = wE(r_1) + (1-w)E(r_2)$. Enter **=B23*$B$6+(1-B23)*$B$7** in cell **D23** and copy the cell to the range **D24:D43**.

6. **Optimal Combination of Risky Assets.** Using the notation that $E_1 = E(r_1) - r_f$ and $E_2 = E(r_2) - r_f$, then the formula for the optimal proportion in the first asset is $w_1 = \left(E_1\sigma_2^2 - E_2\rho\sigma_1\sigma_2\right) / \left(E_1\sigma_2^2 + E_2\sigma_1^2 - (E_1 + E_2)\rho\sigma_1\sigma_2\right)$. In cell **B44**, enter **=(D6*C7^2-D7*C8*C6*C7) /(D6*C7^2+D7*C6^2-(D6+D7)*C8*C6*C7)** Calculate the corresponding Mean and Standard Deviation by copying the range **C43:D43** to the range **C44:D44**. We want to create a separate column for the Efficient Trade-Off Line, so move the formula in cell **D44** to cell **E44**. To do this, select cell **D44**, click on **Edit Cut**, select cell **E44**, and click on **Edit Paste**.

7. **Efficient Trade-Off Line.** The Efficient Trade-Off Line is a combination of the Riskless Asset and the Risky Asset Optimal Combination. It can be calculated as follows:

   - Enter **0.0%** in cell **B45**, **100.0%** in cell **B46**, and **200.0%** in cell **B47**.

   - Since the Riskless Asset has a standard deviation of zero, the standard deviation formula simplifies to $\sigma = w\sigma_T$, where σ_T = standard deviation of the Optimal Combination of Risky Assets (or Tangent Portfolio). Enter **=B45*$C$44** in cell **C45** and copy the cell to the range **C46:C47**.

   - The Expected Return formula is $E(r) = wE(r_T) + (1-w)r_f$, were $E(r_T)$ expected return of the Tangent Portfolio. Enter **=$E$44*B45+$B$5*(1-B45)** in cell **E45** and copy to the range **E46:E47**.

8. **Create The Graph.** Highlight the range **C23:E47** and then choose **Insert Chart** from the main menu. Select an **XY(Scatter)** chart type and make other selections to complete the Chart Wizard. Place the graph in the range **E2:J16**.

9. **(Optional) Formatting The Graph.** Here are some tips to make the chart look attractive:

   - Click on one of the Chart curves, then click on **Format Selected Data Series**. In the Format Data Series dialog box under the **Patterns** tab, select **None** for the Marker and click on **OK**. Repeat for the other curve.

   - Highlight individual points, such as the Riskless Asset, Tangent Portfolio, and Risky Assets 1 and 2, by clicking on a chart curve, then click a second time on an individual point (the four-way arrows symbol appears), then click on **Format Selected Data Point**. In the Format Data Point dialog box under the **Patterns** tab under the Marker, select a market Style, Foreground Color, Background Color, and increase the size to **8** pts and click on **OK**.

- Click on the x-axis, then click on **Format Selected Axis**. In the Format Axis dialog box under the **Scale** tab, enter **0.25** for the Maximum and click on **OK**.

Investors prefer points on the graph that yield higher mean returns (further "North") and lower standard deviations (further "West"). The graph shows that best combinations of high return and low risk (furthest in the "Northwest" direction) are given by the Efficient Trade-Off Line. Better combinations are simply not feasible. Since the Efficient Trade-Off Line is a combination of the Riskless Asset and a Tangent Portfolio, then all investors prefer to invest *only* in the Riskless Asset and a Tangent Portfolio.

6.2 Many Assets

Suppose that you had N risky assets, rather than just two risky assets. How would you calculate the Efficient Trade-Off Line and the Risky Asset Trade-Off Curve in this case? It turns out that it is much easier to handle N risky assets in an Excel model than any other way. The figure below shows the results of the N=5 risky assets case, including a bar chart of the portfolio weights of the optimal (tangent) portfolio.

FIGURE 6.3 Excel Model of Portfolio Optimization - Many Assets.

	A	B	C	D	E	F
1	PORTFOLIO OPTIMIZATION					Many Assets
2					One plus	
3	**Inputs**		Expected	Standard	Exp Ret	
4			Return	Deviation	[1 + E(r)]	Ones
5	Riskless Rate (r)		4.0%	0.0%	104.0%	
6	Risky Asset 1		8.0%	20.0%	108.0%	100.0%
7	Risky Asset 2		9.0%	20.0%	109.0%	100.0%
8	Risky Asset 3		10.0%	20.0%	110.0%	100.0%
9	Risky Asset 4		11.0%	20.0%	111.0%	100.0%
10	Risky Asset 5		12.0%	20.0%	112.0%	100.0%
11						
12			Correlations			
13		1	2	3	4	5
14	1	100.0%	0.0%	0.0%	0.0%	0.0%
15	2	0.0%	100.0%	0.0%	0.0%	0.0%
16	3	0.0%	0.0%	100.0%	0.0%	0.0%
17	4	0.0%	0.0%	0.0%	100.0%	0.0%
18	5	0.0%	0.0%	0.0%	0.0%	100.0%
19						
20			Standard Deviations			
21		1	2	3	4	5
22		20.0%	20.0%	20.0%	20.0%	20.0%
23						
24			Variances and Covariances			
25		1	2	3	4	5
26	1	4.00%	0.00%	0.00%	0.00%	0.00%
27	2	0.00%	4.00%	0.00%	0.00%	0.00%
28	3	0.00%	0.00%	4.00%	0.00%	0.00%
29	4	0.00%	0.00%	0.00%	4.00%	0.00%
30	5	0.00%	0.00%	0.00%	0.00%	4.00%
31						
32						
33						
34						

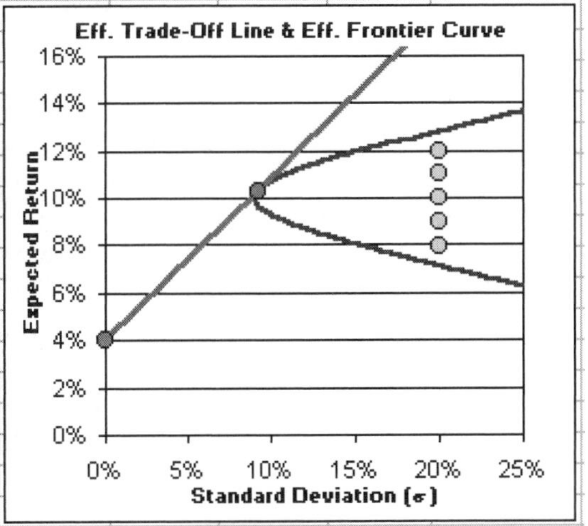

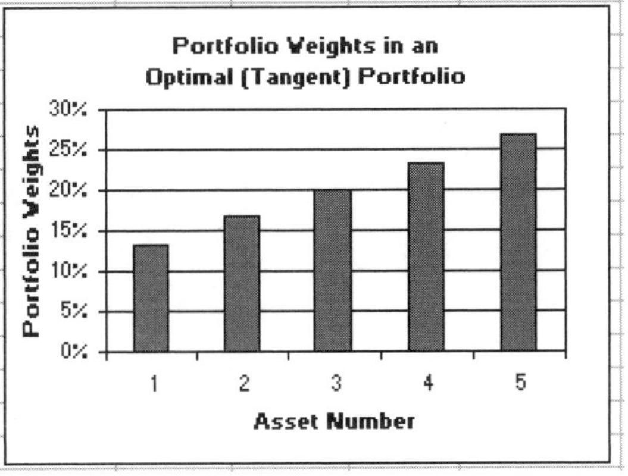

How To Build This Excel Model.

1. **Inputs.** Enter the expected return inputs into the range **C5:C10**, the standard deviation inputs into the range **D6:D10**, the correlation inputs in the triangular range from **B15** to **B18** to **E18**, and **0.0%** in the cell **D5**.

2. **One plus the Expected Return and 100%.** It will be useful to have a column based on one plus the expected return and another column with just the number 100%. Enter **=1+C5** in cell **E5** and copy the cell to the range **E6:E10**. Enter **100%** in cell **F6** and copy the cell to the range **F7:F10**.

3. **Fill Out the Correlations Table (Matrix).** The correlations table (matrix) from **B14:F18** has a simple structure. All of the elements on the diagonal represent the correlation of an asset return with itself. For example, **B14** is the correlation of the Asset 1 return with the Asset 1 return, which is one. **C15** is the correlation of Asset 2 with 2, and so on. Enter **100.0%** into the diagonal cells from **B14** to **F18**. The off-diagonal cells in the *upper* triangular

range from **C14** to **F14** to **F17** are the "mirror image" of the *lower* triangular range from **B15** to **B18** to **E18**. In other words, the correlation of Asset 2 with Asset 1 in **C14** is equal to the correlation of Asset 1 with Asset 2 in **B15**. Enter **=B15** in cell **C14**, **=B16** in **D14**, **=B17** in **E14**, etc. Each cell of the *upper* triangular range from **C14** to **F14** to **F17** should be set equal to its mirror image cell in the *lower* triangular range from **B15** to **B18** to **E18**.

4. **Transposed Standard Deviations.** In addition to the standard deviation input range which runs vertically from top to bottom, it will be useful to have a range of standard deviations that runs horizontally from left-to-right. This can be done easily by using one of Excel's **Matrix** commands to transpose a range. Highlight the range **B22:F22**. Then, type **=TRANSPOSE(D6:D10)**, hold down the **Shift** and **Control** buttons simultaneously, and while continuing to hold them down, press **Enter**. The resulting formula should have braces around it **{=TRANSPOSE(D6:D10)}**.

5. **Variances and Covariance's Table (Matrix).** The Variances and Covariances Table (Matrix) in the range **B26:F30** has a simple structure. All of the elements on the diagonal represent the covariance of an asset return with itself, which equals the variance. For example, **B26** is the covariance of the Asset 1 return with the Asset 1 return, which equals the variance of asset 1. **C27** is the variance of Asset 2, and so on. The off-diagonal cells are covariances. For example, **C26** is the covariance of the Asset 1 return with the Asset 2 return and is calculated with the formula for the Covariance(Asset 1, Asset 2) = (Std Dev 1) * (Std Dev 2) * Correlation(Asset 1, Asset 2). Enter **=C$22*$D6*C14** in cell **C26**. Be very careful to enter the **$** absolute references exactly right. Then copy **C26** to the range **B26:F30**.

FIGURE 6.4 Excel Model Details of Portfolio Optimization - Many Assets.

	A	B	C	D	E	F	G	H	I	J
36	**Outputs**									
37		A	125							
38		B	137.5							
39		C.	151.275		Efficient	Efficient				
40		Delta	3.1E+00		Frontier	Trade-off	Individual			
41		Gamma	0.13333		Curve	Line	Asset	Optimal Combination		
42				Standard	Expected	Expected	Expected	of Risky Assets		
43			Index	Deviation	Return	Return	Return	(Tangent Portfolio)		
44	Risky Asset 1			20.0%			8.0%	1	13.33%	
45	Risky Asset 2			20.0%			9.0%	2	16.67%	
46	Risky Asset 3			20.0%			10.0%	3	20.00%	
47	Risky Asset 4			20.0%			11.0%	4	23.33%	
48	Risky Asset 5			20.0%			12.0%	5	26.67%	
49	Trade-off Curve		0	25.00%	6.31%					
50	Trade-off Curve		1	22.84%	6.68%					
51	Trade-off Curve		2	20.71%	7.05%					
52	Trade-off Curve		3	18.63%	7.42%					
53	Trade-off Curve		4	16.62%	7.79%					
54	Trade-off Curve		5	14.71%	8.15%					
55	Trade-off Curve		6	12.93%	8.52%					
56	Trade-off Curve		7	11.36%	8.89%					
57	Trade-off Curve		8	10.09%	9.26%					
58	Trade-off Curve		9	9.24%	9.63%					
59	Trade-off Curve		10	8.94%	10.00%					
60	Trade-off Curve		11	9.24%	10.37%					
61	Trade-off Curve		12	10.09%	10.74%					
62	Trade-off Curve		13	11.36%	11.11%					
63	Trade-off Curve		14	12.93%	11.48%					
64	Trade-off Curve		15	14.71%	11.85%					
65	Trade-off Curve		16	16.62%	12.21%					
66	Trade-off Curve		17	18.63%	12.58%					
67	Trade-off Curve		18	20.71%	12.95%					
68	Trade-off Curve		19	22.84%	13.32%					
69	Trade-off Curve		20	25.00%	13.69%					
70	Optimal Comb.			9.2%		10.3%				
71	Eff Trade-off Line		0.0%	0.0%		4.0%				
72	Eff Trade-off Line		100.0%	9.2%		10.3%				
73	Eff Trade-off Line		200.0%	18.4%		16.7%				

6. **Hyperbola Coefficients.** In a Mean vs. Standard Deviation graph, the Efficient Frontier is a hyperbola. The exact location of the hyperbola is uniquely determined by three coefficients, unimaginatively called A, B, and C. The derivation of the formulas can be found in Merton (1972).[2] They are easy to implement using Excel's **matrix** functions. In each case, you type the formula and then, hold down the **Shift** and **Control** buttons simultaneously, and while continuing to hold them down, press **Enter**.

---

[2] See Robert C. Merton, "An Analytic Derivation of the Efficient Portfolio Frontier," *Journal of Financial and Quantitative Analysis*, September 1972, pp. 1851-72. His article uses slightly different notation.

- For A: **=MMULT(MMULT(TRANSPOSE(F6:F10), MINVERSE(B26:F30)),F6:F10)** in cell **C37**.

- For B: **=MMULT(MMULT(TRANSPOSE(F6:F10), MINVERSE(B26:F30)),E6:E10)** in cell **C38**.

- For C: **=MMULT(MMULT(TRANSPOSE(E6:E10), MINVERSE(B26:F30)),E6:E10)** in cell **C39**.

7. **Miscellaneous.** It will simplify matters to create range names for various cells. Put the cursor in cell **C37**, click on **Insert Name Define**, enter the name "A" and click on **OK.** Repeat this procedure to give cell **C38** the name "**B**", give cell **C39** the name "**C.**" (Excel does not accept plain "C"), give cell **C40** the name "**Delta**", give cell **C41** the name "**Gamma**", and give cell **E5** the name "**R.**" (again, Excel does not accept plain "**R**"). Enter **=A*C.-(B^2)** in cell **C40** and enter **=1/(B-A*R.)** in cell **C41**. Some restrictions do apply on the range of permissible input values. The variable Delta must always be positive or else the calculations will blow-up or produce nonsense results. Simply avoid entering large negative correlations for multiple assets and this problem will be taken care of.

8. **Individual Risky Assets.** In order to add the individual risky assets to the graph, reference their individual standard deviations and expected returns. Enter **=D6** in cell **D44** and copy down to the range **D45:D48**. Enter **=C6** in cell **G44** and copy down to the range **G45:G48**.

9. **Expected Return.** Using the three Hyperbola coefficients, we can solve for the expected return on the upper and lower branches of the hyperbola which correspond to a standard deviation of **25%** and then fill in intermediate values in order to generate the Efficient Frontier graph.

   - For the upper branch, enter **=(2*B-(4*B^2-4*A*(C.-(0.25^2)*Delta))^(0.5))/(2*A)-1** in cell **E49**.

   - For the lower branch, enter **=(2*B+(4*B^2-4*A*(C.-(0.25^2)*Delta))^(0.5))/(2*A)-1** in cell **E69**.

   - Fill out in index for expected return by entering **0** in cell **C49**, entering **1** in cell **C50**, selecting the range **C49:C50**, and dragging the fill handle (in the lower right corner) down the range **C51:C69**.

   - Fill in the intermediate values by entering **=$E$49+($E$69-$E$49)*(C50/20)** in cell **E50** and copying the cell down the range **E51:E68**.

10. **Standard Deviation.** Again using the three Hyperbola coefficients, we can solve for the Efficient Frontier standard deviation which corresponds to any particular value of expected return. Enter **=((A*(1+E49)^2-(2*B*(1+E49))+C.)/(A*C.-(B^2)))^(1/2)** in cell **D49** and copy it down the range **D50:D69**.

11. **Tangent Portfolio.** The Optimal Combination of Risky Assets (or Tangent Portfolio) can be calculated using Excel's **matrix** functions. In each case, you type the formula and then, hold down the **Shift** and **Control** buttons simultaneously, and while continuing to hold them down, press **Enter**.

    - For the portfolio weights: Select the range **I44:I48**, then type **=Gamma*MMULT(MINVERSE(B26:F30),(E6:E10-R.*F6:F10))**

    - For expected returns: enter **=MMULT(TRANSPOSE(I44:I48),E6:E10)-1** in cell **F70**.

    - For standard deviations: enter **=SQRT(MMULT(MMULT(TRANSPOSE(I44:I48),B26:F30),I44:I48))** in cell **D70**.

12. **Efficient Trade-Off Line.** The Efficient Trade-Off Line is a combination of the Riskless Asset and the Risky Asset Optimal Combination. It can be calculated as follows:

    - Enter **0.0%** in cell **C71**, **100.0%** in cell **C72**, and **200.0%** in cell **C73**.

    - As before, the standard deviation formula simplifies to $\sigma = w\sigma_T$. Enter **=C71*$D$70** in cell **D71** and copy the cell to the range **D72:D73**.

    - The Expected Return formula is $E(r) = wE(r_T) + (1-w)r_f$. Enter **=$F$70*C71+$C$5*(1-C71)** in cell **F71** and copy to the range **F72:F73**.

13. **Create And Locate The Graphs.** Highlight the range **D44:G73** and then choose **Insert Chart** from the main menu. Select an **XY(Scatter)** chart type and make other selections to complete the Chart Wizard. Place the graph in the range **G3:K19**. Highlight the range **I44:I48** and then choose **Insert Chart** from the main menu. Select a **Column** chart type and make other selections to complete the Chart Wizard. Place the graph in the range **G21:K34**. Optionally, one can format the graph as discussed in the previous section.

The graphs show several interesting things. First, look at the Efficient Frontier Curve. At a standard deviation of 20% (same as all of the individual assets), it is possible to achieve a mean return of nearly 13% despite the fact that 12% is the highest mean return offered by any individual asset. How is this possible? The answer is that it is possible to sell (or short sell) low mean return assets and use the proceeds to invest in high mean return assets. Said differently, put a negative portfolio weight (short sell) in low mean assets and "more than 100%" in high mean assets.

Second, the bar chart shows that the optimal (tangent) portfolio represents a trade-off between exploiting higher means vs. lowering risk by diversifying (e.g., spreading the investment across assets). On the one hand it is desirable to put a larger portfolio weight in those assets with higher mean assets (#4 and #5 in this example). On the other hand, spreading assets more (getting closer to 20% per each of the five risky assets) would lower the overall risk of the portfolio. Hence, the optimal portfolio does not put 100% in the high mean assets, nor does it put 20% in each asset, but instead finds the best trade-off possible between theses two goals.

Third, you should be delighted to find any mispriced assets, because these are delightful investment opportunities for you. Indeed, many investors spend money to collect information (do security analysis) which identifies mispriced assets. The bar chart shows you how to optimally exploit any mispriced assets that you find. Below is a list of experiments that you might wish to perform. Notice as you perform these experiments that the optimal portfolio exploits mispriced assets to the *appropriate degree*, but still makes the fundamental trade-off between gaining higher means vs. lowering risk by diversifying.

- What happens when an individual asset is *underpriced* (high mean return)?
- What happens when an individual asset is *overpriced* (low mean return)?
- Is it possible for a very low mean return to optimally generate a negative weight (short sell)?
- What happens when an individual asset is *mispriced* due to a low standard deviation?
- What happens when an individual asset is *mispriced* due to a high standard deviation?
- What happens when the riskless rate is lowered?
- What happens when the riskless rate is raised?
- What happens when risky assets 1 and 2 have a 99% correlation?

Fourth, in general terms the optimal (tangent) portfolio is *not* the same as the market portfolio. Each individual investor should determine his or her *own tangent portfolio* based on his or her own beliefs about asset means, standard deviations, and correlations. If an individual investor believes that a particular asset is mispriced, then this belief should be optimally exploited. Only under the special conditions and the restrictive assumptions of CAPM theory would the tangent portfolio also be the market portfolio.

Here are some additional projects / enhancements you can do:

- Obtain historical data for different asset classes (and/or assets in different countries) and calculate the means, standard deviations, and correlations. Then, forecast future means, standard deviations, and correlations using the historical data as your starting point, but making appropriate adjustments. Input those means, standard deviations, and correlations into the Excel model in order to determine the optimal portfolio. If you have monthly data, you can switch from annual returns to monthly returns by simply entering the appropriate monthly returns numbers and then rescaling the graph appropriately (see how to format the graph scale in the previous section).

- Create a *Dynamic Chart* by adding "spinners" (see other *Dynamic Charts* for examples of how to do this)

- Expand the number of risky assets to any number that you want. For example, expanding to six risky assets simply involves adding a sixth: (1) expected return in cell **C11**, (2) standard deviation in cell **D11**, (3) one plus expected return in cell **E11**, (4) **100%** in cell **F11**, (5) row of correlations in the range **B19:F19** and column in the range **G14:G19**, (6) row of variances / covariances in the range **B31:F31** and column in the range **G26:G31**. Finally, reenter all of the matrix functions changing their references to the expanded ranges. Specifically, reenter matrix functions for: transposed standard deviations, A, B, C, tangent portfolio weights, tangent portfolio expected return, and tangent portfolio standard deviation.

6.3 Dynamic Chart

If you increased the expected return of a risky asset, what would happen to the efficient frontier curve or the efficient trade-off line (tangent line)? What would happen if you increased the standard deviation of a risky asset? What would happen if you increased the correlation between risky assets? You can answer these questions and more by creating a *Dynamic Chart* using "spinners." Spinners are up-arrow / down-arrow buttons that allow you to easily change the inputs to the model with the click of a mouse. Then Excel recalculates the model and instantly redraws the model outputs on the graph.

FIGURE 6.5 Excel Model of Portfolio Optimization - Dynamic Chart.

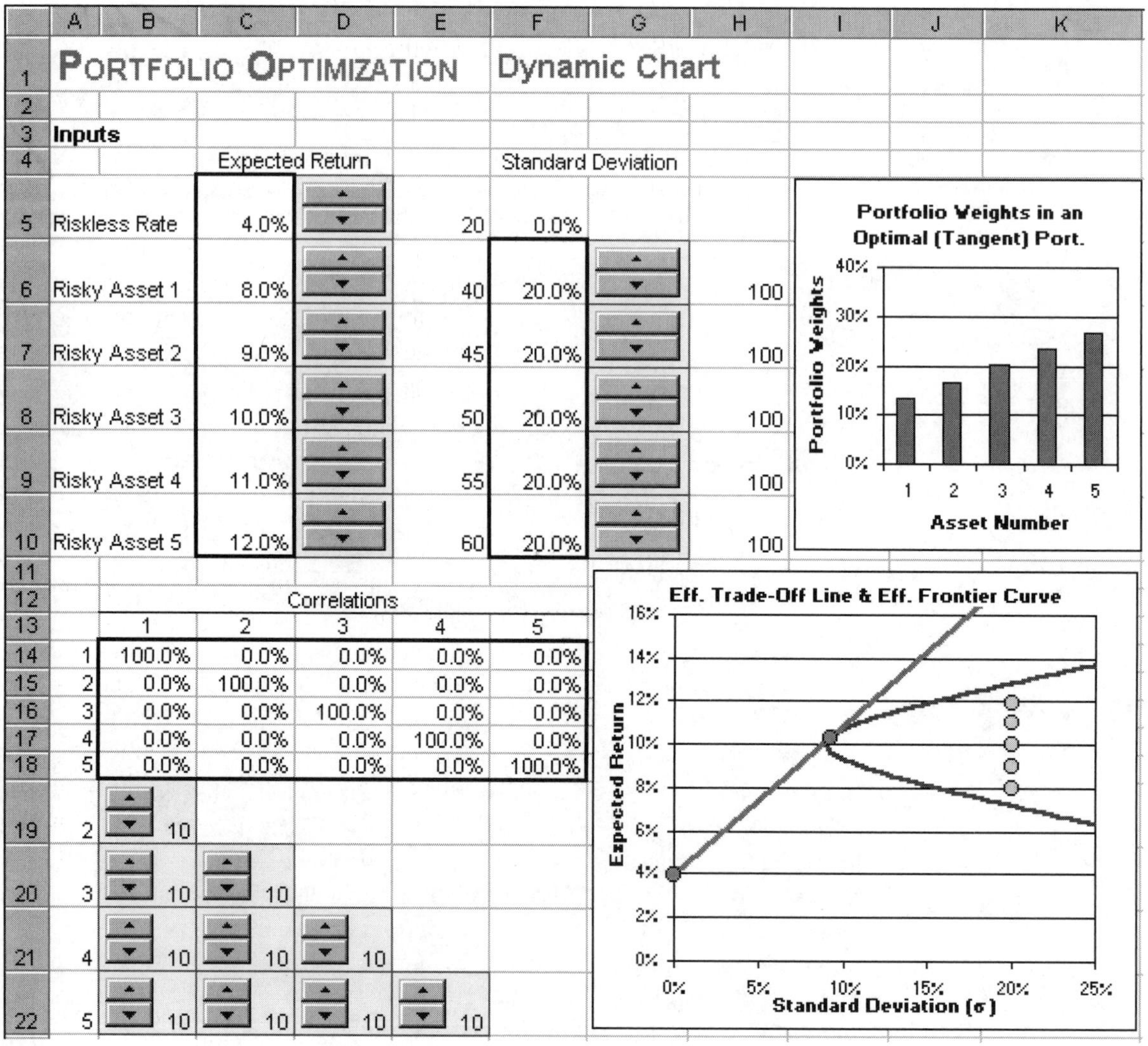

How To Build This Excel Model.

1. **Start with the Many Assets Excel Model, Add Rows, and Rearrange A Bit.** Open the Excel model that you created for Portfolio Optimization - Many Assets and immediately save the file under a new name using the **File Save As** command. Move both of the graphs out of the way. Select each graph and drag them below row **22** and to the right of column **H**. Add four rows by selecting the range **A19:A22**, clicking on **Insert**, **Rows**. Select the range **E2:F10** and drag the range (hover the cursor over the lower highlighted line, click on the left mouse button, and hold it down while you move it) to cell **H26**. Select the range **D5:D10** and drag the range to cell **F5**.

2. **Increase Row Height for the Spinners.** Select the range **A5:A10**. Then click on **Format Row Height** from the main menu. Enter a height of **30** and click on **OK**. Select the range **A19:A22**. Then click on **Format Row Height** from the main menu. Enter a height of **30** and click on **OK**.

3. **Display the Forms Toolbar.** Select **View Toolbars Forms** from the main menu.

4. **Create the Spinners.** Look for the up-arrow / down-arrow button on the **Forms** toolbar (which will display the word "**Spinner**" if you hover the cursor over it) and click on it. Then draw the box for a spinner from the upper left corner of cell **D5** down to the lower right corner of the cell. Then a spinner appears in the cell **D5**. Right click on the spinner (press the right mouse button while the cursor is above the spinner) and a small menu pops up. Click on **Copy**. Then select the cell **D6** and click on **Paste**. This creates an identical spinner in the cell **D6**. Repeat the process four times more in cells **D7**, **D8**, **D9**, and **D10**. Repeat the process five times more in cells **G6**, **G7**, **G8**, **G9**, and **G10**. Click on the spinner button on the **Forms** toolbar and draw the box for a spinner covering the *left half* of cell **B19**. Click on Copy. Then select the cell **B20** and click on **Paste**. Repeat the process eight times more in cells **B21**, **B22**, **C20**, **C21**, **C22**, **D21**, **D22**, and **E22**.

5. **Create The Cell Links.** Right click on the first spinner in the cell **D5** and a small menu pops up. Click on **Format Control** and a dialog box pops up. Click on the **Control** tab, then enter the cell link **E5** in the **Cell link** edit box and click on **OK**. Repeat this procedure for the spinners in the range **D6:D10** and in the range **G6:G10** to link each one to the cell immediately to the right of each spinner. Right click on the spinner in the cell **B19** and a small menu pops up. Click on **Format Control** and a dialog box pops up. Click on the **Control** tab, then enter the *same cell* **B19** as the cell link in the **Cell link** edit box and click on **OK**. Repeat this *same cell* procedure for the spinners in the range **B20:B22** and in the triangle **C20** to **C22** to **E22** (linking each one to the same cell as the spinner). Test your spinners by clicking on the up-arrows and down-arrows of the spinners to see how they change the values in the linked cells.

6. **Create Scaled Inputs.** The values in the linked cells are always integers, but they can be scaled appropriately to the problem at hand. In cell **C5**, enter **=E5/500** and copy this cell to the range **C6:C10** and to the range **F6:F10**. In cell **B15**, enter **=B19/10-1** and copy the cell to the range **B16:B18** and to the triangle **C16** to **C18** to **E18**.

7. **Relocate The Graphs.** Move both of the graphs back into place. Move the Efficient Frontier graph into the range **G11:K22**. Move the Portfolio Weights graph into the range **I5:K10**.

Your *Dynamic Chart* allows you to change Portfolio Optimization inputs and instantly see the impact on graphs of the efficient frontier and portfolio weights. This allows you to perform instant experiments on the efficient frontier and portfolio weights. The portfolio weights of the optimal (tangent) portfolio are a trade-off between putting more in assets with higher expected returns vs. spreading investment out evenly to lower portfolio risk by diversification. You can see how this trade-off works by doing some of the experiments listed below:

- What happens to the optimal portfolio weight of an individual asset that is *underpriced* (e.g., the expected return is raised)?

- What happens to the optimal portfolio weight of an individual asset that is *overpriced* (e.g., the expected return is lowered)?
- What happens to the optimal portfolio weight of an individual asset that is *mispriced* due to the standard deviation of the asset being raised?
- What happens to the optimal portfolio weight of an individual asset that is *mispriced* due to the standard deviation of the asset being lowered?
- What happens to the optimal portfolio weights of two risky assets when the correlation between them is raised?
- What happens to the optimal portfolio weights of two risky assets when the correlation between them is lowered?
- What happens to the efficient trade-off (tangent) line when the riskfree rate is raised?
- What happens to the efficient trade-off (tangent) line when the riskfree rate is lowered?

6.4 Full-Scale Real Data

The mean-variance optimization technique is a very general technique that can be used to find the optimal portfolio investment for any number of risky assets and any type of risky asset: stocks, corporate bonds, international bonds, real estate, commodities, etc.

Problem Using Real Data. The key inputs required are the means, standard deviations, and correlations of the risky assets. These inputs must be estimated from historical data. Typically, one would use five years of monthly data. Using only one or two years worth of data provide enough observations to have reliable estimates. Another difficulty is that means, standard deviations, and correlations evolve over time. So using ten years of data would produce unstable estimates because you are averaging across different "regimes". Five years of data is a good compromise. What are the portfolio weights of the optimal (tangent) portfolio?

Solution Strategy. Collect historical stock prices for 20 companies from Yahoo Finance! and calculate the sample means, standard deviations, and correlations. Expand the Portfolio Optimization - Many Assets model from 5 risky assets to 20 risky assets. Then copy the estimated values of means, standard deviations, and correlations into the input area.

FIGURE 6.6 Excel Model of Portfolio Optimization - Estimating Avg, Std Devs, Corrs, and Covs.

	A	B	C	D	E	V	W	X	Y	Z	AA
1	PORTFOLIO OPTIMIZATION					Estimating Avg, Std Devs, Corrs, & Covs					
2											
3	Date	COG	CSG	CDN	CDMS		COG	CSG	CDN	CDMS	CAE.TO
4	10/1/03	$26.59	$25.14	$13.26	$11.25		2.27%	0.20%	-1.04%	-0.18%	8.09%
5	9/2/03	$26.00	$25.09	$13.40	$11.27		-3.53%	3.00%	-5.77%	4.84%	-15.78%
6	8/1/03	$26.95	$24.36	$14.22	$10.75		7.76%	0.95%	4.02%	6.86%	-1.63%
7	7/1/03	$25.01	$24.13	$13.67	$10.06		-9.25%	0.71%	13.35%	13.67%	7.37%
8	6/2/03	$27.56	$23.96	$12.06	$8.85		1.89%	0.97%	-13.24%	-4.43%	24.45%
9	5/1/03	$27.05	$23.73	$13.90	$9.26		10.77%	5.65%	21.61%	3.93%	31.99%
10	4/1/03	$24.42	$22.46	$11.43	$8.91		2.09%	7.00%	14.30%	12.50%	14.14%
11	3/3/03	$23.92	$20.99	$10.00	$7.92		-0.29%	7.86%	-5.57%	-5.83%	-35.04%
12	2/3/03	$23.99	$19.46	$10.59	$8.41		2.52%	-10.94%	6.75%	-15.73%	-7.51%
13	1/2/03	$23.40	$21.85	$9.92	$9.98		-5.11%	-11.65%	-15.86%	-8.78%	-1.75%
14	12/2/02	$24.66	$24.73	$11.79	$10.94		7.26%	-1.71%	-18.24%	6.52%	-7.54%
15	11/1/02	$22.99	$25.16	$14.42	$10.27		5.90%	-0.55%	42.35%	16.84%	4.50%
59	3/1/99	$13.84	$24.91	$25.75	$12.83		31.94%	-2.50%	7.02%	-0.85%	-4.12%
60	2/1/99	$10.49	$25.55	$24.06	$12.94		-16.15%	-2.33%	-24.81%	-12.21%	4.82%
61	1/4/99	$12.51	$26.16	$32.00	$14.74		-12.52%	-7.59%	7.56%	-11.89%	1.03%
62	12/1/98	$14.30	$28.31	$29.75	$16.73		-2.79%	14.48%	5.80%	17.07%	-6.92%
63	11/2/98	$14.71	$24.73	$28.12	$14.29		-8.80%	-0.20%	33.90%	-6.66%	-5.84%
64	10/1/98	$16.13	$24.78	$21.00	$15.31						
65											
66						Average Return	1.59%	0.22%	0.75%	0.17%	1.57%
67						Standard Deviation	13.15%	6.35%	17.28%	11.89%	15.69%

How To Build This Excel Model.

1. **Collect Historical Stock Price Data For 20 Firms.** Go to **Yahoo Finance!** (**finance.yahoo.com**), click on **Symbol Lookup**, click on **Company and Fund Index**, and click on a letter (such as **C**) to get a list of company names and their corresponding ticker symbols. For example, the stock symbol for Cabot Corp is **CBT**. Click back to the home page of Yahoo Finance! and enter a ticker symbol, such as **CBT**, in the **Enter Symbol(s)** box. Click on **Historical Prices** in the left column of the page. Enter a **Start Date** and **End Date** to give you a five year span of time, click on the **Monthly** radio button, and click on **Get Prices**. It displays five years of monthly data on the firm (if available). Importantly, the monthly data includes the "Adjusted Close" price, which is adjusted for stock splits and dividends. Verify that the data goes back for the full five years, then scroll to the bottom of the page and click on **Download to Spreadsheet**, enter a name for the comma-delimited csv file, such as **cbt.csv**, and click on **Save**. Repeat this process for 20 Firms. Launch Excel and open each csv file. Copy the "Adj. Close*" column from each csv file to a common Excel file and label each column with the corresponding ticker symbol. In the figure above, columns **B** through **U** are the monthly adjusted close price for 20 firms.

2. **Monthly Returns.** The formula for a Monthly Return = (Price Now - Price Last Month) / (Price Last Month). Enter **=(B4-B5)/B5** in cell **W4** and copy the cell to the range **W4:AP63**.

3. **Expected Returns and Standard Deviations.** Estimate the expected returns and standard deviations next period by calculating the sample average returns and sample standard deviation from the historical data. Enter **=AVERAGE(W4:W63)** in cell **W66** and copy it across. Enter **=STDEV(W4:W63)** in cell **W67** and copy it across.

FIGURE 6.7 Excel Model of Portfolio Optimization - Estimating Avg, Std Devs, Corrs, and Covs (Continued).

	AR	AS	AT	AU	AV	AW	AX	AY
4	COG	2.27%	-3.53%	7.76%	-9.25%	1.89%	10.77%	2.09%
5	CSG	0.20%	3.00%	0.95%	0.71%	0.97%	5.65%	7.00%
6	CDN	-1.04%	-5.77%	4.02%	13.35%	-13.24%	21.61%	14.30%
7	CDMS	-0.18%	4.84%	6.86%	13.67%	-4.43%	3.93%	12.50%
8	CAE.TO	8.09%	-15.78%	-1.63%	7.37%	24.45%	31.99%	14.14%
9	CGLA	0.23%	31.54%	32.65%	3.16%	3.71%	-18.65%	4.07%
10	CPT	0.78%	2.56%	2.10%	6.78%	2.44%	-0.59%	7.86%
11	CCC	4.97%	-10.35%	-2.18%	12.24%	0.00%	13.27%	4.12%
12	CPB	1.66%	9.50%	0.21%	-0.78%	-1.82%	13.25%	5.70%
13	CWT	2.32%	2.42%	-9.90%	0.43%	-0.29%	3.10%	7.33%
14	ELY	4.06%	-5.06%	-2.34%	16.95%	-7.84%	3.48%	17.35%
15	CPE	-1.47%	5.36%	5.82%	-5.90%	-11.00%	71.67%	9.39%
16	CLWY	-3.33%	-14.29%	-13.58%	1.25%	6.67%	-9.64%	3.75%
17	CHP	2.75%	-5.12%	32.51%	4.81%	-3.24%	11.67%	11.04%
18	BCR	0.21%	5.97%	-2.28%	-3.53%	1.66%	10.67%	0.86%
19	CCJ	2.75%	1.42%	11.08%	-4.30%	10.67%	13.95%	-5.90%
20	CPN	0.41%	-13.30%	-1.23%	-13.48%	26.92%	-3.17%	62.73%
21	CBJ	-2.89%	23.66%	34.13%	24.63%	8.06%	-8.15%	8.00%
22	CBM	2.95%	7.33%	0.00%	-8.00%	8.60%	22.02%	-27.56%
23	CLWY	0.98%	4.46%	1.07%	2.34%	10.93%	-2.19%	1.45%

4. **Transposed Returns.** The simplest way to calculate the stock return correlations and covariances is to start by transposing the returns. Notice that the returns are currently in the range **W4:AP63**, which is 20 columns wide and 61 rows tall (including the title row). To transpose the returns, select the range **AR4:CZ23**, which is 20 rows tall and 61 columns wide. To edit this selection, press the function key **F2**. Enter **=TRANSPOSE(W3:AP63)**. Then, hold down the **Shift** and **Control** buttons simultaneously, and while continuing to hold them down, press **Enter**. Entering it this way applies a common formula to the entire range as a "matrix." The resulting formula should have braces around it **{=TRANSPOSE(W3:AP63)}**.

FIGURE 6.8 Excel Model of Portfolio Optimization - Estimating Avg, Std Devs, Corrs, and Covs (Continued).

	V	W	X	Y	Z	AA	AB	AC
69	Correlations	COG	CSG	CDN	CDMS	CAE.TO	CGLA	CPT
70	COG	100.00%	13.10%	12.43%	36.20%	6.94%	-12.59%	26.96%
71	CSG	13.10%	100.00%	9.34%	40.27%	5.32%	3.64%	31.03%
72	CDN	12.43%	9.34%	100.00%	24.57%	14.44%	-24.69%	9.62%
73	CDMS	36.20%	40.27%	24.57%	100.00%	30.17%	5.62%	32.48%
74	CAE.TO	6.94%	5.32%	14.44%	30.17%	100.00%	-9.71%	28.61%
75	CGLA	-12.59%	3.64%	-24.69%	5.62%	-9.71%	100.00%	3.65%
76	CPT	26.96%	31.03%	9.62%	32.48%	28.61%	3.65%	100.00%
77	CCC	12.01%	-10.96%	10.51%	20.06%	17.16%	-4.70%	10.65%
78	CPB	35.70%	26.24%	27.20%	11.90%	0.23%	6.93%	7.93%
79	CWT	-3.26%	4.83%	-0.09%	5.28%	4.81%	-4.92%	20.70%
80	ELY	27.37%	12.12%	19.70%	13.51%	16.44%	-1.19%	11.01%
81	CPE	40.68%	-1.15%	21.47%	19.12%	17.04%	-10.65%	20.40%
82	CLWY	-19.75%	-11.23%	9.14%	-4.31%	26.46%	-2.43%	-2.68%
83	CHP	20.96%	-8.07%	43.25%	20.46%	20.33%	-5.86%	3.53%
84	BCR	-1.21%	16.45%	2.81%	1.88%	11.22%	-4.72%	19.40%
85	CCJ	20.56%	-4.67%	13.21%	4.97%	9.75%	24.89%	-14.49%
86	CPN	29.10%	-1.07%	38.18%	21.72%	27.95%	-8.05%	34.49%
87	CBJ	-17.51%	12.42%	4.99%	21.44%	-13.18%	42.53%	12.72%
88	CBM	32.29%	-4.50%	19.04%	20.05%	23.93%	-12.44%	2.84%
89	CLWY	10.38%	7.59%	13.52%	17.99%	-7.45%	32.37%	8.33%
90								
91	Covariances	COG	CSG	CDN	CDMS	CAE.TO	CGLA	CPT
92	COG	1.70%	0.11%	0.28%	0.56%	0.14%	-0.21%	0.16%
93	CSG	0.11%	0.40%	0.10%	0.30%	0.05%	0.03%	0.09%
94	CDN	0.28%	0.10%	2.94%	0.50%	0.38%	-0.54%	0.08%
95	CDMS	0.56%	0.30%	0.50%	1.39%	0.55%	0.09%	0.18%
96	CAE.TO	0.14%	0.05%	0.38%	0.55%	2.42%	-0.19%	0.21%
97	CGLA	-0.21%	0.03%	-0.54%	0.09%	-0.19%	1.65%	0.02%
98	CPT	0.16%	0.09%	0.08%	0.18%	0.21%	0.02%	0.21%
99	CCC	0.17%	-0.07%	0.19%	0.25%	0.29%	-0.06%	0.05%
100	CPB	0.39%	0.14%	0.39%	0.12%	0.00%	0.07%	0.03%
101	CWT	-0.03%	0.02%	0.00%	0.04%	0.05%	-0.04%	0.07%
102	ELY	0.55%	0.12%	0.52%	0.24%	0.39%	-0.02%	0.08%
103	CPE	1.07%	-0.01%	0.74%	0.46%	0.54%	-0.28%	0.19%
104	CLWY	-0.29%	-0.08%	0.18%	-0.06%	0.46%	-0.04%	-0.01%
105	CHP	0.47%	-0.09%	1.27%	0.41%	0.54%	-0.13%	0.03%
106	BCR	-0.01%	0.09%	0.04%	0.02%	0.14%	-0.05%	0.07%
107	CCJ	0.28%	-0.03%	0.24%	0.06%	0.16%	0.33%	-0.07%
108	CPN	1.06%	-0.02%	1.83%	0.72%	1.22%	-0.29%	0.45%
109	CBJ	-0.49%	0.17%	0.19%	0.55%	-0.44%	1.18%	0.13%
110	CBM	0.45%	-0.03%	0.35%	0.25%	0.40%	-0.17%	0.01%
111	CLWY	0.14%	0.05%	0.23%	0.21%	-0.12%	0.42%	0.04%

5. **Correlations.** Using the original returns and the transposed returns, it is easy to calculate the correlations with Excel's **CORREL** function. Enter **=CORREL(W$4:W$63,$AS4:$CZ4)** in cell W70 and copy it to the range W70:AP89.

6. **Covariances.** Similarly, the original returns and transposed returns can be used to calculate the covariances with Excel's **COVAR** function. Enter **=COVAR(W$4:W$63,$AS4:$CZ4)** in cell W92 and copy it to the range W92:AP111.

FIGURE 6.9 Excel Model of Portfolio Optimization - Full-Scale Real Data.

	A	B	C	D	E	F
1	PORTFOLIO OPTIMIZATION					Full-Scale Real Data
2					One plus	
3	Inputs		Expected	Standard	Exp Ret	
4			Return	Deviation	[1 + E(r)]	Ones
5	Riskless Rate (r)		0.1%	0.0%	100.1%	
6	Risky Asset 1		1.6%	13.2%	101.6%	100.0%
7	Risky Asset 2		0.2%	6.4%	100.2%	100.0%
8	Risky Asset 3		0.8%	17.3%	100.8%	100.0%
9	Risky Asset 4		0.2%	11.9%	100.2%	100.0%
10	Risky Asset 5		1.6%	15.7%	101.6%	100.0%
11	Risky Asset 6		-0.5%	13.0%	99.5%	100.0%
12	Risky Asset 7		1.5%	4.7%	101.5%	100.0%
13	Risky Asset 8		0.6%	10.8%	100.6%	100.0%
14	Risky Asset 9		-0.5%	8.4%	99.5%	100.0%
15	Risky Asset 10		0.7%	6.9%	100.7%	100.0%
16	Risky Asset 11		1.9%	15.5%	101.9%	100.0%
17	Risky Asset 12		1.0%	20.4%	101.0%	100.0%
18	Risky Asset 13		-0.5%	11.3%	99.5%	100.0%
19	Risky Asset 14		2.3%	17.3%	102.3%	100.0%
20	Risky Asset 15		1.4%	8.3%	101.4%	100.0%
21	Risky Asset 16		1.9%	10.6%	101.9%	100.0%
22	Risky Asset 17		4.3%	28.3%	104.3%	100.0%
23	Risky Asset 18		1.5%	21.8%	101.5%	100.0%
24	Risky Asset 19		0.5%	10.8%	100.5%	100.0%
25	Risky Asset 20		1.6%	10.1%	101.6%	100.0%

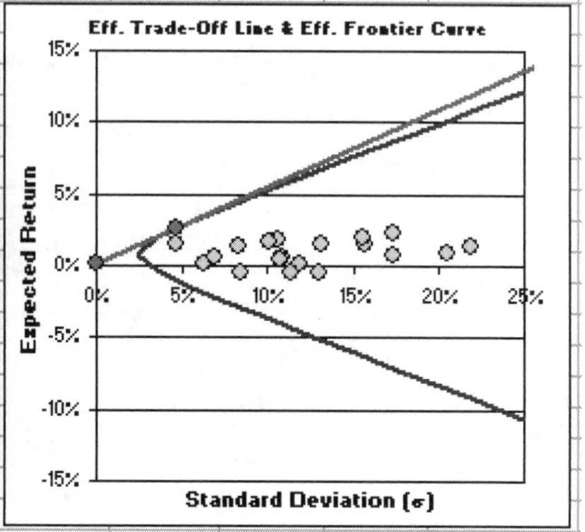

	A	B	C	D	E	F	G	H	I	J	K
26											
27		Correlations									
28		1	2	3	4	5	6	7	8	9	10
29	1	100.0%	13.1%	12.4%	36.2%	6.9%	-12.6%	27.0%	12.0%	35.7%	-3.3%
30	2	13.1%	100.0%	9.3%	40.3%	5.3%	3.6%	31.0%	-11.0%	26.2%	4.8%
31	3	12.4%	9.3%	100.0%	24.6%	14.4%	-24.7%	9.6%	10.5%	27.2%	-0.1%
32	4	36.2%	40.3%	24.6%	100.0%	30.2%	5.6%	32.5%	20.1%	11.9%	5.3%
33	5	6.9%	5.3%	14.4%	30.2%	100.0%	-9.7%	28.6%	17.2%	0.2%	4.8%
34	6	-12.6%	3.6%	-24.7%	5.6%	-9.7%	100.0%	3.6%	-4.7%	6.9%	-4.9%
35	7	27.0%	31.0%	9.6%	32.5%	28.6%	3.6%	100.0%	10.7%	7.9%	20.7%
36	8	12.0%	-11.0%	10.5%	20.1%	17.2%	-4.7%	10.7%	100.0%	11.8%	4.7%
37	9	35.7%	26.2%	27.2%	11.9%	0.2%	6.9%	7.9%	11.8%	100.0%	18.8%
38	10	-3.3%	4.8%	-0.1%	5.3%	4.8%	-4.9%	20.7%	4.7%	18.8%	100.0%
39	11	27.4%	12.1%	19.7%	13.5%	16.4%	-1.2%	11.0%	-3.3%	26.8%	-22.7%
40	12	40.7%	-1.2%	21.5%	19.1%	17.0%	-10.6%	20.4%	19.8%	12.6%	16.4%
41	13	-19.7%	-11.2%	9.1%	-4.3%	26.5%	-2.4%	-2.7%	-16.8%	-19.9%	-9.6%
42	14	21.0%	-8.1%	43.3%	20.5%	20.3%	-5.9%	3.5%	25.5%	9.7%	-15.6%
43	15	-1.2%	16.4%	2.8%	1.9%	11.2%	-4.7%	19.4%	3.0%	17.2%	12.1%
44	16	20.6%	-4.7%	13.2%	5.0%	9.8%	24.9%	-14.5%	-16.7%	14.9%	-10.3%
45	17	29.1%	-1.1%	38.2%	21.7%	28.0%	-8.1%	34.5%	42.9%	20.7%	19.6%
46	18	-17.5%	12.4%	5.0%	21.4%	-13.2%	42.5%	12.7%	0.9%	-10.7%	-22.7%
47	19	32.3%	-4.5%	19.0%	20.1%	23.9%	-12.4%	2.8%	29.5%	17.3%	-27.5%
48	20	10.4%	7.6%	13.5%	18.0%	-7.4%	32.4%	8.3%	11.6%	-0.1%	-17.8%

7. **Open the Many Assets Excel Model, Add Rows, and Update the Riskless Rate.** Open the Excel model that you created for Portfolio Optimization - Many Assets and immediately save the file under a new name using the **File | Save As** command. Move the Efficient Frontier graph out of the way by clicking on it and dragging it below row **32** and to the right of column **V**. Delete the Portfolio Weights graph by clicking on it and pressing the **Delete**

button. Add fifteen rows to the Outputs area by selecting the range **A49:A63** and clicking on **Insert | Rows**. Add fifteen rows for the Variances and Covariances by selecting the range **A31:A45** and clicking on **Insert | Rows**. Add fifteen rows for the Correlations by selecting the range **A19:A33** and clicking on **Insert | Rows**. Add fifteen rows for the Expected Returns and Standard Deviations by selecting the range **A11:A25** and clicking on **Insert | Rows**. Lookup the yield to maturity of a Treasury Bill with one month to maturity in the financial press. To convert this annualized yield to maturity to a monthly rate, divide by 12. (The *Wall Street Journal* and most financial press use the annual percentage rate convention.) Enter this value in cell **C5**.

8. **Copy the Means, Standard Deviations, and Correlations Over.** Copy the estimated values of the Means, Standard Deviations, and Correlations from the estimation Excel model to the Full-Scale Real Data Excel model. Select the range **W66:AP67** of the **Estimating Means, Std Devs, and Corrs** Excel model, click on **Edit | Copy**, select the cell **C6**, of the **Full-Scale Real Data** Excel model, click on **Edit | Paste Special**, in the **Paste** section of the dialog box click on **Values** and near the bottom click on **Transpose** and **OK**. Select the range **W70:AP89** of the **Estimating Means, Std Devs, and Corrs** Excel model, click on **Edit | Copy**, select the cell **B29**, of the **Full-Scale Real Data** Excel model, click on **Edit | Paste Special**, in the **Paste** section of the dialog box click on **Values** and **OK**.

9. **One plus the Expected Return and 100%.** Copy the formulas for One plus the Expected Return and 100% down the columns. Select the range **E6:F6** and copy it to the range **E7:F25**.

FIGURE 6.10 Excel Model Details of Portfolio Optimization - Full-Scale Real Data.

	A	B	C	D	E	F	G	H	I	J	K
50		Standard Deviations									
51		1	2	3	4	5	6	7	8	9	10
52		13.2%	6.4%	17.3%	11.9%	15.7%	13.0%	4.7%	10.8%	8.4%	6.9%
53											
54		Variances and Covariances									
55		1	2	3	4	5	6	7	8	9	10
56	1	1.73%	0.11%	0.28%	0.57%	0.14%	-0.21%	0.17%	0.17%	0.39%	-0.03%
57	2	0.11%	0.40%	0.10%	0.30%	0.05%	0.03%	0.09%	-0.08%	0.14%	0.02%
58	3	0.28%	0.10%	2.99%	0.50%	0.39%	-0.55%	0.08%	0.20%	0.39%	0.00%
59	4	0.57%	0.30%	0.50%	1.41%	0.56%	0.09%	0.18%	0.26%	0.12%	0.04%
60	5	0.14%	0.05%	0.39%	0.56%	2.46%	-0.20%	0.21%	0.29%	0.00%	0.05%
61	6	-0.21%	0.03%	-0.55%	0.09%	-0.20%	1.68%	0.02%	-0.07%	0.08%	-0.04%
62	7	0.17%	0.09%	0.08%	0.18%	0.21%	0.02%	0.22%	0.05%	0.03%	0.07%
63	8	0.17%	-0.08%	0.20%	0.26%	0.29%	-0.07%	0.05%	1.17%	0.11%	0.04%
64	9	0.39%	0.14%	0.39%	0.12%	0.00%	0.08%	0.03%	0.11%	0.71%	0.11%
65	10	-0.03%	0.02%	0.00%	0.04%	0.05%	-0.04%	0.07%	0.04%	0.11%	0.48%
66	11	0.56%	0.12%	0.53%	0.25%	0.40%	-0.02%	0.08%	-0.06%	0.35%	-0.24%
67	12	1.09%	-0.01%	0.76%	0.46%	0.55%	-0.28%	0.19%	0.44%	0.22%	0.23%
68	13	-0.29%	-0.08%	0.18%	-0.06%	0.47%	-0.04%	-0.01%	-0.21%	-0.19%	-0.08%
69	14	0.48%	-0.09%	1.29%	0.42%	0.55%	-0.13%	0.03%	0.48%	0.14%	-0.19%
70	15	-0.01%	0.09%	0.04%	0.02%	0.15%	-0.05%	0.08%	0.03%	0.12%	0.07%
71	16	0.29%	-0.03%	0.24%	0.06%	0.16%	0.34%	-0.07%	-0.19%	0.13%	-0.08%
72	17	1.08%	-0.02%	1.86%	0.73%	1.24%	-0.29%	0.46%	1.31%	0.49%	0.38%
73	18	-0.50%	0.17%	0.19%	0.56%	-0.45%	1.20%	0.13%	0.02%	-0.20%	-0.34%
74	19	0.46%	-0.03%	0.35%	0.26%	0.40%	-0.17%	0.01%	0.34%	0.16%	-0.21%
75	20	0.14%	0.05%	0.24%	0.22%	-0.12%	0.42%	0.04%	0.13%	0.00%	-0.12%

10. **Transposed Standard Deviations.** Extend the range of standard deviations that runs horizontally from left-to-right. Highlight the range **B52:U52**. Press the **F2** key, edit the formula so that it reads **=TRANSPOSE(D6:D25)**, hold down the **Shift** and **Control** buttons simultaneously, and while continuing to hold them down, press **Enter**. The resulting formula should have braces around it **{=TRANSPOSE(D6:D25)}**.

11. **Variances and Covariance's Table (Matrix).** Extend the Variances and Covariances Table (Matrix). Select the cell **B56** and copy the cell to the range **B56:U75**.

FIGURE 6.11 Excel Model Details of Portfolio Optimization - Full-Scale Real Data.

	A	B	C	D	E	F	G	H	I	J
81	**Outputs**									
82		A	1662.1							
83		B	1675.5							
84		C.	1689.22		Efficient	Efficient				
85		Delta	3.5E+02		Frontier	Trade-off	Individual			
86		Gamma	0.08518		Curve	Line	Asset	Optimal Combination		
87				Standard	Expected	Expected	Expected	of Risky Assets		
88			Index	Deviation	Return	Return	Return	(Tangent Portfolio)		
89	Risky Asset 1			13.2%			1.6%	1	3.2%	
90	Risky Asset 2			6.4%			0.2%	2	5.5%	
91	Risky Asset 3			17.3%			0.8%	3	-6.8%	
92	Risky Asset 4			11.9%			0.2%	4	-15.1%	
93	Risky Asset 5			15.7%			1.6%	5	-0.2%	
94	Risky Asset 6			13.0%			-0.5%	6	-15.2%	
95	Risky Asset 7			4.7%			1.5%	7	67.2%	
96	Risky Asset 8			10.8%			0.6%	8	0.2%	
97	Risky Asset 9			8.4%			-0.5%	9	-19.2%	
98	Risky Asset 10			6.9%			0.7%	10	26.3%	
99	Risky Asset 11			15.5%			1.9%	11	-0.8%	
100	Risky Asset 12			20.4%			1.0%	12	-10.0%	
101	Risky Asset 13			11.3%			-0.5%	13	-9.2%	
102	Risky Asset 14			17.3%			2.3%	14	14.7%	
103	Risky Asset 15			8.3%			1.4%	15	4.5%	
104	Risky Asset 16			10.6%			1.9%	16	28.5%	
105	Risky Asset 17			28.3%			4.3%	17	1.7%	
106	Risky Asset 18			21.8%			1.5%	18	5.0%	
107	Risky Asset 19			10.8%			0.5%	19	7.8%	
108	Risky Asset 20			10.1%			1.6%	20	11.9%	
109	Trade-off Curve		0	25.00%	-10.63%					
110	Trade-off Curve		1	22.53%	-9.49%					
111	Trade-off Curve		2	20.05%	-8.34%					
112	Trade-off Curve		3	17.59%	-7.20%					
113	Trade-off Curve		4	15.13%	-6.06%					
114	Trade-off Curve		5	12.68%	-4.91%					
115	Trade-off Curve		6	10.25%	-3.77%					
116	Trade-off Curve		7	7.86%	-2.62%					
117	Trade-off Curve		8	5.55%	-1.48%					
118	Trade-off Curve		9	3.49%	-0.34%					
119	Trade-off Curve		10	2.45%	0.81%					
120	Trade-off Curve		11	3.49%	1.95%					
121	Trade-off Curve		12	5.55%	3.09%					
122	Trade-off Curve		13	7.86%	4.24%					
123	Trade-off Curve		14	10.25%	5.38%					
124	Trade-off Curve		15	12.68%	6.52%					
125	Trade-off Curve		16	15.13%	7.67%					
126	Trade-off Curve		17	17.59%	8.81%					
127	Trade-off Curve		18	20.05%	9.96%					
128	Trade-off Curve		19	22.53%	11.10%					
129	Trade-off Curve		20	25.00%	12.24%					

12. **Hyperbola Coefficients.** Extend the ranges in the three hyperbola coefficients, A, B, and C. They are implemented using Excel's **matrix** functions. In each case, you type the formula and then, hold down the **Shift** and **Control** buttons simultaneously, and while continuing to hold them down, press **Enter**.

- For A: **=MMULT(MMULT(TRANSPOSE(F6:F25), MINVERSE(B56:U75)),F6:F25)** in cell **C82**.

- For B: **=MMULT(MMULT(TRANSPOSE(F6:F25), MINVERSE(B56:U75)),E6:E25)** in cell **C83**.

- For C: **=MMULT(MMULT(TRANSPOSE(E6:E25), MINVERSE(B56:U75)),E6:E25)** in cell **C84**.

13. **Individual Risky Assets.** Extend the individual risky assets in the Outputs section. Select the range **D93:G93** and copy it to the range **D94:D108**.

FIGURE 6.12 Excel Model Details of Portfolio Optimization - Full-Scale Real Data.

	A B	C	D	E	F
109	Trade-off Curve	0	25.00%	-10.63%	
110	Trade-off Curve	1	22.53%	-9.49%	
111	Trade-off Curve	2	20.05%	-8.34%	
112	Trade-off Curve	3	17.59%	-7.20%	
113	Trade-off Curve	4	15.13%	-6.06%	
114	Trade-off Curve	5	12.68%	-4.91%	
115	Trade-off Curve	6	10.25%	-3.77%	
116	Trade-off Curve	7	7.86%	-2.62%	
117	Trade-off Curve	8	5.55%	-1.48%	
118	Trade-off Curve	9	3.49%	-0.34%	
119	Trade-off Curve	10	2.45%	0.81%	
120	Trade-off Curve	11	3.49%	1.95%	
121	Trade-off Curve	12	5.55%	3.09%	
122	Trade-off Curve	13	7.86%	4.24%	
123	Trade-off Curve	14	10.25%	5.38%	
124	Trade-off Curve	15	12.68%	6.52%	
125	Trade-off Curve	16	15.13%	7.67%	
126	Trade-off Curve	17	17.59%	8.81%	
127	Trade-off Curve	18	20.05%	9.96%	
128	Trade-off Curve	19	22.53%	11.10%	
129	Trade-off Curve	20	25.00%	12.24%	
130	Optimal Comb.		4.6%		2.6%
131	Eff Trade-off Line	0.0%	0.0%		0.1%
132	Eff Trade-off Line	100.0%	4.6%		2.6%
133	Eff Trade-off Line	600.0%	27.7%		15.1%

14. **Tangent Portfolio.** The Optimal Combination of Risky Assets (or Tangent Portfolio) can be calculated using Excel's **matrix** functions. In each case, you type the formula and then, hold down the **Shift** and **Control** buttons simultaneously, and while continuing to hold them down, press **Enter**.

- For the portfolio weights: Select the range **I89:I108**, then type **=Gamma*MMULT(MINVERSE(B56:U75),(E6:E25-R.*F6:F25))**

- For expected returns: enter **=MMULT(TRANSPOSE(I89:I108),E6:E25)-1** in cell **F130**.

- For standard deviations: enter **=SQRT(MMULT(MMULT(TRANSPOSE(I89:I108),B56:U75),I89:I108))** in cell **D130**.

15. **Efficient Trade-Off Line.** Extend the Efficient Trade-Off Line. Enter **600.0%** in cell **C133**.

16. **Relocate The Graphs.** Move the graph back into place. Move the Efficient Frontier graph into the range **G6:K22**.

The portfolio weights of the optimal (tangent) portfolio are listed in the range **I89:I108**. You will notice large positive weights on those assets with high expected returns ("past winners") and/or low standard deviation. Similarly, there are large negative weights (meaning short selling) on those assets with low expected returns ("past losers") and/or high standard deviation. One problem with directly using the estimates from historical data is that you get rather extreme portfolio weights (for example, 67.2% in asset 7 and -19.2% in asset 9). Essentially, this assumes that past winners will win just as big in future and past losers will lose just as big in the future. A standard "Bayesian" technique for dealing with this estimation problem is to lower the future expected returns on past winners and raise the future expected returns on past losers. Shifting all of the estimates in the direction of the middle will yield much more reasonable portfolio weights for the optimal (tangent) portfolio.

Problems

Skill-Building Problems.

1. The riskless rate is 5.1%. Risky Asset 1 has a mean return of 11.3% and a standard deviation of 23.2%. Risky Asset 2 has a mean return of 6.9% and a standard deviation of 18.7%. The correlation between Risky Asset 1 and 2 is 24.5%. Graph the Efficient Trade-Off Line and the Risky Asset Trade-Off Curve.

2. The riskless rate is 4.7%. There are five risky assets. Their expected returns are 11.3%, 7.8%, 9.2%, 13.6%, and 10.5%. Their standard deviations are16.6%, 24.3%, 19.7%, 22.9%, and 18.3%. All of the correlations are 0.0%, except the correlation between risky assets 2 and 5 which is 18.2%. Graph the Efficient Trade-Off Line and the Risky Asset Trade-Off Curve and a bar chart of the portfolio weights of the optimal (tangent) portfolio.

3. Perform instant experiments on the efficient frontier and portfolio weights. The portfolio weights of the optimal (tangent) portfolio are a trade-off between putting more in assets with higher expected returns vs. spreading investment out evenly to lower portfolio risk by diversification. You can see how this trade-off works by doing some of the experiments listed below:

    a. What happens to the optimal portfolio weight of an individual asset that is underpriced (e.g. the expected return is raised)?

b. What happens to the optimal portfolio weight of an individual asset that is overpriced (e.g. the expected return is lowered)?

c. What happens to the optimal portfolio weight of an individual asset that is mispriced due to the standard deviation of the asset being raised?

d. What happens to the optimal portfolio weight of an individual asset that is mispriced due to the standard deviation of the asset being lowered?

e. What happens to the optimal portfolio weights of two risky assets when the correlation between them is raised?

f. What happens to the optimal portfolio weights of two risky assets when the correlation between them is lowered?

g. What happens to the efficient trade-off (tangent) line when the riskfree rate is raised?

h. What happens to the efficient trade-off (tangent) line when the riskfree rate is lowered?

4. Collect historical stock prices for 20 companies of your own choosing from Yahoo Finance! and calculate the sample means, standard deviations, and correlations. Determine the portfolio weights of the optimal (tangent) portfolio.

Live In-class Problems.

5. Given the partial Two Asset file **PopttwoZ.xls**, do step **6 Optimal Combination of Risky Assets** and complete step **7 Efficient Trade-Off Line**.

6. Given the partial Many Asset file **PoptmanZ.xls**, do step **11 Tangent Portfolio** and complete step **12 Efficient Trade-Off Line**.

7. Given the partial Dynamic Chart file **PoptdynZ.xls**, complete step **5 Create The Cell Links** and complete step **6 Create Scaled Inputs**.

8. Given the partial Full-Scale Real Data file **PoptfulZ.xls**, do step **14 Tangent Portfolio**.

Chapter 7 Portfolio Diversification Lowers Risk

7.1 Basics

Problem. For simplicity, suppose that all risky assets have a standard deviation of 30% and all pairs of risky assets have a correlation coefficient of 40%. In this simple setting, consider a portfolio diversification strategy of investing in equally-weighted portfolios (e.g., put an equal about in each risky asset). As you increase the number of assets in your portfolio (that you are diversifying across), how much does this lower the risk of your portfolio?

Solution Strategy. Calculate the portfolio standard deviation of an equally-weighted portfolio as the number of assets increases. As a benchmark, compare with the portfolio standard deviation in the limiting case as the number of assets goes to infinity.

FIGURE 7.1 Excel Model of Portfolio Diversification Lowers Risk - Basics.

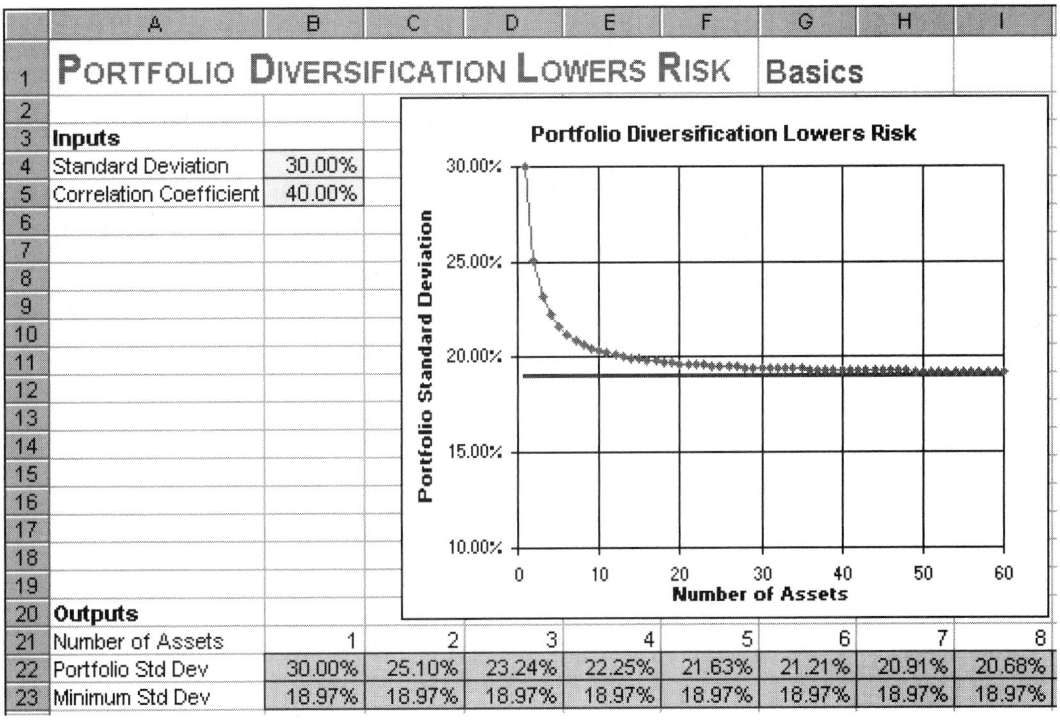

	A	B	C	D	E	F	G	H	I
21	Number of Assets	1	2	3	4	5	6	7	8
22	Portfolio Std Dev	30.00%	25.10%	23.24%	22.25%	21.63%	21.21%	20.91%	20.68%
23	Minimum Std Dev	18.97%	18.97%	18.97%	18.97%	18.97%	18.97%	18.97%	18.97%

How To Build This Excel Model.

1. **Enter The Inputs.** Enter the inputs into the range **B4:B5**.

2. **Number of Assets.** Enter Number of Asset values **1, 2, 3, 4, …, 60** in the range **B21:BI21**.

3. **Portfolio Standard Deviation.** The formula for the standard deviation of an equally-weighted portfolio in this simple setting is

$$\sqrt{\frac{1+(\text{Number of risky assets}-1)\cdot\text{Correlation Coefficient}}{\text{Number of risky assets}}}\cdot\text{Risky Asset Standard Deviation.}$$

Enter **=SQRT((1+(B21-1)*$B$5)/B21)*$B$4** in cell **B22** and copy the cell to the range **B22:BI22**.

4. **Minimum Standard Deviation.** In the limit as the number of assets goes to infinity, the formula above reduces to

$$\sqrt{\text{Correlation Coefficient}}\cdot\text{Risky Asset Standard Deviation,}$$

Enter **=SQRT($B$5)*$B$4** in cell **B23** and copy the cell to the range **B23:BI23**.

5. **Graph the Standard Deviations By The Number Of Risky Assets.** Highlight the range **B21:BI23**. Next choose **Insert Chart** from the main menu. Select an **XY(Scatter)** chart type and make other selections to complete the Chart Wizard. Place the graph in the range **C2:I20**.

This graph shows how diversifying across many assets can reduce risk from 30% to as low as 18.97%. Most of the risk reduction is accomplished with a relatively small number of assets. Increasing the number of assets from one to ten accomplishes more that 85% of the potential risk reduction. Increasing to thirty assets accomplishes more than 95% of the potential risk reduction. In summary, very significant risk reduction can be accomplished by diversifying across thirty assets, but relatively little risk reduction is accomplished by increasing the number of assets further.

7.2 International

Problem. There is a lot of evidence that international correlation coefficients are dramatically lower than local (same country) correlation coefficients. We can explore the benefits of international diversification by extending the Basics example. Suppose there are two countries and all risky assets in both countries have a standard deviation of 30%. All pairs of risky assets *within* the same country have a local correlation coefficient of 40%, but all pairs of risky assets *between* countries have an international correlation coefficient of 10%. Consider an international diversification strategy of investing half of your money in an equally-weighted portfolio in country 1 and the other half in an equally-weighted portfolio in country 2. As you increase the number of assets in your total portfolio, how much does this lower the risk of your portfolio?

Solution Strategy. Calculate the portfolio standard deviation of the internationally diversified portfolio as the number of assets increases. As a benchmark, compare with the international portfolio standard deviation in the limiting case as the number of assets goes to infinity.

FIGURE 7.2 Excel Model of Portfolio Diversification Lowers Risk - International.

	A	B	C	D	E	F	G	H	I
1	PORTFOLIO DIVERSIFICATION LOWERS RISK						International		
2									
3	**Inputs**								
4	Standard Deviation	30.00%							
5	Correlation Coefficient	40.00%							
6	International Corr Coeff	10.00%							
7									
8									
9									
10									
11									
12									
13									
14									
15									
16									
17									
18									
19									
20									
21	Number of Assets	1	2	3	4	5	6	7	8
22	Portfolio Std Dev	30.00%	25.10%	23.24%	22.25%	21.63%	21.21%	20.91%	20.68%
23	Minimum Std Dev	18.97%	18.97%	18.97%	18.97%	18.97%	18.97%	18.97%	18.97%
24	International Port Std Dev		22.25%		18.97%		17.75%		17.10%
25	International Min Std Dev		15.00%		15.00%		15.00%		15.00%

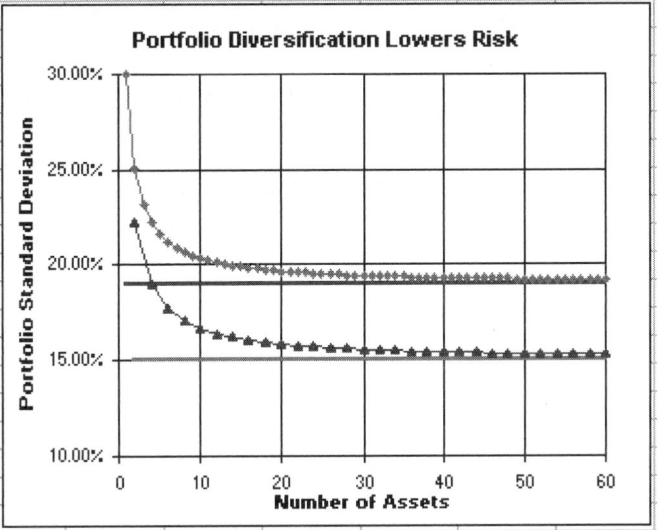

How To Build This Excel Model.

1. **Start with the Basics Excel Model.** Open the Excel model that you created for Portfolio Diversification Lowers Risk – Basics and immediately save the file under a new name using the **File Save As** command. Enter the international correlation coefficient **10.00%** in cell **B6**.

2. **International Portfolio Standard Deviation.** The formula for the standard deviation of the internationally diversified portfolio put half in an equally-weighted portfolio in each country is

$$\sqrt{\frac{1+\left(\#\text{ of assets}/2-1\right)\cdot\text{Local Corr Coeff}+\left(\#\text{ of assets}/2\right)\cdot\text{Intrnl Corr Coeff}}{\#\text{ of assets}}}\cdot\text{Asset Std Dev.}$$

Enter **=SQRT((2+(C21-2)*$B$5+C21*$B$6)/(2*C21))*$B$4** in cell **C24** and copy the cell to the range **D24:BI24**. Then delete the formula from all of cells that correspond to an odd number of assets (**D24**, **F24**, **H24**, ..., **BH24**), because you can't evenly divide an odd number of assets.

3. **International Minimum Standard Deviation.** In the limit as the number of assets goes to infinity, the formula above reduces to

$$\sqrt{(1/2)\cdot \text{Local Corr Coeff} + (1/2)\cdot \text{Intrnl Corr Coeff}} \cdot \text{Asset Std Dev.}$$

   Enter **=SQRT(0.5*$B$5+0.5*$B$6)*$B$4** in cell **C25** and copy the cell to the range **D25:BI25**. Then delete the formula from all of cells that correspond to an odd number of assets (**D25, F25, H25, ..., BH25**), because you can't evenly divide an odd number of assets.

4. **Add the International Standard Deviations To The Chart.** Hover the cursor over the Chart and then click on the right mouse button. From the pop-up menu, select **Source Data**, edit the **Data Range** to read **=Sheet1!$B$21:$BI$25**, and click on **OK**. To fill in the gaps between even numbered observations, click on the Chart, then click on **Tools Options**, click on the **Chart** tab, click on the **Interpolated** radio button, and **OK**.

This graph shows how international diversification can significantly reduce risk beyond local (one country) diversification. In this example, local diversification reduces risk from 30% to as low as 18.57%, but international diversification can reduce risk as low as 15%. International diversification works by getting rid of some country-specific sources of risk. Again, most of the risk reduction is accomplished with a relatively small number of assets. Beyond 30 assets (15 in each country), there is not much risk reduction potential left.

Problems

Live In-class Problems.

1. Given the partial Basics file **PdivbasZ.xls**, do steps **3 Portfolio Standard Deviation** and **4 Minimum Standard Deviation**.

2. Given the partial International file **PdivintZ.xls**, do steps **2 International Portfolio Standard Deviation** and **3 International Minimum Standard Deviation**.

Chapter 8 Life-Cycle Financial Planning

8.1 Basics

Problem. Suppose that you are currently 30 years old and expect to earn a constant real salary of $75,000 starting next year. You are planning to work for 35 years and then retire. You currently have $0 in financial capital. You are limited to investing in the riskfree asset. The real riskfree rate is 2.1%. Develop a financial plan for real savings and real consumption over your lifetime.

Solution Strategy. Develop a financial plan on a year-by-year basis over an entire lifetime. During your working years, divide your salary each year between current consumption and savings to provide for consumption during your retirement years. Put savings in a retirement fund that is invested at the riskfree rate. During your retirement years, your salary is zero, but you are able to consume each year by withdrawing money from your retirement fund. Calculate a constant level of real consumption that can be sustained in both working years and retirement years. Since there is substantial uncertainty about how long you will actually live and since it's not a good idea to run out of money, calculate real consumption based on infinite annuity. This level of real consumption can be sustained indefinitely. Finally, analyze human capital, financial capital, and total wealth over your lifetime.

Life Expectancy. How long will you live? For today's US population of 65 year olds, average life expectancy is 82. To determine your individual life expectancy, add to (or subtract from) 82 based your individual health-conscious practices. Not smoking adds nine years. Aerobic exercising and getting seven to eight hours of sleep per night adds three years. A healthy diet and maintaining a desirable weight based on your height adds three years. A thorough annual medical exam to catch cancer and other health problems early adds two years. The following six items add one year each: (1) daily aspirin to reduce fatal heart attacks, (2) preventing high blood pressure, (3) avoiding accidents, (4) getting immunized against pneumonia and influenza, (5) avoiding suicide and AIDS, and (6) avoiding heavy alcohol consumption. For the subset of today's US 65 year olds who follow all of these health-conscious practices, life expectancy is 105! These life expectancy figures are very conservative in the sense that they do not take into account future scientific/medical progress. For more information on the factors effecting longevity and the long-run impact of scientific and medical progress, read "Hello Methuselah! Living to 100 and Beyond" by George Webster, Ph.D. or visit http://www.george-webster.com/Subindex.html.

FIGURE 8.1 Excel Model of Life-Cycle Financial Planning - Basics.

	A	B	C	D	E	F	G
1	LIFE-CYCLE FINANCIAL PLANNING				Basics		
2							
3	**Inputs**						
4	Real Riskfree Rate	2.1%					
5	Working Years	35					
6							
7							
8							
9							
10							
11							
12							
13							
14							
15							
16							
17							
18							
19							
20							
21							
22							
23							
24	**Outputs**						
25	PV of Work Yrs $1 Annuity	$24.61					
26	PV of $1 Infinite Annuity	$47.62					
27	Working PV / Infinite PV	51.68%					
28							
29	Date	0	1	2	3	4	5
30	Age	30	31	32	33	34	35
31	Real Salary		$75,000	$75,000	$75,000	$75,000	$75,000
32	Real Savings		$36,238	$36,238	$36,238	$36,238	$36,238
33	Real Consumption		$38,762	$38,762	$38,762	$38,762	$38,762
34							
35	Real Human Capital	$1,845,825	$1,809,587	$1,772,589	$1,734,813	$1,696,244	$1,656,865
36	Real Financial Capital	$0	$36,238	$73,236	$111,012	$149,581	$188,960
37	Real Total Wealth	$1,845,825	$1,845,825	$1,845,825	$1,845,825	$1,845,825	$1,845,825

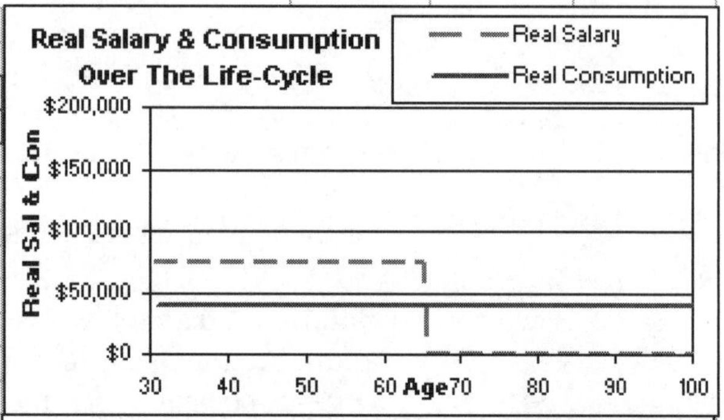

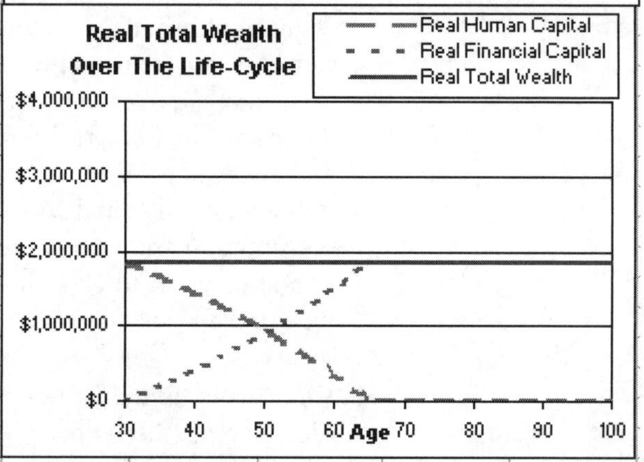

How To Build This Excel Model.

1. **Inputs.** Enter the *inputs* described in the problem into the range **B4:5** and the cells **B30**, **C31**, and **B36**. Lock in the left column of titles by selecting the cell **B1** and clicking on **Window Freeze Panes**.

2. **Date and Age.** For the Date row, enter **0, 1, 2,..., 70** in the range **B29:BT29**. The easy way to do this is enter **0** in cell **B29**, **1** in cell **C29**, highlight the range **B29:C29**, put the cursor over the lower right corner of cell **C29** until it becomes a "plus" icon, and drag the cursor all the way across to cell **BT29**. For the Age row, enter **=B30+1** in cell **C30** and copy it across

3. **Real Salary.** Your real salary is assumed to be constant during working years and zero after you retire. Enter **=IF(D29<=$B$5,C31,0)** in cell **D31**

and copy it across. As can be seen in the figure below, the **IF** statement causes the Real Salary to drop to zero at age 66.

FIGURE 8.2 Working Years vs. Retirement Years.

	A	AI	AJ	AK	AL	AM	AN	AO
29	Date	33	34	35	36	37	38	39
30	Age	63	64	65	66	67	68	69
31	Real Salary	$75,000	$75,000	$75,000	$0	$0	$0	$0
32	Real Savings	$36,238	$36,238	$36,238	-$38,762	-$38,762	-$38,762	-$38,762
33	Real Consumption	$38,762	$38,762	$38,762	$38,762	$38,762	$38,762	$38,762
34								
35	Real Human Capital	$145,404	$73,457	$0	$0	$0	$0	$0
36	Real Financial Capital	$1,700,421	$1,772,368	$1,845,825	$1,845,825	$1,845,825	$1,845,825	$1,845,825
37	Real Total Wealth	$1,845,825	$1,845,825	$1,845,825	$1,845,825	$1,845,825	$1,845,825	$1,845,825

4. **Working PV / Infinite PV.** The key challenge is to translate a constant annuity (real salary) earned over 35 working years into an infinite annuity (real consumption) to be consumed over an infinite horizon. To do this, first calculate the present value of a $1 annuity received over 35 working years using the **PV** function. The format is PV(Real Riskfree Rate, Working Years, -$1). Enter **=PV(B4,B5,-1)** in cell **B25**. Next calculate the present value of a $1 annuity over an infinite horizon = ($1) / (Real Riskfree Rate). Enter **=1/B4** in cell **B26**. Then calculate the working PV / infinite PV ratio. Enter **=B25/B26** in cell **B27**.

5. **Real Consumption and Real Savings.** Applying the ratio just calculated, Real Consumption = (Working PV / Infinite PV)*(Salary in Working Years). Enter **=B27*C31** in cell **C33**. Enter **=C33** in cell **D33** and copy it across. The remainder is Real Savings = (Real Salary) – (Real Consumption). Enter **=C31-C33** in cell **C32** and copy it across.

6. **Real Human Capital, Real Financial Capital, and Real Total Wealth.** By definition, Real Human Capital is the present value of all future real labor income. It can be calculated using the **NPV** function in the format NPV(Real Riskfree Rate, Range containing Future Real Salary). Enter **=NPV($B$4,C31:$BT$31)** in cell **B35** and copy it across. Real Financial Capital starts at zero. Enter **0** in cell **B36**. Then the formula for (This Period's Real Financial Capital) = (Last Period's Real Financial Capital) * (1 + Real Riskfree Rate) + (This Period's Real Savings). Enter **=B36*(1+$B4)+C32** in cell **C36** and copy it across. Sum to get (Real Total Wealth) = (Real Human Capital) + (Real Financial Capital). Enter **=B35+B36** in cell **C37** and copy it across.

7. **Graph Real Salary and Consumption Over The Life-cycle.** Highlight the range **B30:BT31** and then while holding down the **Ctrl** button highlight the ranges **B33:BT33**. Next choose **Insert Chart** from the main menu. Select an **XY(Scatter)** chart type and make other selections to complete the Chart Wizard.

8. **Graph Real Total Wealth Over The Life-cycle.** Highlight the range **B30:BT30** and then while holding down the **Ctrl** button highlight the ranges

B35:BT37. Next choose **Insert Chart** from the main menu. Select an **XY(Scatter)** chart type and make other selections to complete the Chart Wizard.

From the first graph, we see that your Real Salary from working years only is used to support a constant level of Real Consumption over an "infinite" lifetime. By using this approach, the same level of Real Consumption can be sustained even if you end up living much longer than originally anticipated. From the second graph, we see that Real Total Wealth is constant over a lifetime. At date 0, Real Total Wealth comes entirely from Real Human Capital, which is the present value of all future Real Salary. Over time Real Human Capital declines and Real Financial Capital builds up. After retirement, Real Total Wealth comes entirely from Real Financial Capital.

8.2 Full-Scale

Problem. Suppose that you are currently 30 years old and expect to earn a constant real salary of $75,000 starting next year. You are planning to work for 35 years and then retire. You currently have $0 in financial capital. You can invest in the riskfree asset or a broad stock portfolio. The inflation rate is 2.0% and the real riskfree rate is 2.1%. A broad stock portfolio offers an average real return of 6.0% and a standard deviation of 17.0%. Suppose that federal income taxes have six brackets with the following rates: 10.0%, 15.0%, 27.0%, 30.0%, 35.0%, and 38.6%. For current year, the upper cutoffs on the first five brackets are $6,000, $27,950, $67,700, $141,250, and $307,050 and these cutoffs are indexed to inflation. The state tax rate is 3.0%, federal FICA-SSI tax rate on salary up to $87,000 is 6.2%, and the federal FICA-Medicare tax rate on any level of salary is 1.45%. You will start receiving social security benefits at age 66. The current level of social security benefits is $24,204 per year and this is indexed to inflation. Develop a financial plan for real savings and real consumption over your lifetime.

Solution Strategy. The full-scale Excel model of life-cycle financial planning adds consideration of inflation, taxes, social security, and the opportunity to invest in a broad stock index. It is assumed that your savings are put in a tax-deferred retirement fund. You pay zero taxes on contributions to the retirement fund during your working years. But you have to pay taxes on withdrawals from the retirement fund during your retirement years. This Excel model includes several *choice variables*. You need to choose your Real Growth Rate in Salary. You need to choose your Taxable Income / Total Wealth. Specifying taxable income as a percentage of total wealth indirectly determines your consumption and savings as a percentage of total wealth. You also need to choose your Asset Allocation: Stock Portfolio %, that is, what percentage of your savings to invest in the broad stock portfolio. Investing in the broad stock portfolio will give you higher average returns than the riskfree asset, but also more risk. The balance of your savings will be invested in the riskfree asset and will grow at the riskfree rate.

FIGURE 8.3 Excel Model of Life-Cycle Financial Planning – Full-Scale.

	A	B	C	D	E	F	G
1	LIFE-CYCLE FINANCIAL PLANNING			Full-Scale			
2							
3	**Inputs**						
4	Real Riskfree Rate	2.1%					
5	Working Years	35					
6	Inflation Rate	2.4%					
7	Average Real Return of Stock Port	6.0%					
8	Standard Deviation of Stock Port	0.0001%					
9	Federal Income Bracket 1 Tax Rate	10.0%					
10	Federal Income Bracket 2 Tax Rate	15.0%					
11	Federal Income Bracket 3 Tax Rate	27.0%					
12	Federal Income Bracket 4 Tax Rate	30.0%					
13	Federal Income Bracket 5 Tax Rate	35.0%					
14	Federal Income Bracket 6 Tax Rate	38.6%					
15	Federal FICA-SSI Tax Rate on Salary	6.2%					
16	Federal FICA-Medicare Tax on Salary	1.45%					
17	State Income Tax Rate	3.0%					
18	Adjustment for Social Security	2.50%					
19							
20							
21							
22							
23							
24							
25							
26							
27							
28							
29	Date	0	1	2	3	4	5
30	Age	30	31	32	33	34	35
31	**Choice Variables**						
32	Real Growth Rate in Salary			2.0%	2.0%	2.0%	2.0%
33	Asset Allocation: Stock Port %		100.0%	100.0%	100.0%	100.0%	100.0%
34	Taxable Income / Total Wealth		4.4%	4.5%	4.5%	4.6%	4.7%

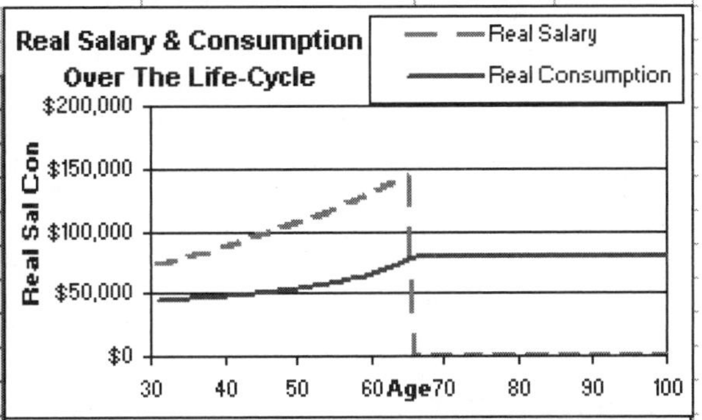

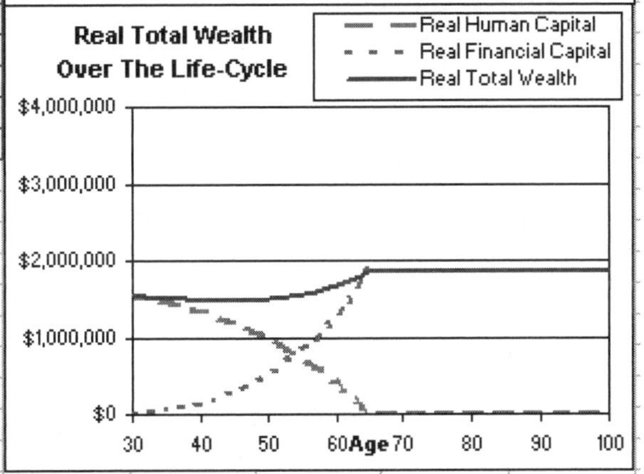

How To Build This Excel Model.

1. **Start with the Basics Excel Model, Insert Rows, and Delete Rows.** Open the Excel model that you created for Life-Cycle Financial Planning – Basics and immediately save the Excel model under a new name using the **File Save As** command. Insert twenty three rows below row **30** by selecting the range **A31:A53** and clicking **Insert | Rows**. Delete one row below row **54** by selecting the cell **A55**, clicking on **Edit | Delete**, selecting the **Entire Row** radio button on the **Delete** dialog box, and clicking on **OK**. Repeat this process to delete row **57**. Don't worry about the error messages created by deleting rows. We will update the formulas later.

2. **Inputs.** Enter the *inputs* described in the problem into the range **B4:B17**, the cells **B30**, **C40**, **B51**, **C60**, and the range **B61:B66**. For the time being, enter **0.0001%** in cell **B8** as the standard deviation rather than 17%. For the time being, enter a dummy value, such as **2.50%**, in cell **B18** as the social security adjustment.

FIGURE 8.4 Early Working Years.

	A	B	C	D	E	F	G
29	Date	0	1	2	3	4	5
30	Age	30	31	32	33	34	35
31	**Choice Variables**						
32	Real Growth Rate in Salary			2.0%	2.0%	2.0%	2.0%
33	Asset Allocation: Stock Port %		100.0%	100.0%	100.0%	100.0%	100.0%
34	Taxable Income / Total Wealth		4.4%	4.5%	4.5%	4.6%	4.7%
35	**Outputs**						
36	Nominal Riskfree Rate	4.55%					
37	Nominal Return on Stock Port		8.54%	8.54%	8.54%	8.54%	8.54%
38	Nominal Return on Retirement Fund		8.54%	8.54%	8.54%	8.54%	8.54%
39							
40	Salary		$75,000	$78,336	$81,820	$85,460	$89,261
41	Retire. Fund Contribution (Withdrawl)		$7,255	$8,209	$9,245	$10,367	$11,575
42	Taxable Income		$67,745	$70,127	$72,575	$75,093	$77,686
43	Less Taxes		$22,319	$23,199	$24,108	$25,068	$26,064
44	After-Tax Income		$45,426	$46,928	$48,467	$50,025	$51,622
45	Plus Social Security Benefits		$0	$0	$0	$0	$0
46	Consumption		$45,426	$46,928	$48,467	$50,025	$51,622
47							
48	Savings / Salary (%)		9.7%	10.5%	11.3%	12.1%	13.0%
49							
50	Human Capital	$1,539,666	$1,562,965	$1,585,244	$1,606,363	$1,626,175	$1,644,519
51	Financial Capital	$0	$7,255	$16,083	$26,702	$39,351	$54,287
52	Total Wealth	$1,539,666	$1,570,220	$1,601,327	$1,633,066	$1,665,526	$1,698,806
53							
54	Real Salary		$73,242	$74,707	$76,201	$77,725	$79,280
55	Real Consumption		$44,361	$44,754	$45,138	$45,498	$45,850
56	Real Human Capital	$1,539,666	$1,526,333	$1,511,806	$1,496,043	$1,478,998	$1,460,626
57	Real Financial Capital	$0	$7,085	$15,338	$24,869	$35,789	$48,217
58	Real Total Wealth	$1,539,666	$1,533,418	$1,527,144	$1,520,911	$1,514,787	$1,508,843
59							
60	Social Security Benefit Level		$24,204	$24,785	$25,380	$25,989	$26,613
61	Federal Income Tax Bracket 1 Cutoff	$6,000	$6,144	$6,291	$6,442	$6,597	$6,755
62	Federal Income Tax Bracket 2 Cutoff	$27,950	$28,621	$29,308	$30,011	$30,731	$31,469
63	Federal Income Tax Bracket 3 Cutoff	$67,700	$69,325	$70,989	$72,692	$74,437	$76,223
64	Federal Income Tax Bracket 4 Cutoff	$141,250	$144,640	$148,111	$151,666	$155,306	$159,033
65	Federal Income Tax Bracket 5 Cutoff	$307,050	$314,419	$321,965	$329,692	$337,605	$345,708
66	Federal FICA-SSI Wage Cap	$87,000	$89,088	$91,226	$93,416	$95,658	$97,953

3. **Choice Variables.** Each year, starting with age 31 (column **C**) and continuing through age 100 (column **BT**), you need to make certain decisions. Each decision is called a choice variable. Here are some initial values for the choice variables to get you started. Feel free to change these values and explore the consequences of alternative decisions. Suppose that your Real Salary Rate in Salary will be 2.0% during your working years and drop by -100.0% to nothing during your first year of retirement. Enter **2.0%** into the range **D32:AK32**, **-100.0%** into cell **AL32**, and **0.0%** into the range **AM32:BT32**. Suppose that you will invest 100.0% of your retirement fund in the Broad Stock Portfolio during working years and 50.0% during retirement years. Enter **100.0%** into the range **C33:AK33** and **50.0%** into the range **AL33:BT33**. Suppose that you want to maintain a steady state ratio of Taxable Income out of Total Wealth (approximately a constant ratio of Consumption out of Total Wealth). In retirement years, steady state consumption is obtained by consuming the average real increase of your

retirement portfolio. So set Taxable Income / Total Wealth = (Average Real Return on the Retirement Fund) * (1 + Inflation Rate) = [(Broad Stock Portfolio Percentage) * (Average Real Return on the Broad Stock Portfolio) + (1 - Broad Stock Portfolio Percentage) * (Real Riskfree Rate)] * (1 + Inflation Rate).[3] Enter **=(AL33*$B$7+(1-AL33)*$B$4)*(1+$B$6)** in cell **AL34** and copy it across. Suppose that you want to want Taxable Income out of Total Wealth to start at 4.4% and then rise steady throughout working years so that there is a smooth transition in Real Consumption between working years and retirement years. Enter **4.4%** in cell **C34**, enter **=$C$34+((D29-1)/($B$5-1))*($AL$34+$B$18-$C$34)** in cell **D34** and copy it to the range **E34:AK34**.

---

[3] The last term "(1 + Inflation Rate)" takes care of the cross-product between (1 + real return) and (1 + inflation rate), so that your retirement fund can grow at the inflation rate.

FIGURE 8.5 Transition From Working To Retirement Years.

	A	AJ	AK	AL	AM	AN
29	Date	34	35	36	37	38
30	Age	64	65	66	67	68
31	**Choice Variables**					
32	Real Growth Rate in Salary	2.0%	2.0%	-100.0%	0.0%	0.0%
33	Asset Allocation: Stock Port %	100.0%	100.0%	50.0%	50.0%	50.0%
34	Taxable Income / Total Wealth	6.6%	6.6%	4.1%	4.1%	4.1%
35	**Outputs**					
36	Nominal Riskfree Rate					
37	Nominal Return on Stock Port	8.54%	8.54%	8.54%	8.54%	8.54%
38	Nominal Return on Retirement Fund	8.54%	8.54%	6.55%	6.55%	6.55%
39						
40	Salary	$315,330	$329,356	$0	$0	$0
41	Retire. Fund Contribution (Withdrawl)	$60,378	$59,895	-$176,124	-$180,351	-$184,679
42	Taxable Income	$254,953	$269,461	$176,124	$180,351	$184,679
43	Less Taxes	$88,055	$93,031	$44,769	$45,844	$46,944
44	After-Tax Income	$166,898	$176,431	$131,354	$134,507	$137,735
45	Plus Social Security Benefits	$0	$0	$55,512	$56,844	$58,208
46	Consumption	$166,898	$176,431	$186,866	$191,351	$195,944
47						
48	Savings / Salary (%)	19.1%	18.2%	0.0%	0.0%	0.0%
49						
50	Human Capital	$196,416	$0	$0	$0	$0
51	Financial Capital	$3,857,343	$4,246,811	$4,348,733	$4,453,107	$4,559,985
52	Total Wealth	$4,053,759	$4,246,811	$4,348,733	$4,453,107	$4,559,985
53						
54	Real Salary	$140,788	$143,604	$0	$0	$0
55	Real Consumption	$74,516	$76,927	$79,567	$79,567	$79,567
56	Real Human Capital	$87,696	$0	$0	$0	$0
57	Real Financial Capital	$1,722,224	$1,851,674	$1,851,673	$1,851,675	$1,851,676
58	Real Total Wealth	$1,809,920	$1,851,674	$1,851,673	$1,851,675	$1,851,676
59						
60	Social Security Benefit Level	$52,940	$54,211	$55,512	$56,844	$58,208
61	Federal Income Tax Bracket 1 Cutoff	$13,438	$13,761	$14,091	$14,429	$14,776
62	Federal Income Tax Bracket 2 Cutoff	$62,601	$64,103	$65,642	$67,217	$68,830
63	Federal Income Tax Bracket 3 Cutoff	$151,631	$155,270	$158,996	$162,812	$166,720
64	Federal Income Tax Bracket 4 Cutoff	$316,364	$323,957	$331,732	$339,693	$347,846
65	Federal Income Tax Bracket 5 Cutoff	$687,714	$704,219	$721,120	$738,427	$756,149
66	Federal FICA-SSI Wage Cap	$194,858	$199,534	$204,323	$209,227	$214,248

As you adapt this model to your own situation, it is not necessary to go from full-time work to zero work. You could consider retiring to part-time work and then gradually tapering off. For example, you could drop to half-time work by entering **-50%** in your first retirement year and then enter **-100.0%** in the year that you stop working entirely.

4. **Nominal Returns.** The formula for (Nominal Riskfree Rate) = (1 + Inflation Rate) * (1 + Real Riskfree Rate) - 1. Enter **=(1+$B$6)*(1+$B$4)-1** in cell **B36**. The formula for (Nominal Return on Broad Stock Portfolio) = (1 + Inflation Rate) * (1 + Real Return on Broad Stock Portfolio) - 1. Assume that the Real Return on Broad Stock Portfolio is normally distributed with the average return given in cell **B7** and the standard deviation given in cell **B8**. The Excel function **RAND()** generates a random variable with a uniform distribution over the interval from 0 to 1 (that is, with an equal chance of getting any number between 0 and 1). To transform this uniformly

distributed random variable into a normally distributed one, just place **RAND()** inside the Excel function **NORMINV**.[4] Enter **=(1+$B$6)*(1+NORMINV(RAND(),$B$7,$B$8))-1** in cell **C37** and copy it across. The nominal return that you get depends on how much you have placed in the Broad Stock Portfolio vs. the Riskfree Asset. Nominal Return on Retirement Fund = (Broad Stock Portfolio Percentage) * (Nominal Return on Broad Stock Portfolio) + (1 – Broad Stock Portfolio Percentage) * (Nominal Return on Riskfree Asset). Enter **=C33*C37+(1-C33)*$B$36** in cell **C38** and copy it across.

---

[4] The "Transformation Method" for converting a uniform random variable x into some other random variable y based on a cumulative distribution F is $y(x) = F^{-1}(x)$. See Press, W., B. Flannery, S. Teukolsky, and W. Vetterling, 1987, Numerical Recopies: The Art of Scientific Computing, Cambridge University Press, chapter on Random Numbers, subsection on the Transformation Method, page 201.

FIGURE 8.6 Late Retirement Years.

	A	BP	BQ	BR	BS	BT
29	Date	66	67	68	69	70
30	Age	96	97	98	99	100
31	**Choice Variables**					
32	Real Growth Rate in Salary	0.0%	0.0%	0.0%	0.0%	0.0%
33	Asset Allocation: Stock Port %	50.0%	50.0%	50.0%	50.0%	50.0%
34	Taxable Income / Total Wealth	4.1%	4.1%	4.1%	4.1%	4.1%
35	**Outputs**					
36	Nominal Riskfree Rate					
37	Nominal Return on Stock Port	8.54%	8.54%	8.54%	8.54%	8.54%
38	Nominal Return on Retirement Fund	6.55%	6.55%	6.55%	6.55%	6.55%
39						
40	Salary	$0	$0	$0	$0	$0
41	Retire. Fund Contribution (Withdrawl)	-$358,771	-$367,381	-$376,198	-$385,227	-$394,472
42	Taxable Income	$358,771	$367,381	$376,198	$385,227	$394,472
43	Less Taxes	$91,197	$93,386	$95,627	$97,922	$100,272
44	After-Tax Income	$267,574	$273,996	$280,571	$287,305	$294,200
45	Plus Social Security Benefits	$113,080	$115,794	$118,573	$121,418	$124,332
46	Consumption	$380,653	$389,789	$399,144	$408,723	$418,533
47						
48	Savings / Salary (%)	0.0%	0.0%	0.0%	0.0%	0.0%
49						
50	Human Capital	$0	$0	$0	$0	$0
51	Financial Capital	$8,858,537	$9,071,141	$9,288,842	$9,511,772	$9,740,065
52	Total Wealth	$8,858,537	$9,071,141	$9,288,842	$9,511,772	$9,740,065
53						
54	Real Salary	$0	$0	$0	$0	$0
55	Real Consumption	$79,567	$79,567	$79,567	$79,567	$79,567
56	Real Human Capital	$0	$0	$0	$0	$0
57	Real Financial Capital	$1,851,675	$1,851,675	$1,851,674	$1,851,674	$1,851,676
58	Real Total Wealth	$1,851,675	$1,851,675	$1,851,674	$1,851,674	$1,851,676
59						
60	Social Security Benefit Level	$113,080	$115,794	$118,573	$121,418	$124,332
61	Federal Income Tax Bracket 1 Cutoff	$28,704	$29,393	$30,099	$30,821	$31,561
62	Federal Income Tax Bracket 2 Cutoff	$133,715	$136,924	$140,210	$143,575	$147,021
63	Federal Income Tax Bracket 3 Cutoff	$323,881	$331,654	$339,614	$347,765	$356,111
64	Federal Income Tax Bracket 4 Cutoff	$675,749	$691,967	$708,574	$725,580	$742,994
65	Federal Income Tax Bracket 5 Cutoff	$1,468,947	$1,504,202	$1,540,303	$1,577,270	$1,615,125
66	Federal FICA-SSI Wage Cap	$416,214	$426,203	$436,432	$446,906	$457,632

5. **The Rest Of The Outputs.** Below are the formulas for the rest of the outputs and the suggested, but not required, order for entering them.

   - **Salary** = (Last Year's Salary) * (1 + Inflation Rate) * (1 + Real Growth Rate in Salary) in working year. Enter **=C40*(1+$B$6)*(1+D32)** in cell **D40** and copy it across.

   - **Human Capital** = Net Present Value of Future After-Tax Salary = Net Present Value of Future Before-Tax Salary * (1 + Federal Income Tax Rate + Federal FICA-SSI Tax Rate + Federal FICA-Medicare Tax Rate

+ State Income Tax Rate). Enter **=NPV($B$36,C40:$BT$40)*(1-$B$11-$B$15-$B$16-$B$17)** in cell B50 and copy it across.[5]

- **Total Wealth** = (Human Capital) + (Financial Capital). Enter **=B50+B51** in cell B52 and copy it across.

- **Taxable Income** = (This Year's Taxable Income / Total Wealth) * (Last Year's Total Wealth). Enter **=C34*B52** in cell C42 and copy it across.

- **Retirement Fund Contribution (Withdrawal)** = Salary – (Taxable Income). Enter **=C40-C42** in cell C41 and copy it across.

- **Financial Capital** = (Last Year's Financial Capital) * (1 + Nominal Return on Retirement Fund) + [Retirement Fund Contribution (Withdrawal)]. Enter **=B51*(1+C38)+C41** in cell C51 and copy it across.

- **Social Security Benefit Level** = Last Year's Social Security Benefit Level * (1 + Inflation Rate). Enter **=C60*(1+$B$6)** in cell D60 and copy it across. To check your social security eligibility and benefit level, surf the Social Security Administration's web site www.socialsecurity.gov.

- **Federal Income Tax Bracket Cutoffs.** = Last Year's Federal Income Tax Bracket Cutoff * (1 + Inflation Rate). Enter **=B61*(1+$B$6)** in cell C61 and copy it to the range C61:BT65.

- **Federal FICA-SSI Wage Cap.** = Last Year's Federal FICA-SSI Wage Cap * (1 + Inflation Rate). Enter **=B66*(1+$B$6)** in cell C66 and copy it across.

- **Taxes** = (Bracket 1 Tax Rate) * MIN(Taxable Income, Bracket 1 Cutoff)

+ (Bracket 2 Tax Rate) * MAX(MIN(Taxable Income, Bracket 2 Cutoff) - Bracket 1 Cutoff, 0)

+ (Bracket 3 Tax Rate) * MAX(MIN(Taxable Income, Bracket 3 Cutoff) - Bracket 2 Cutoff, 0)

+ (Bracket 4 Tax Rate) * MAX(MIN(Taxable Income, Bracket 4 Cutoff) - Bracket 3 Cutoff, 0)

+ (Bracket 5 Tax Rate) * MAX(MIN(Taxable Income, Bracket 5 Cutoff) - Bracket 4 Cutoff, 0)

+ (Bracket 6 Tax Rate) * MAX(Taxable Income - Bracket 5 Cutoff, 0)

---

[5] This is a fairly rough adjustment for taxes, but the year-by-year cash flows have a more sophisticated calculation of taxes. The reason for doing it this way (as opposed to present valuing the After-Tax Income row) is that this approach avoids generating circular references.

+ (Federal FICA-SSI Tax Rate) * MIN(Salary, Federal FICA-SSI Wage Cap)

+ (Federal FICA-Medicare Tax Rate) * Salary

+ (State Income Tax Rate) * Taxable Income

Enter **=$B$9*MIN(C42,C61)**
+$B$10*MAX(MIN(C42,C62)-C61,0)
+$B$11*MAX(MIN(C42,C63)-C62,0)
+$B$12*MAX(MIN(C42,C64)-C63,0)
+$B$13*MAX(MIN(C42,C65)-C64,0)
+$B$14*MAX(C42-C65,0)
+$B$15*MIN(C40,C66)
+$B$16*C40
+$B$17*C42

in cell C43 and copy it across.

- **After-Tax Income** = Taxable Income - Taxes. Enter **=C42-C43** in cell C44 and copy it across.

- **Social Security Benefits** = 0 in working years
  = Social Security Benefit Level in retirement years.
  Enter **=IF(C29>$B$5,C60,0)** in cell C45 and copy it across.

- **Consumption** = After-Tax Income + Social Security Benefits. Enter **=C44+C45** in cell C46 and copy it across.

- **Savings / Salary**
  = (Retirement Fund Contribution) / (Salary) when Salary > 0
  = 0 when Salary = 0
  Enter **=IF(C40>0,C41/C40,0)** in cell C48 and copy it across.

- **Real Salary** = (Nominal Salary) / ((1 + Inflation Rate) ^ Number of periods). Enter **=C40/((1+$B$6)^C$29)** in cell C54 and copy it across.

- **Real Consumption** = (Nominal Consumption) / ((1 + Inflation Rate) ^ Number of periods). Enter **=C46/((1+$B$6)^C$29)** in cell C55 and copy it across.

- **Real Human Capital, Real Financial Capital, and Real Total Wealth.** (Real Human Capital) = (Nominal Human Capital) / ((1 + Inflation Rate) ^ Number of periods). Real Financial Capital and Real Total Wealth are calculated in a similar manner. Enter **=B50/((1+$B$6)^B$29)** in cell B56 and copy it to the range B56:BT58.

- **Clean up.** Eliminate the leftover formulas from the Basics Excel model. Select the range A24:B27 and press the **Delete** key.

6. **Adjustment for Social Security.** It doesn't make any sense to live like a king in your working years and the live in poverty in your retirement years. Similarly, it doesn't make sense to live in poverty in your working years and live like a king in your retirement years. The key idea is that you want to have a smooth pattern of real consumption over the life-cycle. Setting Taxable Income as a percentage of Total Wealth does a good job of delivering a smooth pattern. The only tricky part is when social security kicks in. By default, social security payments start at 66.There are also other options (see www.socialsecurity.gov). Looking at the graph of Real Consumption, you should see a smooth pattern with no jump up or down at your retirement date. Notice that Taxable Income / Total Wealth is 6.6% in cell **AK34** and 4.1% the next year in cell **AL34**, which is an adjustment of 2.5%. In other words, the drop in Taxable Income is offset by addition of Social Security Benefits (which are NOT taxable). Notice that Real Consumption transitions smoothly from $76,927 in cell **AK55** to $79,567 in cell **AL55**. An adjustment of 2.5% works well for the default input values of this Excel model. When you change input values, you may need to change the adjustment. Manually adjust the value in cell **B18** in small increments until the graph of Real Consumption shows a smooth pattern with no jump at the retirement date.

Since the standard deviation (risk) in cell **B8** is virtually zero, the results we see in the two graphs are based on *average returns*. Starting with the second graph, we see that Real Human Capital starts at $1.5 million and declines smoothly to $0 at retirement. Real Financial Capital starts at $0, rises smoothly to $1.9 million at retirement, and then stays constant at that level. Turning to the first graph, Real Consumption starts at $44,361, rises smoothly to $79,567 at retirement, and then stays constant at that level.

How much saving does it take to reach such a comfortable lifestyle? Savings starts at 9.7% of salary at age 31, rises to 23.5% of salary at age 55, and tapers off to 18.2% of salary at age 65. Clearly, a lot of saving is required to live so well in retirement.

Now let's consider the risk involved.

7. **Adjust The Standard Deviation and View The Risk Involved.** Change the standard deviation to a realistic figure. Enter **17.0000%** in cell **B8**. The random variables in rows **37** and **38** spring to life and the graph of real consumption over the life-cycle reflect the high or low realizations of the broad stock portfolio. Press the function key **F9** and the Excel model is recalculated. You see a new realization of real consumption on the first graph. The three figures below show: (a) a low real consumption case due to low stock returns, (b) a medium real consumption case due to medium stock returns, and (c) a high real consumption case due to high stock returns.

FIGURE 8.7 Low Real Consumption Due To Low Stock Returns.

	A	B	C	D	E	F	G
1	LIFE-CYCLE FINANCIAL PLANNING			Full-Scale			
2							
3	**Inputs**						
4	Real Riskfree Rate	2.1%					
5	Working Years	35					
6	Inflation Rate	2.4%					
7	Average Real Return of Stock Port	6.0%					
8	Standard Deviation of Stock Port	17.0000%					
9	Federal Income Bracket 1 Tax Rate	10.0%					
10	Federal Income Bracket 2 Tax Rate	15.0%					
11	Federal Income Bracket 3 Tax Rate	27.0%					
12	Federal Income Bracket 4 Tax Rate	30.0%					
13	Federal Income Bracket 5 Tax Rate	35.0%					
14	Federal Income Bracket 6 Tax Rate	38.6%					
15	Federal FICA-SSI Tax Rate on Salary	6.2%					
16	Federal FICA-Medicare Tax on Salary	1.45%					
17	State Income Tax Rate	3.0%					
18	Adjustment for Social Security	2.50%					
19							
20							
21							
22							
23							
24							
25							
26							
27							
28							

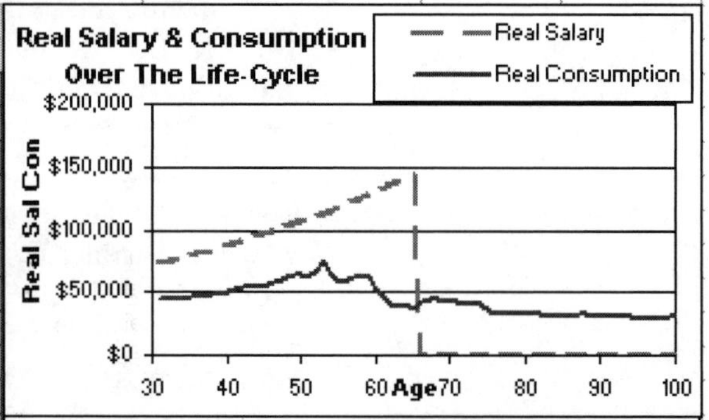

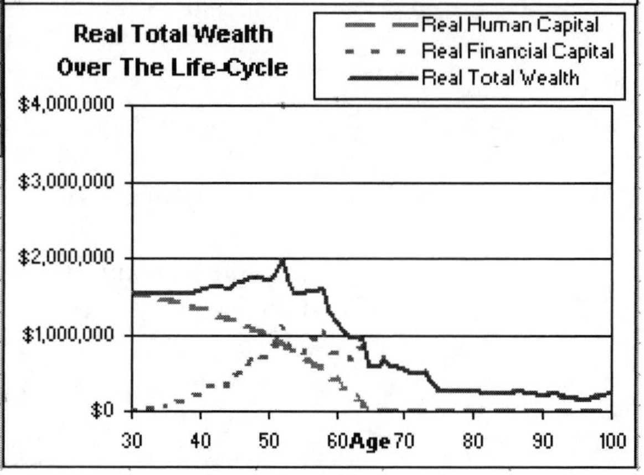

FIGURE 8.8 Medium Real Consumption Due To Medium Stock Returns.

	A	B	C	D	E	F	G
1	LIFE-CYCLE FINANCIAL	PLANNING		Full-Scale			
2							
3	**Inputs**						
4	Real Riskfree Rate	2.1%					
5	Working Years	35					
6	Inflation Rate	2.4%					
7	Average Real Return of Stock Port	6.0%					
8	Standard Deviation of Stock Port	17.0000%					
9	Federal Income Bracket 1 Tax Rate	10.0%					
10	Federal Income Bracket 2 Tax Rate	15.0%					
11	Federal Income Bracket 3 Tax Rate	27.0%					
12	Federal Income Bracket 4 Tax Rate	30.0%					
13	Federal Income Bracket 5 Tax Rate	35.0%					
14	Federal Income Bracket 6 Tax Rate	38.6%					
15	Federal FICA-SSI Tax Rate on Salary	6.2%					
16	Federal FICA-Medicare Tax on Salary	1.45%					
17	State Income Tax Rate	3.0%					
18	Adjustment for Social Security	2.50%					
19							
20							
21							
22							
23							
24							
25							
26							
27							
28							

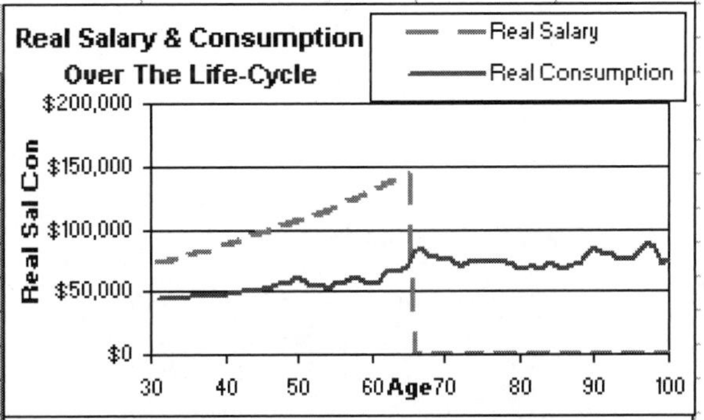

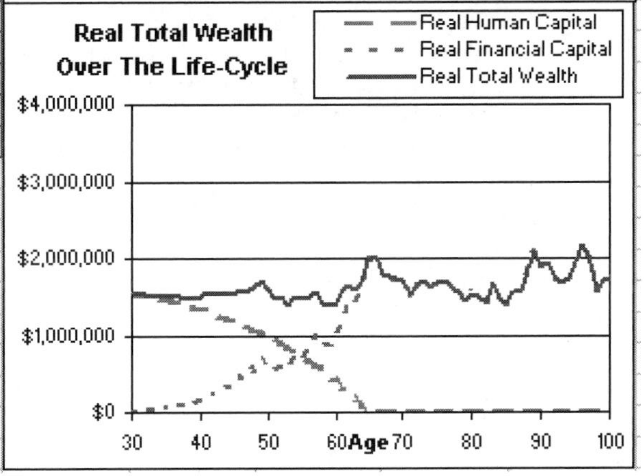

FIGURE 8.9 High Real Consumption Due To High Stock Returns.

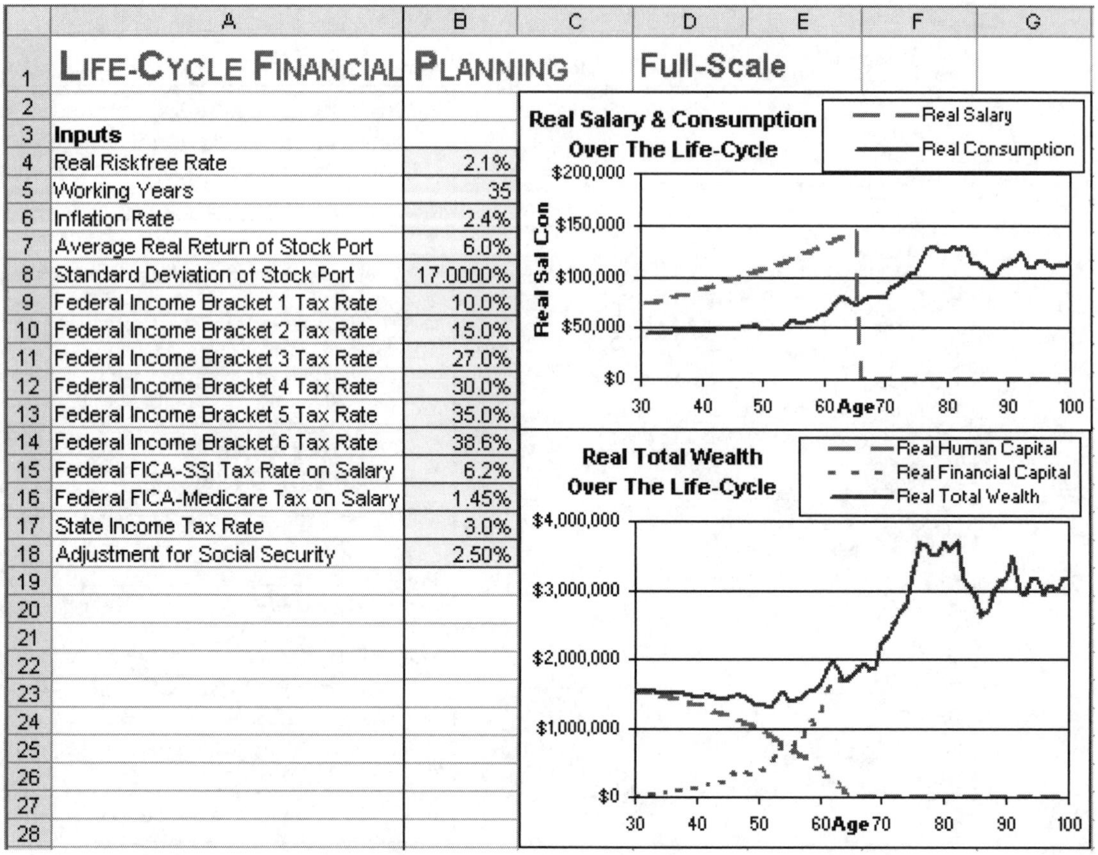

These three graphs are "representative" of the risk you face from being heavily investing in the broad stock portfolio. In the low case, real consumption drops to about $35,000. In the medium case, real consumption fluctuates between $50,000 and $100,000. In the high case, real consumption fluctuates between $100,000 and $150,000. Clearly, there is substantial risk from being so heavily exposed to the broad stock portfolio.

Now that we have completed the Excel model, it is time for you to explore. Change the values of the choice variables and see the implications for lifetime real consumption and real total wealth. For example, if you are uncomfortable with the amount of risk implied by the three figures above, consider more conservative strategies. Many investors reduce stock exposure in retirement years to little or nothing.

A key driver in the model is the initial value for Taxable Income / Total wealth in cell C34. Raise this value and there will be more real consumption in early working years and less real consumption retirement years. Lower this value and it will tilt in the opposite direction.

Play around with the choice variables and have fun exploring your lifetime opportunities. Enjoy!

Problems

Skill-Building Problems.

1. Suppose that you are currently 28 years old and expect to earn a constant real salary of $64,000 starting next year. You are planning to work for 32 years and then retire. You currently have $0 in financial capital. You are limited to investing in the riskfree asset. The real riskfree rate is 2.8%. Develop a financial plan for real savings and real consumption over your lifetime.

2. Suppose that you are currently 32 years old and expect to earn a constant real salary of $85,000 starting next year. You are planning to work for 25 years and then retire. You currently have $10,000 in financial capital. You can invest in the riskfree asset or a broad stock portfolio. The inflation rate is 3.4% and the real riskfree rate is 2.5%. A broad stock portfolio offers an average real return of 7.3% and a standard deviation of 25.0%. Suppose that federal income taxes have six brackets with the following rates: 10.0%, 15.0%, 27.0%, 30.0%, 35.0%, and 38.6%. For current year, the upper cutoffs on the first five brackets are $6,000, $27,950, $67,700, $141,250, and $307,050 and these cutoffs are indexed to inflation. The state tax rate is 4.5%, federal FICA-SSI tax rate on salary up to $87,000 is 6.2%, and the federal FICA-Medicare tax rate on any level of salary is 1.45%. You will start receiving social security benefits at age 66. The current level of social security benefits is $24,204 per year and this is indexed to inflation. Develop a financial plan for real savings and real consumption over your lifetime.

Skill-Extending Problems.

3. Extend the model above by converting the Excel model into a Dynamic Chart by adding spinners to drive the inputs. See **Black Scholes Option Pricing - Dynamic Chart** for details on how to implement spinners. After you click on the spinners to change the inputs, then adjust the Savings Percentage to have a smooth consumption pattern.

Live In-class Problems.

4. Given the partial Basics file **LifebasZ.xls**, do step **4 Working PV / Infinite PV**.

5. Given the partial Full-Scale file **LifefulZ.xls**, do step **3 Choice Variables**.

Chapter 9 Dividend Discount Models

9.1 Two Stage

Problem. Given the historical data, we can see that over last two years Hot Prospects Inc. has generated a very high real Return On Investment (Real ROI) of 22.3% and 20.7%. Over the last three years, its dividends per share have increased rapidly from $5.10 to $5.84 to $6.64. As the competition catches up over the next five years, the Hot Prospects Real ROI is expected to gradually slow down. The long-run forecast calls for the firm's Real ROI to match the firm's real discount rate (Real k), which is 9.0% per year. Hot Prospects follows a policy of retaining 50.0% of its earnings and paying out the rest as dividends. Going forward, the inflation rate is expected to be 3.0% per year indefinitely. What is the firm's intrinsic value / share?

Solution Strategy. Construct a two-stage discounted dividend model. In stage one, explicitly forecast the firm's dividend over a five-year horizon. In stage two, forecast the firm's dividend from year six to infinity and calculate its continuation value as the present value of this constant growth annuity. Then, discount the future dividends and the date 5 continuation value back to the present to get the intrinsic value per share.

FIGURE 9.1 Excel Model of Dividend Discount Models - Two Stage.

	A	B	C	D	E	F	G	H	I	J
1	DIVIDEND DISCOUNT MODELS			Two Stage						
2										
3	**Inputs**									
4	Inflation Rate	3.0%								
5	Real Discount Rate (Real k)	9.0%								
6	Earnings Retention Rate	50.0%								
7										
8	**Outputs**									**Stage 2:**
9	Nominal Discount Rate (k)	12.3%								**Infinite**
10						**Stage 1: Explicit Forecast**				**Horizon**
11			**Historical Data**			**Horizon (ROI > k)**				**(ROI = k)**
12	Period	-2	-1	0	1	2	3	4	5	6
13	Inflation Rate		2.8%	3.1%	3.0%	3.0%	3.0%	3.0%	3.0%	3.0%
14	Real Return on Investment (Real ROI)		22.3%	20.7%	19.0%	17.0%	15.0%	13.0%	11.0%	9.0%
15	Nominal Return on Investment (ROI)		25.7%	24.4%	22.6%	20.5%	18.5%	16.4%	14.3%	12.3%
16	Real Growth Rate in Dividend (Real g)		11.2%	10.4%	9.5%	8.5%	7.5%	6.5%	5.5%	4.5%
17	Nominal Growth Rate in Dividend (g)		14.5%	13.7%	12.8%	11.8%	10.7%	9.7%	8.7%	7.6%
18	Nominal Dividend / Share	$5.10	$5.84	$6.64	$7.49	$8.37	$9.27	$10.17	$11.05	$11.89
19	Continuation Value / Share								$256.51	
20	Sum of Future Div. & Cont. Value/Shr				$7.49	$8.37	$9.27	$10.17	$267.56	
21	PV of Future Div. & Cont. Value / Shr				$6.67	$6.64	$6.55	$6.40	$150.00	
22	Intrinsic Value / Share			$176.26						

How To Build This Excel Model.

1. **Inputs.** Enter the inflation rate, real discount rate, and earnings retention rate into the range **B4:B6**. Enter the historical data in the range **C13:D18** and the cell **B18**. Input the projected inflation rate by entering **=$B$4** in cell **E13** and copy the cell to the range **F13:J13**.

2. **Calculate The Nominal Discount Rate.** The Nominal Discount Rate = (1 + Inflation Rate) * (1 + Real Discount Rate) - 1. Enter **=(1+B4)*(1+B5)-1** in cell **B9**.

3. **Forecast Future Real and Nominal ROI.** In the long-run, the firm's Real ROI is forecast to equal the firm's real discount rate. Enter **=B5** in cell **J14**. Given the Real ROI of 20.7% on date 0 and a forecast of 9.0% per year starting in year 6, forecast the intermediate years by entering a smooth declining pattern, such as **19.0%**, **17.0%**, **15.0%**, etc. from date 1 to date 5 in the range **E14:I14**. For date 6, enter **=B5** in cell **J14**. Calculate the Nominal Return On Investment (ROI) = (1 + Inflation Rate) * (1 + Real ROI) - 1. Enter **=(1+E13)*(1+E14)-1** in cell **E15** and copy the cell to the range **F15:J15**.

4. **Real and Nominal Growth Rate in Dividends.** Calculate the Real Growth Rate in Dividend (Real g) = (Real ROI) * (Earnings Retention Rate). Enter **=E14*$B$6** in cell **E16** and copy the cell to the range **F16:J16**. Calculate the Nominal Growth Rate in Dividend (g) = (1 + Inflation Rate) (1 + Real g) - 1. Enter **=(1+$B$4)*(1+E16)-1** in cell **E17** and copy the cell to the range **F17:J17**.

5. **Nominal Dividend / Share.** Calculate the Date t Nominal Dividend = (Date t-1 Nominal Dividend) * (1 + Date t Nominal Growth Rate in Dividend). Enter **=D18*(1+E17)** in cell **E18** and copy the cell to the range **F18:J18**.

6. **Date 5 Continuation Value.** The Date 5 Continuation Value is the present value of the stream of dividends from date 6 to infinity. Using the present value of an infinitely growing annuity formula, calculate Date 5 Continuation Value = (Date 6 Dividend) / (Nominal Discount Rate – Date 6 Nominal Growth Rate in Dividends). Enter **=J18/(B9-J17)** in cell **I19**.

7. **Sum and PV of Future Dividends and the Continuation Value / Share.** On each date, sum the future dividend and continuation value / share. Enter **=SUM(E18:E19)** in cell **E20** and copy the cell to the range **F20:J20**. Calculate the Present Value of the Future Dividend and Continuation Value / Share = (Date t Sum) / ((1 + Nominal Discount Rate) ^ t). Enter **=E20/((1+$B$9)^E12)** in cell **E21** and copy it across the range **F21:I21**.

8. **Intrinsic Value Per Share.** Sum the PV of Future Dividends and Continuation Value. Enter **=SUM(E21:I21)** in cell **D22**.

Hot Prospects Inc. is estimated to have an intrinsic value per share of $176.26.

9.2 Dynamic Chart

Problem. How sensitive is the Intrinsic Value to changes in: (1) the Inflation Rate, (2) Earnings Retention Rate, and (3) Real Discount Rate (k)? Said differently, how important is it to be very accurate in forecasting these three inputs?

Solution Strategy. First, we vary the Real Discount Rate input and use Excel's **Data Table** feature to generate the corresponding Intrinsic Value / Share outputs. Second, we construct a **Dynamic Chart** by graphing the Data Table inputs and outputs and by adding spinners to the Inflation Rate and Earnings Retention Rate inputs.

FIGURE 9.2 Excel Model of Dividend Discount Models - Dynamic Chart.

	A	B	C	D	E	F	G	H	I	J
1	DIVIDEND DISCOUNT MODELS			Dynamic Chart						
2										
3	**Inputs**									
4	Inflation Rate	3.0%		6						
5	Earnings Retention Rate	50.0%		5						
6										
7										
8										
9										
10										
11										
12										
13										
14	**Outputs**									
15	Real Discount Rate (Real k)	9.0%	7.0%	8.0%	9.0%	10.0%	11.0%	12.0%		
16	Intrinsic Value / Share	$176	$235	$202	$176	$156	$139	$125		
17										
18										**Stage 2:**
19	Nominal Discount Rate (k)	12.3%								**Infinite**
20					**Stage 1: Explicit Forecast**					**Horizon**
21		**Historical Data**			**Horizon (ROI > k)**					**(ROI = k)**
22	Period	-2	-1	0	1	2	3	4	5	6
23	Inflation Rate		2.8%	3.1%	3.0%	3.0%	3.0%	3.0%	3.0%	3.0%
24	Real Return on Investment (Real ROI)		22.3%	20.7%	19.0%	17.0%	15.0%	13.0%	11.0%	9.0%
25	Nominal Return on Investment (ROI)		25.7%	24.4%	22.6%	20.5%	18.5%	16.4%	14.3%	12.3%
26	Real Growth Rate in Dividend (Real g)		11.2%	10.4%	9.5%	8.5%	7.5%	6.5%	5.5%	4.5%
27	Nominal Growth Rate in Dividend (g)		14.5%	13.7%	12.8%	11.8%	10.7%	9.7%	8.7%	7.6%
28	Nominal Dividend / Share	$5.10	$5.84	$6.64	$7.49	$8.37	$9.27	$10.17	$11.05	$11.89
29	Continuation Value / Share								$256.51	
30	Sum of Future Div. & Cont. Value/Shr				$7.49	$8.37	$9.27	$10.17	$267.56	
31	PV of Future Div. & Cont. Value / Shr				$6.67	$6.64	$6.55	$6.40	$150.00	
32	Intrinsic Value / Share			$176.26						

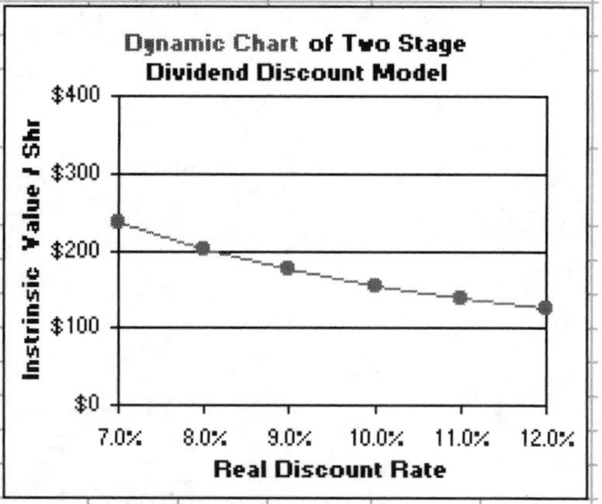

How To Build This Excel Model.

1. **Open the Two Stage Excel Model and Move A Few Things.** Open the Excel model that you created for Dividend Discount Models – Two Stage and immediately save the file under a new name using the **File Save As** command. Insert ten rows above the **Outputs**, by selecting the range **A8:A17** and clicking on **Insert Rows**. Move The Label "Outputs," by selecting the cell **A18**, clicking on **Edit Cut**, selecting the cell **A14** and clicking on **Edit Paste**. Using the same steps, move the range **A5:B5** to the range **A15:B15** and move the range **A6:B6** to the range **A5:B5**.

2. **Increase Row Height for the Spinners.** Select the range **A4:A5**. Then click on **Format Row Height** from the main menu. Enter a height of **30** and click on **OK**.

3. **Display the Forms Toolbar.** Select **View Toolbars Forms** from the main menu.

4. **Create the Spinners.** Look for the up-arrow / down-arrow button on the Forms toolbar (which will display the word "Spinner" if you hover the cursor over it) and click on it. Then draw the box for a spinner from the upper left corner of cell **C4** down to the lower right corner of the cell. Then a spinner appears in the cell **C4**. Right click on the spinner (press the right mouse button while the cursor is above the spinner) and a small menu pops up. Click on Copy. Then select the cell **C5** and click on Paste. This creates an identical spinner in cell **C5**. You now have two spinners down column **C**.

5. **Create The Cell Links.** Right click on the first spinner in the cell **C4** and a small menu pops up. Click on **Format Control** and a dialog box pops up. Enter the cell link **D4** in the **Cell link** edit box and click on **OK**. Repeat this procedure for the other spinner. Link the spinner in cell **C5** to cell **D5**. Click on the up-arrows and down-arrows of the spinners to see how they change the values in the linked cells.

6. **Create Scaled Inputs.** The values in the linked cells are always integers, but they can be scaled appropriately to the problem at hand. In cell **B4**, enter **=D4/200**. In cell **B5**, enter **=D5/10**.

7. **Enter Real Discount Rate Values.** In the range **C15:H15**, enter the values **7%**, **8%**, **9%**, **10%**, **11%**, and **12%**.

8. **Create A Data Table To Calculate Intrinsic Value / Share.** Use Excel's Data Table feature to calculate the Intrinsic Value / Share for each corresponding Real Discount Rate. Specify the output cell by entering **=D32** in cell **B16**. Select the range **B15:H16**, click on **Data Table**, enter **$B$15** in the **Row Input Cell** box, and click on **OK**.

9. **Graph the Infinitely-long Rate and Yield to Maturity.** Select the range **C15:H16**, then click on **Insert Chart** from the main menu. Select an **XY(Scatter)** chart type and make other selections to complete the Chart Wizard. Place the graph in the range **E2:J13**.

The Data Table and the graph indicate that decreasing the Real Discount Rate from 12% to 7% causes the Intrinsic Value / Share to jump from \$125 / Share to \$235 / Share. Thus, the Intrinsic Value / Share is *very sensitive* to Real Discount Rate. Clicking on the spinner for the Inflation Rate causes no change at all in the Intrinsic Value / Share. This makes sense because the Inflation Rate contributes equally to the Nominal Return on Investment and to the Nominal Discount Rate. The two effects cancel each other out, leaving zero net impact on Intrinsic Value / Share. Clicking on the spinner for the Earnings Retention Rate causes a huge movement in the Intrinsic Value / Share. Hence, it is important to be as accurate as possible about both the Real Discount Rate and the Earnings Retention Rates.

Problems

Skill-Building Problems.

1. Suppose that a firm has generated a real Return On Investment (Real ROI) of 14.6% and 11.9% of the last two year, while the inflation rate as been 3.5% and 2.4%, respectively. Over the last three years, the firm's dividends per share have increased from \$15.92 to \$16.23 to \$17.36. Over the next five years, the firm's Real ROI is expected to gradually slow down. The long-run forecast calls for the firm's Real ROI to match the firm's real discount rate (Real k), which is 6.2% per year. The firm follows a policy of retaining 34.0% of its earnings and paying out the rest as dividends. Going forward, the inflation rate is expected to be 4.1% per year indefinitely. Determine the firm's intrinsic value / share.

2. Perform instant experiments on whether changing various inputs causes an increase or decrease in the firm's intrinsic value / share and by how much.

   a. What happens when the inflation rate is increased?

   b. What happens when the earnings retention rate is increased?

Live In-class Problems.

3. Given the partial Two Stage file **DivtwosZ.xls**, do steps **4 Real and Nominal Growth Rate in Dividends, 5 Nominal Dividend / Share, 6 Date 5 Continuation Value, 7 Sum and PV of Future Dividends and Continuation Value / Share,** and **8 Intrinsic Value Per Share**.

4. Given the partial Dynamic Chart file **DivdynaZ.xls**, complete steps **7 Enter Real Discount Rate Values** and **8 Create A Data Table To Calculate Intrinsic Value / Share**.

PART 3 OPTIONS / FUTURES / DERIVATIVES

Chapter 10 Option Payoffs and Profits

10.1 Basics

Problem. A call option has an exercise price of $40.00 and an option price of $5.00. A put option has the same exercise price and option price. Graph the option payoffs and profits for buying or selling a call option and for buying or selling a put option.

Solution Strategy. We will create a switch that can be used to select buying or selling an option and another switch for a call vs. a put. For a range of stock prices at maturity, calculate the corresponding option payoffs and profits. Then graph it.

FIGURE 10.1 Excel Model of Option Payoffs and Profits - Basics.

	A	B	C	D	E	F	G	H	I
1	OPTION PAYOFFS AND PROFITS				Basics		Buy	Call	
2									
3	**Inputs**								
4	Buy or Sell: 1 = Buy, -1 = Sell	1							
5	Option Type: 1=Call, 2=Put	1							
6	Exercise Price	$40.00							
7	Option Price	$5.00							
8									
9									
10									
11									
12									
13									
14									
15									
16									
17									
18									
19									
20									
21	**Outputs**								
22	Stock Price At Maturity	$0.00	$8.00	$16.00	$24.00	$32.00	$40.00	$48.00	$56.00
23	Option Payoff	$0.00	$0.00	$0.00	$0.00	$0.00	$0.00	$8.00	$16.00
24	Option Profit	-$5.00	-$5.00	-$5.00	-$5.00	-$5.00	-$5.00	$3.00	$11.00

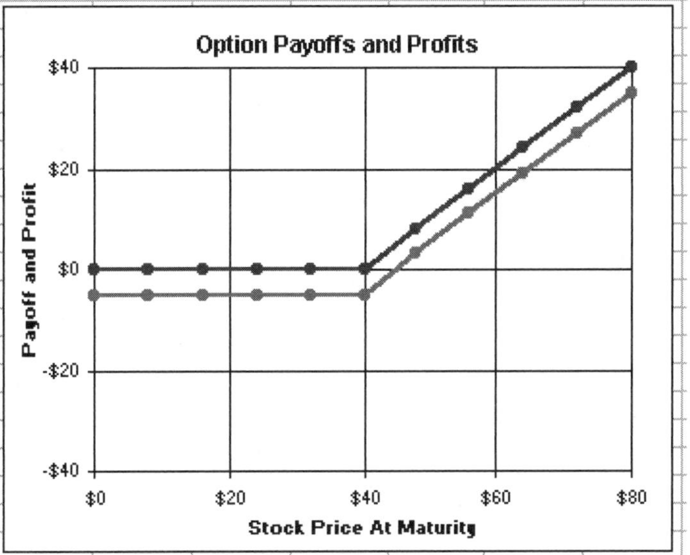

How To Build This Excel Model.

1. **Enter The Inputs.** Enter **1** in cell **B4**. This will serve as a switch with **1** for Buying and. **-1** for Selling. Enter **1** in cell **B5**. This will serve as a switch

with **1** for a Call and **2** for a Put. To highlight which case is being considered, enter **=IF($B$4=1,"Buy","Sell")** in cell **G1** and **=IF($B$5=1,"Call","Put")** in cell **H1** Enter the other inputs into the range **B6:B7**.

2. **Enter Stock Price At Maturity.** Enter Stock Price At Maturity values **$0.00, $8.00, $16.00, $24.00, …, $80.00** in the range **B22:L22**.

3. **Option Payoff.** The formulas for option payoffs are:

   - For a Call, the Payoff At Maturity = Max (Stock Price At Maturity – Exercise Price, 0).

   - For a Put, the Payoff At Maturity = Max (Exercise Price – Stock Price At Maturity, 0).

We need to multiply these payoffs by the Buy or Sell switch in cell **B4**. Enter **=IF($B$5=1,$B$4*MAX(B22-$B$6,0),$B$4*MAX($B$6-B22,0))** in cell **B23** and copy this cell to the range **C23:L23**.

4. **Option Profit.** The formula for an Option Profit = Option Payoff - (Buy or Sell switch) * (Option Price). Enter **=B23-$B$4*$B$7** in cell **B24** and copy this cell to the range **C24:L24**.

5. **Graph the Option Payoffs and Profits.** Highlight the range **B22:L24**. Next choose **Insert Chart** from the main menu. Select an **XY(Scatter)** chart type and make other selections to complete the Chart Wizard. Place the graph in the range **C2:I21**.

The graph displays the "hockey stick" payoffs and profits that characterize options. Change the switches between buy vs. sell and call vs. put to see all four graphs.

Problems

Skill-Building Problems.

1. A call option has an exercise price of $32.54 and an option price of $4.71. A put option has the same exercise price and option price. Graph the option payoffs and profits for buying or selling a call option and for buying or selling a put option.

2. A call option has an exercise price of $18.23 and an option price of $2.96. A put option has the same exercise price and option price. Graph the option payoffs and profits for buying or selling a call option and for buying or selling a put option.

Live In-class Problems.

1. Given the partial Basics file **OpaybasZ.xls**, do steps **3 Option Payoff** and **4 Option Profit**.

Chapter 11 Option Trading Strategies

11.1 Two Assets

Problem. There are three types of trading strategies involving options: (1) strategies involving a single option and a stock, (2) spreads involving options of one type (i.e., two or more calls or two or more puts), and (3) combinations involving both call(s) and put(s). Construct a chart that can show all of the trading strategies involving two assets.

Solution Strategy. We will create ranges for first asset inputs and for second asset inputs. Then calculate first asset profit, second asset profit, total profit, exercise price lines, and graph them.

FIGURE 11.1 Excel Model of Option Trading Strategies - Two Assets.

	A	B	C	D	E	F	G	H	I
1	OPTION TRADING STRATEGIES			Two Assets		Buying a Bullish Spread			
2						Buy Call		Sell Call	
3	**Inputs**								
4	First Asset								
5	Buy or Sell: 1 = Buy, -1 = Sell	1							
6	Type: 1=Call, 2=Put, 3=Stock	1							
7	Exercise Price	$30.00							
8	Asset Price	$12.00							
9	Second Asset								
10	Buy or Sell: 1 = Buy, -1 = Sell	-1							
11	Type: 1=Call, 2=Put, 3=Stock	1							
12	Exercise Price	$45.00							
13	Asset Price	$6.00							
14									
15									
16									
17									
18									
19									
20									
21									
22									
23									
24									
25	**Outputs**								
26	Stock Price At Maturity	$0.00	$30.00	$45.00	$80.00	$30.00	$30.00	$45.00	$45.00
27	First Asset Profit	-$12.00	-$12.00	$3.00	$38.00				
28	Second Asset Profit	$6.00	$6.00	$6.00	-$29.00				
29	Total Profit	-$6.00	-$6.00	$9.00	$9.00				
30	Lower Exercise Price					-$40.00	$40.00		
31	Higher Exercise Price							-$40.00	$40.00

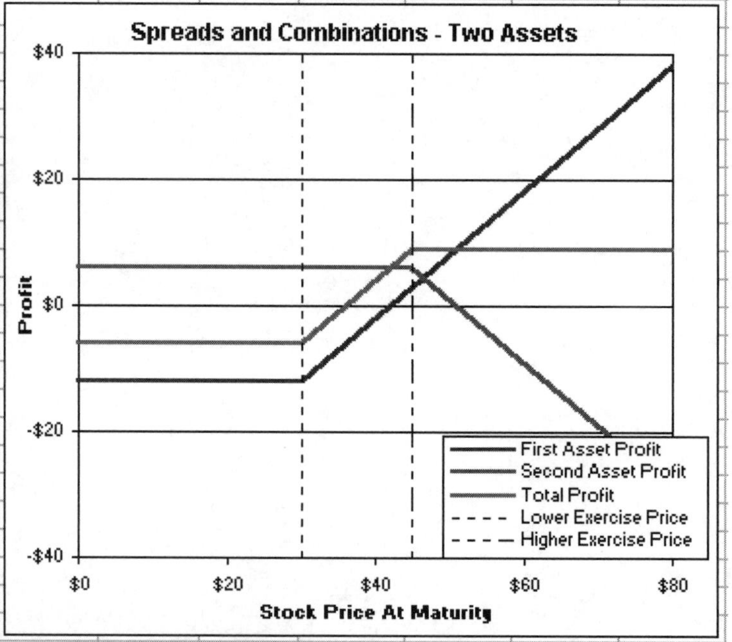

How To Build This Excel Model.

1. **Enter The Inputs.** For the First Asset, enter **1** in cell **B5**. This will serve as a switch with **1** for Buying and. **-1** for Selling. Also for the First Asset, enter **1** in cell **B6**. This will serve as a switch with **1** for a Call, **2** for a Put, and **3** for a Stock. To highlight the First Asset, enter **=IF(B5=1,"Buy ","Sell ")&IF(B6=1,"Call",IF(B6=2,"Put","Stock"))** in cell **F2**. Enter the other First Asset inputs into the range **B7:B8**. Create the Second Asset inputs by copying the range **B5:B8** to the cell **B10** and highlight it by entering **=IF(B10=1,"Buy ","Sell ")&IF(B11=1,"Call",IF(B11=2,"Put","Stock"))** in cell **H2**.

2. **Enter Stock Price At Maturity.** Enter Stock Price At Maturity value **$0.00** in cell **B26**, the lower exercise price **=IF(B7<B12,B7,B12)** in cell **C26**, the higher exercise price **=IF(B7>B12,B7,B12)** in cell **D26**, and **$80.00** in cell **E26**. Reference the lower exercise price **=$C$26** in **F26** and copy the cell to the cell **G26**. Reference the higher exercise price **=$D$26** in **H26** and copy the cell to the cell **I26**.

3. **Asset Profit.** The formulas for asset profits are:

   - For a Call, the Profit = Max (Stock Price At Maturity – Exercise Price, 0) - Asset Price.

   - For a Put, the Profit = Max (Exercise Price – Stock Price At Maturity, 0) - Asset Price.

   - For a Stock, the Profit = Stock Price At Maturity - Asset Price

   We need to multiply these profits by the First Asset Buy or Sell switch in cell **B5** or by the corresponding Second Asset Buy or Sell switch in cell **B10**. For the First Asset, Enter **=IF($B$6=1,$B$5*(MAX(B26-$B$7,0)-$B$8),IF($B$6=2,$B$5*(MAX($B$7-B26,0)-$B$8),$B$5*(B26-$B$8)))** in cell **B27** and copy this cell to the range **C27:E27**. For the Second Asset, Enter **=IF($B$11=1,$B$10*(MAX(B26-$B$12,0)-$B$13),IF($B$11=2,$B$10*(MAX($B$12-B26,0)-$B$13),$B$10*(B26-$B$8)))** in cell **B28** and copy this cell to the range **C28:E28**.

4. **Total Profit.** The Total Profit = First Asset Profit + Second Asset Profit. Enter **=B27+B28** in cell **B29** and copy this cell to the range **C29:E29**.

5. **Exercise Price Lines.** When each asset is an option, it is convenient to have vertical lines on the graph at the corresponding exercise price. To do this enter **-40** in cell **F30**, **=IF(B6=3,-40,40)** in cell **G30**, **-40** in cell **H31**, **=IF(B11=3,-40,40)** in cell **I31**.

6. **Graph the Asset Profits and Exercise Prices.** Highlight the range **B26:I31**. Next choose **Insert Chart** from the main menu. Select an **XY(Scatter)** chart type and make other selections to complete the Chart Wizard. Place the graph in the range **C3:I25**.

FIGURE 11.2 Table of Option Trading Strategies.

	J	K
1		
2	Low-High:	Buy Call, Sell Call
3		
4	No	Buying a Covered Call
5	No	Writing a Covered Call
6	No	Buying a Protective Put
7	No	Writing a Protective Put
8	Yes	Buying a Bullish Spread
9	No	Buying a Bearish Spread
10	No	Buying a Straddle
11	No	Writing a Straddle
12	No	Buying a Strangle
13	No	Writing a Strangle
14	No	Other Strategies

7. **(Optional) Add An Option Trading Strategy Label.** As a nice extra touch, add a label in cell **F1** which identifies the type of option trading strategy. Here are the steps to accomplish this:

   - **Two asset label.** Combine the labels in **F2** and **H2** starting with the asset which has the lowest exercise price. Enter **=IF(B7<B12,F2&", "&H2,H2&", "&F2)** in cell **K2**.

   - **Buying a Covered Call.** Test for Buy Stock and Sell Call. Enter **=IF(OR($K$2="Buy Stock, Sell Call",$K$2="Sell Call, Buy Stock"),"Yes","No")** in cell **J4**.

   - **Writing a Covered Call.** Test for Sell Stock and Buy Call. Enter **=IF(OR($K$2="Sell Stock, Buy Call",$K$2="Buy Call, Sell Stock"),"Yes","No")** in cell **J5**.

   - **Buying a Protected Put.** Test for Buy Stock and Buy Put. Enter **=IF(OR($K$2="Buy Stock, Buy Put",$K$2="Buy Put, Buy Stock"),"Yes","No")** in cell **J6**.

   - **Writing a Protected Put.** Test for Sell Stock and Sell Put. Enter **=IF(OR($K$2="Sell Stock, Sell Put",$K$2="Sell Put, Sell Stock"),"Yes","No")** in cell **J7**.

   - **Buying a Bullish Spread.** Test for Buy Call Low and Sell Call High or Buy Put Low and Sell Put High. Enter **=IF(OR($K$2="Buy Call, Sell Call",$K$2="Buy Put, Sell Put"),"Yes","No")** in cell **J8**.

   - **Buying a Bearish Spread.** Test for Sell Call Low and Buy Call High or Sell Put Low and Buy Put High. Enter **=IF(OR($K$2="Sell Call, Buy Call",$K$2="Sell Put, Buy Put"),"Yes","No")** in cell **J9**.

- **Buying a Straddle.** Test for Buy Call and Buy Put and the same exercise price. In cell **J10**, enter **=IF(AND(OR($K$2="Buy Call, Buy Put",$K$2="Buy Put, Buy Call"),$B$7=$B$12),"Yes","No")**.

- **Writing a Straddle.** Test for Buy Call and Buy Put and the same exercise price. In cell **J11**, enter **=IF(AND(OR($K$2="Sell Call, Sell Put",$K$2="Sell Put, Sell Call"),$B$7=$B$12),"Yes","No")**.

- **Buying a Strangle.** Test for Buy Put Low and Buy Call High. Enter **=IF(OR($K$2="Buy Put, Buy Call"),"Yes","No")** in cell **J12**.

- **Writing a Strangle.** Test for Sell Put Low and Sell Call High. Enter **=IF(OR($K$2="Sell Put, Sell Call"),"Yes","No")** in cell **J13**.

- **Other Strategies.** Test the range **J4:J13** for "Yes" cases. Enter **=IF(COUNTIF(J4:J13,"=Yes")>0,"No","Yes")** in cell **J14**.

- **Option Trading Strategy Label.** Determine which type of option trading strategy applies by looking for "Yes" in the range **J4:J14** using the **VLOOKUP** function. Enter **=VLOOKUP("Yes",J4:K14,2,FALSE)** in cell **F1**.

Incidentally in case you're wondering, Writing a Bullish Spread is the same as Buying a Bearish Spread. Similarly, Writing a Bearish Spread is the same as Buying a Bullish Spread.

11.2 Four Assets

Problem. Construct a chart that can show the trading strategies which involve four assets.

Solution Strategy. We will expand the input ranges to include a place for third asset inputs and fourth asset inputs. Then expand the calculations to include third asset profit, fourth asset profit, total profit, exercise price lines, and graph them.

FIGURE 11.3 Excel Model of Option Trading Strategies - Four Assets.

	A	B	C	D	E	F	G	H	I
1	OPTION TRADING STRATEGIES			Four Assets		Buying a Butterfly Spread			
2		Buy Call		Sell Call		Sell Call		Buy Call	
3	Inputs								
4	First Asset (Lowest Exer Price)								
5	Buy or Sell: 1 = Buy, -1 = Sell	1							
6	Type: 1=Call, 2=Put, 3=Stock	1							
7	Exercise Price	$25.00							
8	Asset Price	$8.00							
9	Second Asset (Med-Low Exer Price)								
10	Buy or Sell: 1 = Buy, -1 = Sell	-1							
11	Type: 1=Call, 2=Put, 3=Stock	1							
12	Exercise Price	$35.00							
13	Asset Price	$10.00							
14	Third Asset (Med-High Exer Price)								
15	Buy or Sell: 1 = Buy, -1 = Sell	-1							
16	Type: 1=Call, 2=Put, 3=Stock	1							
17	Exercise Price	$35.00							
18	Asset Price	$4.00							
19	Fourth Asset (Highest Exer Price)								
20	Buy or Sell: 1 = Buy, -1 = Sell	1							
21	Type: 1=Call, 2=Put, 3=Stock	1							
22	Exercise Price	$45.00							
23	Asset Price	$10.00							
24									
25	Outputs								
26	Stock Price At Maturity	$0.00	$25.00	$35.00	$35.00	$45.00	$80.00	$25.00	$25.00
27	First Asset Profit	-$8.00	-$8.00	$2.00	$2.00	$12.00	$47.00		
28	Second Asset Profit	$10.00	$10.00	$10.00	$10.00	$0.00	-$35.00		
29	Third Asset Profit	$4.00	$4.00	$4.00	$4.00	-$6.00	-$41.00		
30	Fourth Asset Profit	-$10.00	-$10.00	-$10.00	-$10.00	-$10.00	$25.00		
31	Total Profit	-$4.00	-$4.00	$6.00	$6.00	-$4.00	-$4.00		
32	Lowest Exer Price							-$40.00	$40.00
33	Med-Low Exer Price								
34	Med-High Exer Price								
35	Highest Exer Price								

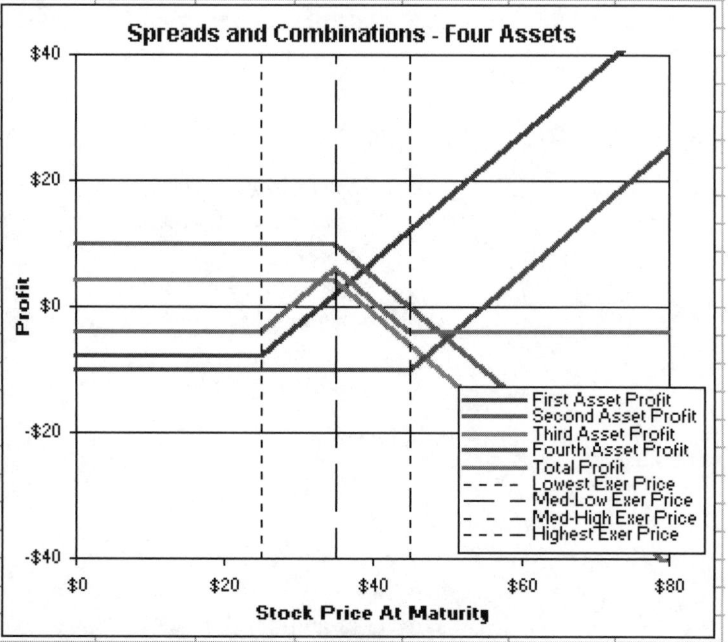

How To Build This Excel Model.

1. **Start with the Two Assets Excel Model.** Open the Excel model that you created for Option Trading Strategies – Two Assets and immediately save the file under a new name using the **File Save As** command.

2. **Inputs for the Third and Fourth Assets.** Create a place for the input information on the third and fourth assets. Copy the range **B5:B13** to the cell **B15**. For each asset, enter the new inputs (buy or sell, type, exercise price, and asset price) as shown in the figure above. Specifically, put the first asset inputs in the range **B5:B8**, second asset inputs in the range **B10:B13**, third asset inputs in the range **B15:B18**, and fourth asset inputs in the range **B20:B23**. Select the range **F2:H2**, click on **Edit Cut**, select the cell **B2**, and click on **Edit Paste**. To highlight the Third Asset, enter **=IF(B15=1,"Buy ","Sell ")&IF(B16=1,"Call",IF(B16=2,"Put","Stock"))** in cell **F2**. To highlight the Fourth Asset, enter

=IF(B20=1,"Buy ","Sell")&IF(B21=1,"Call",IF(B21=2,"Put","Stock")) in cell H2. Note that this Excel model uses the convention that the first asset in the one with the lowest exercise price, the second asset has the second lowest exercise price, the third has the third lowest exercise price, and the fourth asset has the highest exercise prices. Ties in exercise prices can be assigned either way.

3. **Stock Price At Maturity.** Make room and add the additional exercise price columns. Select the range E26:I31, click on **Edit Cut**, select the cell G26, and click on **Edit Paste**. Enter **=B7** in cell C26. Enter **=B12** in cell D26. Enter **=B17** in cell E26. Enter **=B22** in cell F26. Reference the third asset exercise price **=$E$26** in L26 and copy the cell to the cell M26. Reference the fourth asset exercise price **=$F$26** in N26 and copy the cell to the cell O26.

4. **Asset Profits.** Copy the range B27:B28 to the range C27:G27. Insert two rows by selecting A29:A30 and clicking on **Insert Rows**. The formulas for asset profits are:

   - For a Call, the Profit = Max (Stock Price At Maturity – Exercise Price, 0) - Asset Price.

   - For a Put, the Profit = Max (Exercise Price – Stock Price At Maturity, 0) - Asset Price.

   - For a Stock, the Profit = Stock Price At Maturity - Asset Price

   We need to multiply these profits by the Third Asset Buy or Sell switch in cell B15 or by the corresponding Fourth Asset Buy or Sell switch in cell B20. For the Third Asset, Enter **=IF($B$16=1,$B$15*(MAX(B$26-$B$17,0)-$B$18),IF($B$16=2,$B$15*(MAX($B$17-B$26,0)-$B$18),$B$15*(B$26-$B$18)))** in cell B29 and copy this cell to the range C29:G29. For the Fourth Asset, Enter **=IF($B$21=1,$B$20*(MAX(B$26-$B$22,0)-$B$23),IF($B$21=2,$B$20*(MAX($B$22-B$26,0)-$B$23),$B$20*(B$26-$B$23)))** in cell B30 and copy this cell to the range C30:G30.

5. **Total Profit.** The Total Profit = First Asset Profit + Second Asset Profit + Third Asset Profit + Fourth Asset Profit. Enter **=B27+B28+B29+B30** in cell B31 and copy this cell to the range C31:G31.

6. **Exercise Price Lines.** When each asset is an option, add vertical lines on the graph for the third and fourth asset exercise prices. enter **-40** in cell L34, **=IF(B16=3,-40,40)** in cell M34, **-40** in cell N35, **=IF(B21=3,-40,40)** in cell O35.

7. **Graph the Asset Profits and Exercise Prices.** Click on the old graph and press the **Delete** key. Highlight the range **B26:O35**. Next choose **Insert Chart** from the main menu. Select an **XY(Scatter)** chart type and make other selections to complete the Chart Wizard. Place the graph in the range C3:I25.

FIGURE 11.4 Table of Option Trading Strategies.

	J	K	L
1			
2	Low-High:	Buy Call, Sell Call, Sell Call, Buy Call	
3			
4	Yes	Buying a Butterfly Spread	
5	No	Writing a Butterfly Spread	
6	No	Other Strategies	

8. **(Optional) Add An Option Trading Strategy Label.** As a nice extra touch, add a label in cell **F1** which identifies the type of option trading strategy. Here are the steps to accomplish this:

   - **Four asset label.** Combine the labels in **B2**, **D2**, **F2**, and **H2** (which are already in order from the lowest exercise price to the highest). Enter **=B2&", "&D2&", "&F2&", "&H2** in cell **K2**.

   - **Buying a Butterfly Spread.** Test for Buy Call, Sell Call, Sell Call, Buy Call and the same second and third exercise price. Enter **=IF(AND(OR($K$2="Buy Call, Sell Call, Sell Call, Buy Call",$K$2="Buy Put, Sell Put, Sell Put, Buy Put"),$B$12=$B$17),"Yes","No")** in cell **J4**.

   - **Writing a Butterfly Spread.** Test for Sell Call, Buy Call, Buy Call, Sell Call and the same second and third exercise price. Enter **=IF(AND(OR($K$2="Sell Call, Buy Call, Buy Call, Sell Call",$K$2="Sell Put, Buy Put, Buy Put, Sell Put"),$B$12=$B$17),"Yes","No")** in cell **J5**.

   - **Other Strategies.** Test the range **J4:J5** for "Yes" cases. Enter **=IF(COUNTIF(J4:J5,"=Yes")>0,"No","Yes")** in cell **J6**.

   - **Option Trading Strategy Label.** Determine which type of option trading strategy applies by looking for "Yes" in the range **J4:J6** using the **VLOOKUP** function. Enter **=VLOOKUP("Yes",J4:K6,2,FALSE)** in cell **F1**.

Buying a butterfly spread is betting that there will be less volatility than the rest of the market thinks. Writing a butterfly spread is the opposite.

Problems

Skill-Building Problems.

1. There are three types of trading strategies involving options: (1) strategies involving a single option and a stock, (2) spreads involving options of one type (i.e., two or more calls or two or more puts), and (3) combinations

involving both call(s) and put(s). Graph all of the trading strategies involving two assets. In particular, show the following strategies:

a. First asset: Buy a stock for a stock price (asset price) of \$41.25 and
Second asset: Sell a call with an exercise price of \$47.39 for a call price of \$5.83 = Buying a covered call.

b. First asset: Sell a stock for a stock price (asset price) of \$36.47 and
Second asset: Buy a call with an exercise price of \$32.83 for a call price of \$6.74 = Writing a covered call.

c. First asset: Buy a stock for a stock price (asset price) of \$43.72 and
Second asset: Buy a put with an exercise price of \$47.87 for a put price of \$7.31 = Buying a protective put.

d. First asset: Sell a stock for a stock price (asset price) of \$36.93 and
Second asset: Sell a put with an exercise price of \$33.29 for a put price of \$6.36 = Writing a protective put.

e. First asset: Buy a call with an exercise price of \$24.12 for a call price of \$5.31 and
Second asset: Sell a call with an exercise price of \$38.34 for a call price of \$3.27 = Buying a bullish spread = Writing a bearish spread.

f. First asset: Sell a call with an exercise price of \$18.92 for a call price of \$7.39 and
Second asset: Buy a call with an exercise price of \$45.72 with a call price of \$3.78 = Buying a bearish spread = Writing a bullish spread.

g. First asset: Buy a call with an exercise price of \$41.29 for a call price of \$3.81 and
Second asset: Buy a put with an exercise price of \$41.29 for a put price of \$4.94 = Buying a straddle.

h. First asset: Sell a call with an exercise price of \$38.47 for a call price of \$2.93 and
Second asset: Sell a put with an exercise price of \$38.47 for a put price of \$5.63 = Writing a straddle.

i. First asset: Buy a call with an exercise price of \$42.72 for a call price of \$2.93 and
Second asset: Buy a put with an exercise price of \$36.44 for a put price of \$5.63 = Buying a strangle.

j. First asset: Sell a call with an exercise price of \$46.18 for a call price of \$3.58 and
Second asset: Sell a put with an exercise price of \$38.50 for a put price of \$6.39 = Writing a strangle.

2. Graph all of the trading strategies involving four assets. In particular, show:

k. First asset: Buy a call with an exercise price of \$25.73 for a call price of \$7.92 and
Second asset: Sell a call with an exercise price of \$34.07 for a call price of \$10.15
Third asset: Sell a call with an exercise price of \$34.07 for a call price of \$3.96 and
Fourth asset: Buy a call with an exercise price of \$41.83 for a call price of \$9.23 = Buying a butterfly spread using calls.

l. First asset: Buy a call with an exercise price of \$23.84 for a call price of \$5.39 and
Second asset: Sell a call with an exercise price of \$36.19 for a call price of \$6.98
Third asset: Sell a call with an exercise price of \$36.19 for a call price of \$3.36 and
Fourth asset: Buy a call with an exercise price of \$47.28 for a call price of \$8.34 = Writing a butterfly spread using calls.

m. First asset: Buy a put with an exercise price of \$29.33 for a put price of \$4.59 and
Second asset: Sell a put with an exercise price of \$39.54 for a put price of \$2.87
Third asset: Sell a put with an exercise price of \$39.54 for a put price of \$4.56 and
Fourth asset: Buy a put with an exercise price of \$54.78 for a put price of \$10.37 = Buying a butterfly spread using puts.

n. First asset: Buy a put with an exercise price of \$27.49 for a put price of \$3.22 and
Second asset: Sell a put with an exercise price of \$41.38 for a put price of \$5.39
Third asset: Sell a put with an exercise price of \$41.38 for a put price of \$2.74 and
Fourth asset: Buy a put with an exercise price of \$52.86 for a put price of \$9.49 = Writing a butterfly spread using puts.

Live In-class Problems.

2. Given the partial Two Assets file **OtradtwZ.xls**, do steps **3 Asset Profit** and **4 Total Profit**.

3. Given the partial Four Assets file **OtradfoZ.xls**, complete step **4 Asset Profits** and do step **5 Total Profit**.

Chapter 12 Put-Call Parity

12.1 Basics

Problem. Consider a call option and put option on the same underlying stock with the same exercise price and time to maturity. The call price is \$4.00, the underlying stock price is \$43.00, the exercise price on both options is \$40.00, the riskfree rate is 5.00%, the time to maturity on both options is 0.25 years, and the stock pays a \$2.00 / share dividend in 0.10 years. What is the price of the put price now?

FIGURE 12.1 Excel Model of Put-Call Parity - Basics.

	A	B	C
1	PUT-CALL PARITY	Basics	
2			
3	**Inputs**		
4	Call Price Now	$4.00	
5	Stock Price Now	$43.00	
6	Exercise Price	$40.00	
7	Riskfree Rate	5.00%	
8	Time To Maturity	0.25	
9	Dividend	$2.00	
10	Time To Dividend	0.10	
11			
12	**Outputs**		
13	Put Price Now	$2.51	

How To Build This Excel Model.

1. **Inputs.** Enter the inputs into the range **B4:B10**.

2. **Put Price Now.** The Put-Call Parity formula is Put Price Now = Call Price Now - Stock Price Now + Exercise Price / ((1 + Riskfree Rate)^(Time To Maturity)) + Dividend / ((1 + Riskfree Rate)^(Time To Dividend)). Enter **=B4-B5+B6/((1+B7)^B8)+B9/((1+B7)^B10)** in cell **B13**.

Put-Call Parity predicts the Put Price is \$2.51.

12.2 Payoff Diagram

The Put-Call Parity equation claims that one Put Option is equivalent to a replicating portfolio consisting of one Call Option, short one Stock, and a Bond paying a face value equal to the exercise price of the put and call options. Construct a payoff diagram to determine if the payoff at maturity of the replicating portfolio is equivalent to the payoff at maturity of a put option.

FIGURE 12.2 Excel Model of Put-Call Parity - Payoff Diagram.

	A	B	C	D	E	F	G	H	I
1	PUT-CALL PARITY	Payoff Diagram							
2									
3	**Inputs**								
4	Call Price Now	$4.00							
5	Stock Price Now	$43.00							
6	Exercise Price	$40.00							
7	Riskfree Rate	5.00%							
8	Time To Maturity	0.25							
9	Dividend	$2.00							
10	Time To Dividend	0.10							
11									
12									
13									
14									
15									
16									
17									
18									
19	**Outputs**								
20	Stock Price at Maturity	$0.00	$8.00	$16.00	$24.00	$32.00	$40.00	$48.00	$56.00
21	Call Payoff	$0.00	$0.00	$0.00	$0.00	$0.00	$0.00	$8.00	$16.00
22	Short Stock Payoff	$0.00	-$8.00	-$16.00	-$24.00	-$32.00	-$40.00	-$48.00	-$56.00
23	Bond Payoff	$40.00	$40.00	$40.00	$40.00	$40.00	$40.00	$40.00	$40.00
24	Total Payoff	$40.00	$32.00	$24.00	$16.00	$8.00	$0.00	$0.00	$0.00
25	Exercise Price								
26									
27	Put Payoff	$40.00	$32.00	$24.00	$16.00	$8.00	$0.00	$0.00	$0.00

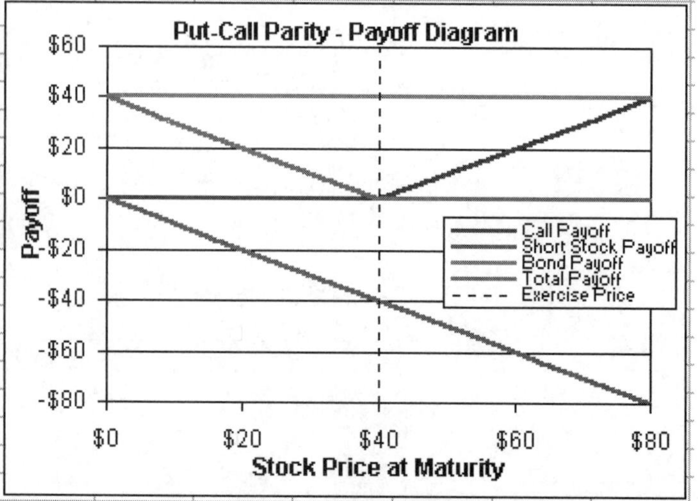

How To Build This Excel Model.

1. **Start with the Basics Excel Model.** Open the Excel model that you created for Put-Call Parity - Basics and immediately save the file under a new name using the **File Save As** command.

2. **Stock Price At Maturity.** Enter **0, 8, 16, ..., 80** in the range **B20:L20**. Enter **=$B$6** in cell **M20** and copy the cell to cell **N20**.

3. **Replicating Portfolio Payoff.** Calculate the payoff on each piece of the replicating portfolio

   - Call Payoff = Max(Stock Price At Maturity - Exercise Price, 0). Enter **=MAX(B20-$B$6,0)** in cell **B21** and copy the cell to the range **C21:L21**.

   - Short Stock Payoff = -(Stock Price At Maturity). Enter **=-B20** in cell **B22** and copy the cell to the range **C22:L22**.

   - Bond Payoff = Face Value = Exercise Price of the put and call options. Enter **=$B$6** in cell **B23** and copy the cell to the range **C23:L23**.

- Total Payoff = Sum of the Payoffs of the Three Replicating Portfolio Components. Enter **=SUM(B21:B23)** in cell **B24** and copy the cell to the range **C24:L24**.

4. **Exercise Price.** For convenience we wish to draw a vertical line at the exercise price by entering the upper and lower bound of the Y-axis. Enter **-80** in **M25** and **60** in **N25**.

5. **Put Payoff** = Max(Exercise Price - Stock Price At Maturity, 0). Enter **=MAX($B$6-B20,0)** in cell **B27** and copy the cell to the range **C27:L27**.

6. **Graph the Payoff on the Replicating Portfolio.** Highlight the range **B20:N25**, click on **Insert Chart** from the main menu, and select an **XY(Scatter)** chart type and make other selections to complete the Chart Wizard. Place the graph in the range **C2:I19**.

Looking at the Total Payoff on the Replicating Portfolio (row **24**), we see that it matches the Put Payoff in row **27**. Looking at the Payoff Diagram we can see the payoff of each of the component of the replicating portfolio: (1) Call Payoff, (2) Short Stock Payoff, and (3) Bond Payoff. At each point on the X-axis, we vertically sum the three components to get the Total Payoff. The Payoff Diagram verifies that the Total Payoff has the same "hockey stick" payoff as a put option.

Problems

Skill-Building Problems.

1. Consider a call option and put option on the same underlying stock with the same exercise price and time to maturity. The call price is $2.59, the underlying stock price is $28.63, the exercise price on both options is $26.18, the riskfree rate is 6.21%, the time to maturity on both options is 0.47 years, and the stock pays a $1.64 / share dividend in 0.28 years. Determine the price of the put price now.

2. The Put-Call Parity equation claims that one Put Option is equivalent to a replicating portfolio consisting of one Call Option, short one Stock, and a Bond paying a face value equal to the exercise price of the put and call options. Determine if the payoff at maturity of the replicating portfolio is equivalent to the payoff at maturity of a put option.

Live In-class Problems

3. Given the partial Basics file PcparbaZ.xls, do step 2 Put Price Now.

4. Given the partial Payoff Diagram file **PcparpaZ.xls**, do steps **3 Replicating Portfolio Payoff** and **5 Put Profit**.

Chapter 13 Binomial Option Pricing

13.1 Single Period

Problem. The current stock price of All-Net is $100.00, the potential up movement / period of All-Net's stock price is 30.00%, the potential down movement / period of All-Net's stock price is -20.00%, the risk-free rate is 2.0% per period, the exercise price of an one-period, European call option on All-Net is $90.00, the exercise price of an one-period, European put option on All-Net is $90.00, the time to maturity for both options is 0.75 years (nine months), and the number of periods for both options is 1. What are the current prices of the call and put?

Solution Strategy. First, calculate the date 1, maturity date items: stock up price, stock down price, and the corresponding call and put payoffs. Second, calculate the shares of stock and money borrowed to create a replicating portfolio that replicates the option payoff at maturity. Finally, calculate the price now of the replicating portfolio and, in the absence of arbitrage, this will be the option price now.

FIGURE 13.1 Excel Model of Binomial Option Pricing - Single Period - Call Option.

	A	B	C	D	E	F	G
1	BINOMIAL OPTION PRICING			Single Period			Call
2							
3	**Inputs**						
4	Option Type: 1=Call, 0=Put	1					
5	Stock Price Now	$100.00					
6	Up Movement / Period	30.00%					
7	Down Movement / Period	-20.00%					
8	Riskfree Rate / Period	2.00%					
9	Exercise Price	$90.00					
10	Time To Maturity (Years)	0.75					
11	Number of Periods	1					
12							
13		**Now**	**Maturity**				
14	**Period**	**0**	**1**				
15	**Time**	**0.000**	**0.750**				
16							
17	**Stock**	$100.00	$130.00				
18			$80.00				
19							
20	**Call**	$17.25	$40.00				
21			$0.00				
22							
23	**Replicating Portfolio**						
24							
25	**Stock Shares Bought** (Sold)						
26		0.800					
27							
28	**Money Lent** (Borrowed)						
29		($62.75)					

How To Build This Excel Model.

1. **Inputs.** Enter 1 in cell **B4**. This will serve as a switch between a call option and a put option. To highlight which type of option is being evaluated, enter **=IF($B$4=1,"Call","Put")** in cell **G1** and copy this cell to cell **A20**. Enter the other inputs into the range **B5:B11**.

2. **Enter Periods and Time.** Enter the periods **0** and **1** in cells **B14** and **C14**. The formula for Time = Time To Maturity * (Period / Number of Periods). Enter **=$B$10*(B14/$B$11)** in cell **B15** and copy the cell to cell **C15**.

3. **Stock Prices.** Set the Date 0 Stock Price equal to the Stock Price Now by entering **=B5** in cell **B17**. Calculate the Date 1 Stock Up Price = Stock Price Now * (1 + Up Movement / Period) by entering **=B17*(1+B6)** in cell **C17**. Calculate the Date 1 Stock Down Price = Stock Price Now * (1 + Down Movement / Period) by entering **=B17*(1+B7)** in cell **C18**.

4. **Option Payoffs At Maturity.** The formulas for option payoffs are:

   - For a Call, the Payoff At Maturity = Max (Stock Price At Maturity – Exercise Price, 0).

   - For a Put, the Payoff At Maturity = Max (Exercise Price – Stock Price At Maturity, 0).

   Enter **=IF($B$4=1,MAX(C17-$B$9,0),MAX($B$9-C17,0))** in cell **C20** and copy this cell to cell **C21**.

5. **Create A Replicating Portfolio.** For the Replicating Portfolio, calculate the Stock Shares Bought **(Sold)** using the Hedge Ratio = (Option Up Payoff – Option Down Payoff) / (Stock Up Price – Stock Down Price). In cell **B26**, enter **=(C20-C21)/(C17-C18)**. For the Replicating Portfolio, calculate the amount of Money Lent **(Borrowed)** = (Call Down Payoff –Hedge Ratio * Stock Down Price) / (1 + Riskfree Rate / Period). In cell **B29**, enter **=(C21-B26*C18)/(1+B8)**. Notice that replicating a Call option requires <u>Buying</u> Shares of Stock and <u>Borrowing</u> Money, whereas a Put option requires <u>Selling</u> Shares of Stock and <u>Lending</u> Money.

6. **Calculate the Option Price Now.** In the absence of arbitrage, the Option Price Now = Replicating Portfolio Price Now = Number of Shares of Stock * Stock Price Now + Money Borrowed. In cell **B20**, enter **=B26*B17+B29**.

We see that the Binomial Option Pricing model predicts a one-period European call price of $17.25. Now let's check the put.

FIGURE 13.2 Excel Model of Binomial Option Pricing - Single Period - Put Option.

	A	B	C	D	E	F	G
1	BINOMIAL OPTION PRICING			Single Period			Put
2							
3	**Inputs**						
4	Option Type: 1=Call, 0=Put	0					
5	Stock Price Now	$100.00					
6	Up Movement / Period	30.00%					
7	Down Movement / Period	-20.00%					
8	Riskfree Rate / Period	2.00%					
9	Exercise Price	$90.00					
10	Time To Maturity (Years)	0.75					
11	Number of Periods	1					
12							
13		**Now**	**Maturity**				
14	**Period**	**0**	**1**				
15	**Time**	**0.000**	**0.750**				
16							
17	**Stock**	$100.00	$130.00				
18			$80.00				
19							
20	**Put**	$5.49	$0.00				
21			$10.00				
22							
23	**Replicating Portfolio**						
24							
25	**Stock Shares Bought (Sold)**						
26		(0.200)					
27							
28	**Money Lent (Borrowed)**						
29		$25.49					

7. **Put Option.** Enter **0** in cell **B4**.

We see that the Binomial Option Pricing model predicts a one-period European put price of $5.49.

13.2 Multi-Period

Problem. The current stock price of Energy Systems is $60.00, the potential up movement / period of Energy Systems' stock price is 10.00%, the potential down movement / period of Energy Systems' stock price is -5.00%, the risk-free rate is 0.5% per period, the exercise price of an one-period, European call option on Energy Systems is $65.00, the exercise price of an one-period, European put option on Energy Systems is $65.00, the time to maturity for both options is 2.00 years, and the number of periods for both options is 8. What are the current prices of the call and put?

Solution Strategy. First, build a multi-period tree of stock prices. Second, calculate call and put payoffs at maturity. Third, build the multi-period trees of the shares of stock and money borrowed to create a replicating portfolio that replicates the option period by period. Finally, build a multi-period tree of the value of the replicating portfolio and, in the absence of arbitrage, this will be value of the option.

FIGURE 13.3 Excel Model of Binomial Option Pricing - Multi-Period - Call Option.

	A	B	C	D	E	F	G	H	I	J
1	BINOMIAL OPTION PRICING			Multi-Period			Call			
2										
3	**Inputs**									
4	Option Type: 1=Call, 0=Put	1								
5	Stock Price Now	$60.00								
6	Up Movement / Period	10.00%								
7	Down Movement / Period	-5.00%								
8	Riskfree Rate / Period	0.50%								
9	Exercise Price	$65.00								
10	Time To Maturity (Years)	2.00								
11	Number of Periods	8								
12										
13		**Now**								**Maturity**
14	**Period**	**0**	**1**	**2**	**3**	**4**	**5**	**6**	**7**	**8**
15	**Time**	**0.000**	**0.250**	**0.500**	**0.750**	**1.000**	**1.250**	**1.500**	**1.750**	**2.000**
16										
17	**Stock**	$60.00	$66.00	$72.60	$79.86	$87.85	$96.63	$106.29	$116.92	$128.62
18			$57.00	$62.70	$68.97	$75.87	$83.45	$91.80	$100.98	$111.08
19				$54.15	$59.57	$65.52	$72.07	$79.28	$87.21	$95.93
20					$51.44	$56.59	$62.25	$68.47	$75.32	$82.85
21						$48.87	$53.76	$59.13	$65.05	$71.55
22							$46.43	$51.07	$56.18	$61.79
23								$44.11	$48.52	$53.37
24									$41.90	$46.09
25										$39.81
26										
27	**Call**	$3.93	$6.73	$10.94	$16.78	$24.13	$32.60	$41.94	$52.25	$63.62
28			$2.34	$4.34	$7.65	$12.66	$19.42	$27.44	$36.30	$46.08
29				$1.20	$2.46	$4.81	$8.84	$14.93	$22.53	$30.93
30					$0.48	$1.12	$2.52	$5.39	$10.64	$17.85
31						$0.12	$0.32	$0.87	$2.39	$6.55
32							$0.00	$0.00	$0.00	$0.00
33								$0.00	$0.00	$0.00
34									$0.00	$0.00
35										$0.00

How To Build This Excel Model.

1. **Start with the Single Period Excel Model, Enter the Inputs, and Delete Rows.** Open the Excel model that you created for Binomial Option Pricing – Single Period and immediately save the file under a new name using the **File Save As** command. Enter the new inputs into the range **B5:B11**. Delete rows **20** through **29** by selecting the range **A20:A29**, clicking on **Edit**, **Delete**, selecting the **Entire Row** radio button on the **Delete** dialog box, and clicking on **OK**.

2. **Enter Periods and Time.** Enter the periods **0, 1, 2, ... , 8** in cells **B14** and **J14**. The formula for Time = Time To Maturity * (Period / Number of Periods). Enter **=$B$10*(B14/$B$11)** in cell **B15** and copy the cell to the range **C15:J15**.

3. **The Stock Price Tree.** As in the single period case, the Period 0 Stock Price is equal to the Stock Price Now. Turning to the rest of the Stock Price Tree, we want to create the entire tree with one copy command to a square range. To do this we have to determine whether a cell in the square area is on the tree or off the tree. Further, there are two different formulas to use on the tree (a Down Price vs. an Up Price). Hence, there are three possibilities:

   - When the cell to the left and the cell diagonally to the upper left are both blank, then show a blank.

   - When the cell to the left is blank and the cell diagonally to the upper left has a number, then you are on the lower edge of the triangle so calculate the Down Price = (Stock Price in the Upper Left) * (1 + Down Movement / Period)

   - When both cells have numbers, then calculate the Up Price = (Stock Price to the Left) * (1 + Up Movement / Period)

   Enter **=IF(B17="",IF(B16="","",B16*(1+$B$7)),B17*(1+$B$6))** in cell **C17** and copy this cell to the 9-by-9 square range **C17:J25**. The nested **IF** statements cause a binomial tree to form in the triangular area from **C17** to **J17** to **J25**. Incidentally, the same procedure could create a binominal tree for any number of periods. For example, if you wished to create a 20 period model, then you would simply copy this cell to a 20-by-21 square range. In the **Binomial Option Pricing - Full-Scale Real Data** Excel model, we will exploit this feature to create a 50 period model!

4. **Option Payoffs At Maturity.** Copy the option type indicator from cell **G1** and copy this cell to cell **A27**. The formulas for option payoffs are:

   - For a Call, the Payoff At Maturity = Max (Stock Price At Maturity – Exercise Price, 0).

   - For a Put, the Payoff At Maturity = Max (Exercise Price – Stock Price Maturity, 0).

   Enter **=IF($B$4=1,MAX(J17-$B$9,0),MAX($B$9-J17,0))** in cell **J27** and copy this cell to the range **J28:J35**.

FIGURE 13.4 Excel Model of Binomial Option Pricing - Multi-Period - Call Option (Continued).

	A	B	C	D	E	F	G	H	I	J
1	BINOMIAL OPTION PRICING			Multi-Period			Call			
2										
3	**Inputs**									
4	Option Type: 1=Call, 0=Put	1								
5	Stock Price Now	$60.00								
6	Up Movement / Period	10.00%								
7	Down Movement / Period	-5.00%								
8	Riskfree Rate / Period	0.50%								
9	Exercise Price	$65.00								
10	Time To Maturity (Years)	2.00								
11	Number of Periods	8								
12										
13		**Now**								**Maturity**
14	**Period**	**0**	**1**	**2**	**3**	**4**	**5**	**6**	**7**	**8**
15	**Time**	**0.000**	**0.250**	**0.500**	**0.750**	**1.000**	**1.250**	**1.500**	**1.750**	**2.000**
37	**Replicating Portfolio**									
38										
39	**Stock Shares Bought (Sold)**									
40		0.487	0.667	0.838	0.958	1.000	1.000	1.000	1.000	
41			0.367	0.552	0.758	0.929	1.000	1.000	1.000	
42				0.244	0.413	0.644	0.882	1.000	1.000	
43					0.130	0.259	0.484	0.803	1.000	
44						0.043	0.108	0.269	0.671	
45							0.000	0.000	0.000	
46								0.000	0.000	
47									0.000	
48										
49	**Money Lent (Borrowed)**									
50		($25.32)	($37.28)	($49.93)	($59.71)	($63.72)	($64.03)	($64.35)	($64.68)	
51			($18.60)	($30.26)	($44.66)	($57.86)	($64.03)	($64.35)	($64.68)	
52				($11.99)	($22.16)	($37.36)	($54.74)	($64.35)	($64.68)	
53					($6.20)	($13.53)	($27.59)	($49.61)	($64.68)	
54						($2.00)	($5.50)	($15.06)	($41.28)	
55							$0.00	$0.00	$0.00	
56								$0.00	$0.00	
57									$0.00	

5. **The Stock Shares Bought (Sold) Tree.** At each point in the 8-by-8 square range, you need to determine if you are on the tree or off the tree. There are two possibilities:

- When the corresponding cell in the Stock Price area is blank, then show a blank.
- When the corresponding cell in the Stock Price area has a number, then use the Hedge Ratio = (Option Up Payoff – Option Down Payoff) / (Stock Up Price – Stock Down Price).

Enter **=IF(C28="","",(C27-C28)/(C17-C18))** in cell **B40** and copy this cell to the 8-by-8 square range **B40:I47**. A binomial tree will form in the triangular area from **B40** to **I40** to **I47**. Again the same procedure could create a binominal tree for any number of periods.

6. **The Money Lent (Borrowed) Tree.** At each point in the 8-by-8 square range, you need to determine if you are on the tree or off the tree. There are two possibilities:

- When the corresponding cell in the Stock Price area is blank, then show a blank.

- When the corresponding cell in the Stock Price area has a number, then calculate the amount of Money Lent (Borrowed) = (Call Down Payoff – Hedge Ratio * Stock Down Price) / (1 + Riskfree Rate / Period).

   Enter **=IF(C28="","",(C28-B40*C18)/(1+$B$8))** in cell **B50** and copy this cell to the 8-by-8 square range **B50:I57**. A binomial tree will form in the triangular area from **B50** to **I50** to **I57**. Again the same procedure could create a binominal tree for any number of periods.

7. **The Option Price Tree.** At each point in the 8-by-8 square range (excluding column **J** containing option payoffs at maturity), you need to determine if you are on the tree or off the tree. There are two possibilities:

- When the corresponding cell in the Stock Price area is blank, then show a blank.

- When the corresponding cell in the Stock Price area has a number, then (in the absence of arbitrage) the Option Price At Each Node = Price Of The Corresponding Replicating Portfolio = Number of Shares of Stock * Stock Price + Money Borrowed.

   Enter **=IF(C28="","",B40*B17+B50)** in cell **B27** and copy this cell to the 8-by-9 range **B27:I34**. **Be sure not to copy over column J containing option payoffs at maturity.** A binomial tree will form in the triangular area from **B27** to **J27** to **J35**. Again the same procedure could create a binominal tree for any number of periods.

We see that the Binomial Option Pricing model predicts an eight-period European call price of $3.93. Now let's check the put.

FIGURE 13.5 Excel Model of Binomial Option Pricing - Multi-Period - Put Option.

	A	B	C	D	E	F	G	H	I	J
1	BINOMIAL OPTION PRICING			Multi-Period			Put			
2										
3	**Inputs**									
4	Option Type: 1=Call, 0=Put	0								
5	Stock Price Now	$60.00								
6	Up Movement / Period	10.00%								
7	Down Movement / Period	-5.00%								
8	Riskfree Rate / Period	0.50%								
9	Exercise Price	$65.00								
10	Time To Maturity (Years)	2.00								
11	Number of Periods	8								
12										
13		**Now**								**Maturity**
14	**Period**	**0**	**1**	**2**	**3**	**4**	**5**	**6**	**7**	**8**
15	**Time**	**0.000**	**0.250**	**0.500**	**0.750**	**1.000**	**1.250**	**1.500**	**1.750**	**2.000**
16										
17	**Stock**	$60.00	$66.00	$72.60	$79.86	$87.85	$96.63	$106.29	$116.92	$128.62
18			$57.00	$62.70	$68.97	$75.87	$83.45	$91.80	$100.98	$111.08
19				$54.15	$59.57	$65.52	$72.07	$79.28	$87.21	$95.93
20					$51.44	$56.59	$62.25	$68.47	$75.32	$82.85
21						$48.87	$53.76	$59.13	$65.05	$71.55
22							$46.43	$51.07	$56.18	$61.79
23								$44.11	$48.52	$53.37
24									$41.90	$46.09
25										$39.81
26										
27	**Put**	$6.39	$3.50	$1.43	$0.32	$0.00	$0.00	$0.00	$0.00	$0.00
28			$8.11	$4.72	$2.08	$0.51	$0.00	$0.00	$0.00	$0.00
29				$10.13	$6.29	$3.01	$0.80	$0.00	$0.00	$0.00
30					$12.44	$8.25	$4.30	$1.27	$0.00	$0.00
31						$14.96	$10.60	$6.09	$2.02	$0.00
32							$17.61	$13.29	$8.50	$3.21
33								$20.25	$16.16	$11.63
34									$22.78	$18.91
35										$25.19

8. **Put Option.** Enter **0** in cell **B4**.

We see that the Binomial Option Pricing model predicts an eight-period European put price of $6.39.

FIGURE 13.6 Excel Model of Binomial Option Pricing - Multi-Period - Put Option (Continued).

	A	B	C	D	E	F	G	H	I	J
1	BINOMIAL OPTION PRICING			Multi-Period			Put			
2										
3	**Inputs**									
4	Option Type: 1=Call, 0=Put	0								
5	Stock Price Now	$60.00								
6	Up Movement / Period	10.00%								
7	Down Movement / Period	-5.00%								
8	Riskfree Rate / Period	0.50%								
9	Exercise Price	$65.00								
10	Time To Maturity (Years)	2.00								
11	Number of Periods	8								
12										
13		**Now**								**Maturity**
14	**Period**	**0**	**1**	**2**	**3**	**4**	**5**	**6**	**7**	**8**
15	**Time**	**0.000**	**0.250**	**0.500**	**0.750**	**1.000**	**1.250**	**1.500**	**1.750**	**2.000**
37	**Replicating Portfolio**									
38										
39	**Stock Shares Bought (Sold)**									
40		(0.513)	(0.333)	(0.162)	(0.042)	0.000	0.000	0.000	0.000	
41			(0.633)	(0.448)	(0.242)	(0.071)	0.000	0.000	0.000	
42				(0.756)	(0.587)	(0.356)	(0.118)	0.000	0.000	
43					(0.870)	(0.741)	(0.516)	(0.197)	0.000	
44						(0.957)	(0.892)	(0.731)	(0.329)	
45							(1.000)	(1.000)	(1.000)	
46								(1.000)	(1.000)	
47									(1.000)	
48										
49	**Money Lent (Borrowed)**									
50		$37.14	$25.49	$13.16	$3.69	$0.00	$0.00	$0.00	$0.00	
51			$44.17	$32.83	$18.74	$5.85	$0.00	$0.00	$0.00	
52				$51.09	$41.24	$26.35	$9.29	$0.00	$0.00	
53					$57.20	$50.19	$36.44	$14.74	$0.00	
54						$61.71	$58.54	$49.29	$23.39	
55							$64.03	$64.35	$64.68	
56								$64.35	$64.68	
57									$64.68	

As in the single period case, replicating a Call option requires **Buying** Shares of Stock and **Borrowing** Money, whereas a Put option requires **Selling** Shares of Stock and **Lending** Money. Notice that the quantity of Money Borrowed or Lent and the quantity of Shares Bought or Sold changes over time and differs for up nodes vs. down nodes. This process of changing the replicating portfolio every period based on the realized up or down movement in the underlying stock price is called dynamic replication.

Price accuracy can be increased by subdividing the interval into more periods (15, 30, etc.). Typically, from 30 subperiods to 100 periods are required in order to achieve price accuracy to the penny.

13.3 Risk Neutral

The previous Excel model, **Binomial Option Pricing Multi-Period**, determined the price of an option by constructing a replicating portfolio, which combines a stock and a bond to replicate the payoffs of the option. An alternative way to price an option is the Risk Neutral method. Both techniques give you the same answer. The main advantage of the Risk Neutral method is that it is faster and easier to implement. The Replicating Portfolio method required the construction of four trees (stock prices, shares of stock **bought** **(sold)**, money **lent** **(borrowed)**, and option prices). The Risk Neutral method will only require two trees (stock prices and option prices).

FIGURE 13.7 Excel Model of Binomial Option Pricing - Risk Neutral - Call Option.

	A	B	C	D	E	F	G	H	I	J
1	BINOMIAL OPTION PRICING			Risk Neutral			Call			
2										
3	**Inputs**				**Outputs**					
4	Option Type: 1=Call, 0=Put	1			Risk Neutral Probability	36.67%				
5	Stock Price Now	$60.00								
6	Up Movement / Period	10.00%								
7	Down Movement / Period	-5.00%								
8	Riskfree Rate / Period	0.50%								
9	Exercise Price	$65.00								
10	Time To Maturity (Years)	2.00								
11	Number of Periods	8								
12										
13		**Now**								**Maturity**
14	**Period**	**0**	**1**	**2**	**3**	**4**	**5**	**6**	**7**	**8**
15	**Time**	**0.000**	**0.250**	**0.500**	**0.750**	**1.000**	**1.250**	**1.500**	**1.750**	**2.000**
16										
17	**Stock**	$60.00	$66.00	$72.60	$79.86	$87.85	$96.63	$106.29	$116.92	$128.62
18			$57.00	$62.70	$68.97	$75.87	$83.45	$91.80	$100.98	$111.08
19				$54.15	$59.57	$65.52	$72.07	$79.28	$87.21	$95.93
20					$51.44	$56.59	$62.25	$68.47	$75.32	$82.85
21						$48.87	$53.76	$59.13	$65.05	$71.55
22							$46.43	$51.07	$56.18	$61.79
23								$44.11	$48.52	$53.37
24									$41.90	$46.09
25										$39.81
26										
27	**Call**	$3.93	$6.73	$10.94	$16.78	$24.13	$32.60	$41.94	$52.25	$63.62
28			$2.34	$4.34	$7.65	$12.66	$19.42	$27.44	$36.30	$46.08
29				$1.20	$2.46	$4.81	$8.84	$14.93	$22.53	$30.93
30					$0.48	$1.12	$2.52	$5.39	$10.64	$17.85
31						$0.12	$0.32	$0.87	$2.39	$6.55
32							$0.00	$0.00	$0.00	$0.00
33								$0.00	$0.00	$0.00
34									$0.00	$0.00
35										$0.00

How To Build This Excel Model.

1. **Start with the Multi-Period Excel Model.** Open the Excel model that you created for Binomial Option Pricing – Multi-Period and immediately save the file under a new name using the **File Save As** command.

2. **Risk Neutral Probability.** Calculate the Risk Neutral Probability = (Riskfree Rate / Period - Down Movement / Period) / (Up Movement / Period - Down Movement / Period). Enter **=(B8-B7)/(B6-B7)** in cell **F4**.

3. **The Option Price Tree.** At each point in the 8-by-9 range, you need to determine if you are on the tree or off the tree. There are two possibilities:

   - When the corresponding cell in the Stock Price area is blank, then show a blank.

   - When the corresponding cell in the Stock Price area has a number, then (in the absence of arbitrage) the Option Price At Each Node = Expected Value of the Option Price Next Period (using the Risk Neutral Probability) Discounted At The Riskfree Rate = [(Risk Neutral Probability) * (Stock Up Price) + (1 - Risk Neutral Probability) * (Stock Down Price)] / (1+ Riskfree Rate / Period).

   Enter **=IF(C28="","",($F$4*C27+(1-$F$4)*C28)/(1+$B$8))** in cell **B27** (yielding a blank output at first) and then copy this cell to the 8-by-8 range **B27:I34**. **Be sure not to copy over column J containing option payoffs at maturity**. A binomial tree will form in the triangular area from **B27** to **J27** to **J35**. Again the same procedure could create a binominal tree for any number of periods. For appearances, delete rows **37** through **57** by selecting the range **A37:A57**, clicking on **Edit**, **Delete**, selecting the **Entire Row** radio button on the **Delete** dialog box, and clicking on **OK**.

We see that the Risk Neutral method predicts an eight-period European call price of $3.93. This is identical to Replicating Portfolio Price. Now let's check the put.

FIGURE 13.8 Excel Model of Binomial Option Pricing - Risk Neutral - Put Option.

	A	B	C	D	E	F	G	H	I	J
1	BINOMIAL OPTION PRICING			Risk Neutral			Put			
2										
3	**Inputs**				**Outputs**					
4	Option Type: 1=Call, 0=Put	0			Risk Neutral Probability	36.67%				
5	Stock Price Now	$60.00								
6	Up Movement / Period	10.00%								
7	Down Movement / Period	-5.00%								
8	Riskfree Rate / Period	0.50%								
9	Exercise Price	$65.00								
10	Time To Maturity (Years)	2.00								
11	Number of Periods	8								
12										
13		**Now**								**Maturity**
14	**Period**	**0**	**1**	**2**	**3**	**4**	**5**	**6**	**7**	**8**
15	**Time**	**0.000**	**0.250**	**0.500**	**0.750**	**1.000**	**1.250**	**1.500**	**1.750**	**2.000**
16										
17	**Stock**	$60.00	$66.00	$72.60	$79.86	$87.85	$96.63	$106.29	$116.92	$128.62
18			$57.00	$62.70	$68.97	$75.87	$83.45	$91.80	$100.98	$111.08
19				$54.15	$59.57	$65.52	$72.07	$79.28	$87.21	$95.93
20					$51.44	$56.59	$62.25	$68.47	$75.32	$82.85
21						$48.87	$53.76	$59.13	$65.05	$71.55
22							$46.43	$51.07	$56.18	$61.79
23								$44.11	$48.52	$53.37
24									$41.90	$46.09
25										$39.81
26										
27	**Put**	$6.39	$3.50	$1.43	$0.32	$0.00	$0.00	$0.00	$0.00	$0.00
28			$8.11	$4.72	$2.08	$0.51	$0.00	$0.00	$0.00	$0.00
29				$10.13	$6.29	$3.01	$0.80	$0.00	$0.00	$0.00
30					$12.44	$8.25	$4.30	$1.27	$0.00	$0.00
31						$14.96	$10.60	$6.09	$2.02	$0.00
32							$17.61	$13.29	$8.50	$3.21
33								$20.25	$16.16	$11.63
34									$22.78	$18.91
35										$25.19

4. **Put Option.** Enter **0** in cell **B4**.

We see that the Risk Neutral method predicts an eight-period European put price of $6.39. This is identical to Replicating Portfolio Price. Again, we get the same answer either way. The advantage of the Risk Neutral method is that we only have to construct two trees, rather than four trees.

13.4 Full-Scale Real Data

The binomial model can be used to price real-world European calls and puts. Further, the Binomial Tree / Risk Neutral method can be extended to price *any* type of derivative security (European vs. American vs. other, on any underlying asset(s), with any underlying dividends or cash flows, with any derivative payoffs at maturity and/or payoffs before maturity). Indeed, it is one of the most popular techniques on Wall Street for pricing and hedging derivatives.

Problem Using Real Data. In the afternoon of September 29, 2003, the stock price of Amazon.com was \$48.89, the yield on a risk-free Treasury Bill maturing on January 15, 2004 was 0.96%, the exercise price of an January 50 call on Amazon.com was \$50.00, the exercise price of an January 50 put on Amazon.com was \$50.00, and the time to maturity for both January 16, 2004 maturity options was 0.2972 years. What is the annual standard deviation of Amazon.com stock? What are the current prices of the call and put under the *continuous* annualization convention? What are the current prices of the call and put under the *discrete* annualization convention?

Solution Strategy. Collect Amazon.com's historical stock prices from Yahoo Finance! and calculate the annual standard deviation. Use the annual standard deviation and the annual riskfree rate to calculate the up movement / period, down movement / period, and riskfree rate / period. Extend the Binomial Option Pricing - Risk Neutral model to full-scale (50 periods) in order to achieve greater price accuracy.

FIGURE 13.9 Excel Model of Binomial Option Pricing - Estimating Volatility.

	A	B	C	D	E	F	G	H	I
1	BINOMIAL OPTION PRICING					Estimating Volatility			
2									
3	Date	Open	High	Low	Close	Volume	Adj. Close*	Discrete Return	Continuous Return
4	29-Sep-03	\$48.88	\$49.97	\$48.40	\$49.86	9,039,300.00	\$49.86	2.68%	2.64%
5	26-Sep-03	\$49.90	\$50.46	\$48.30	\$48.56	13,438,500.00	\$48.56	-2.98%	-3.02%
6	25-Sep-03	\$49.66	\$50.95	\$49.28	\$50.05	11,033,300.00	\$50.05	0.89%	0.88%
7	24-Sep-03	\$50.35	\$51.30	\$49.60	\$49.61	15,330,200.00	\$49.61	-1.65%	-1.66%
8	23-Sep-03	\$47.41	\$50.92	\$47.35	\$50.44	20,295,900.00	\$50.44	6.26%	6.07%
9	22-Sep-03	\$46.56	\$47.53	\$46.20	\$47.47	9,240,000.00	\$47.47	-0.23%	-0.23%
10	19-Sep-03	\$47.87	\$47.97	\$47.35	\$47.58	6,249,500.00	\$47.58	-0.65%	-0.65%
11	18-Sep-03	\$46.16	\$48.24	\$45.94	\$47.89	9,038,500.00	\$47.89	3.75%	3.68%
12	17-Sep-03	\$46.21	\$46.86	\$45.54	\$46.16	7,334,100.00	\$46.16	-0.17%	-0.17%
13	16-Sep-03	\$45.40	\$46.25	\$45.05	\$46.24	7,755,200.00	\$46.24	1.60%	1.59%
14	15-Sep-03	\$45.36	\$45.77	\$45.23	\$45.51	4,427,000.00	\$45.51	-0.37%	-0.37%
61	9-Jul-03	\$40.54	\$40.73	\$39.87	\$40.50	7,832,200.00	\$40.50	-0.02%	-0.02%
62	8-Jul-03	\$38.76	\$40.83	\$38.75	\$40.51	12,145,400.00	\$40.51	3.74%	3.67%
63	7-Jul-03	\$38.30	\$39.10	\$37.95	\$39.05	6,697,300.00	\$39.05	2.98%	2.94%
64	3-Jul-03	\$37.02	\$38.16	\$37.02	\$37.92	3,846,000.00	\$37.92	0.18%	0.18%
65	2-Jul-03	\$37.60	\$37.89	\$37.14	\$37.85	6,086,100.00	\$37.85	1.61%	1.60%
66	1-Jul-03	\$36.33	\$37.29	\$35.70	\$37.25	7,242,800.00	\$37.25	2.56%	2.53%
67	30-Jun-03	\$36.63	\$36.82	\$36.02	\$36.32	5,143,900.00	\$36.32	0.06%	0.06%
68	27-Jun-03	\$36.69	\$37.09	\$36.18	\$36.30	6,756,500.00	\$36.30		
69									
70									
71						Standard Deviation (Daily)		3.00%	2.91%
72						Standard Deviation (Annual)		57.23%	55.56%

How To Build This Excel Model.

1. **Collect Historical Stock Price Data.** Go to **Yahoo Finance!** (**finance.yahoo.com**), enter **AMZN** (the ticker symbol for Amazon.com) in the **Enter Symbol(s)** box, in the left column click on **Historical Prices**,

scroll to the bottom of the page, click on **Download To Spreadsheet**, and save the **csv** file. Launch Excel, open the **csv** file, and save it as an Excel workbook file by clicking on **File | Save As**, in the **Save as type** drop-down list at the bottom of the dialog box select **Microsoft Excel Workbook (*.xls)**, and click **Save**.

2. **Calculate Discrete and Continuous Returns.** As key sequence of prices is the Adjust Closing Price (in column **G**), which accounts for any dividend payments or stock slits. There are two conventions for calculating stock returns. A simple percent change yields the Discrete Return = [(Price on date t) - (Price on date t-1)] / (Price on date t-1). Enter **=(G4-G5)/G5** in cell **H4** and copy it down. The Continuous Return = LN[(Price on date t) / (Price on date t-1)]. Enter **=LN(G4/G5)** in cell **I4** and copy it down.

3. **Calculate the Daily and Annual Standard Deviation.** Use Excel's function **STDEV** to calculate the sample standard deviation of daily discrete returns and daily continuous returns. Enter **=STDEV(H4:H67)** in cell **H71** and copy the cell to **I71**. Convert the daily standard deviation to annual standard deviation by multiplying by the square root of the number of days in the year. Enter **=H71*SQRT(365)** in cell **H72** and copy the cell to **I72**.

We find that Amazon.com's annual standard deviation is 57.23% based on discrete returns and is 55.56% based on continuous returns.

FIGURE 13.10 Excel Model of Binomial Option Pricing - Full-Scale Real Data - Call Option.

	A	B	C	D	E	F	AX	AY	AZ
1	BINOMIAL OPTION PRICING			Full-Scale Real Data					
2				Call	Continuous				
3	Inputs				Outputs				
4	Option Type: 1=Call, 0=Put	1			Time / Period	0.006			
5	Stock Price Now	$48.89			Riskfree Rate / Period	0.01%			
6	Standard Dev (Annual)	55.56%			Up Movement / Period	4.38%			
7	Riskfree Rate (Annual)	0.96%			Down Movement / Period	-4.19%			
8	Exercise Price	$50.00			Risk Neutral Probability	49.00%			
9	Time To Maturity (Years)	0.2972							
10	Number of Periods	50							
11	Annualization Convention: 1=Discrete, 0=Continuous	0							
12									
13		Now							Maturity
14	Period	0	1	2	3	4	48	49	50
15	Time	0.000	0.006	0.012	0.018	0.024	0.285	0.291	0.297
16									
17	Stock	$48.89	$51.03	$53.26	$55.59	$58.03	$382.09	$398.82	$416.27
18			$46.84	$48.89	$51.03	$53.26	$350.72	$366.07	$382.09
19				$44.88	$46.84	$48.89	$321.93	$336.02	$350.72
20					$42.99	$44.88	$295.50	$308.43	$321.93
21						$41.19	$271.23	$283.11	$295.50
22							$248.97	$259.86	$271.23
23							$228.52	$238.53	$248.97
24							$209.76	$218.94	$228.52
25							$192.54	$200.97	$209.76
26							$176.73	$184.47	$192.54
27							$162.22	$169.32	$176.73
28							$148.90	$155.42	$162.22
29							$136.68	$142.66	$148.90
30							$125.46	$130.95	$136.68
31							$115.15	$120.19	$125.46
32							$105.70	$110.33	$115.15
33							$97.02	$101.27	$105.70
34							$89.06	$92.95	$97.02
35							$81.74	$85.32	$89.06
36							$75.03	$78.32	$81.74

4. **Start with the Risk Neutral Excel Model and Freeze Panes.** Open the Excel model that you created for Binomial Option Pricing – Risk Neutral and immediately save the file under a new name using the **File Save As** command. It will be helpful for navigation purposes to lock in both column titles and row titles. Select cell **G16** and click on **Window Freeze Panes**.

5. **Rearrange the Inputs.** Select the range **A6:B7** and drag the range (hover the cursor over the lower highlighted line, click on the left mouse button, and hold it down while you move it) to cell **E6**. Select the range **A8:B8** and drag the range to cell **E5**. Select the range **A9:B11** and drag the range to cell **A8**. Select the range **E4:F4** and drag the range to cell **E8**.

6. **Enter the New Inputs.** Enter the Full-Scale Real Data inputs in the range **B4:B11** as shown in the figure above. The value in cell **B11** serves as a

switch between the Discrete and Continuous Annualization Conventions. To accommodate both annualization conventions, enter **=IF(B11=1,90.23%,86.07%)** in cell **B6** for the Annual Standard Deviation. To highlight which annualization convention is in use, enter **=IF($B$11=1,"Discrete","Continuous")** in cell **E2**.

7. **Calculate the New Outputs.** Calculate four new "per period" outputs:

- **Time / Period** = (Time To Maturity) / (Number of Periods). Enter **=B9/B10** in cell **F4**.

- **Riskfree Rate / Period** = (Annual Riskfree Rate) * (Time / Period) under the discrete annualization convention or = exp[(Annual Riskfree Rate) * (Time / Period)] -1 under the continuous annualization convention. Enter **=IF($B$11=1,B7*F4,EXP(B7*F4)-1)** in cell **F5**.

- **Up Movement / Period** = (Annual Standard Deviation) * Square Root (Time / Period) under the discrete annualization convention or = exp[(Annual Standard Deviation) * Square Root (Time / Period)] -1 under the continuous annualization convention. Enter **=IF($B$11=1,B6*SQRT(F4),EXP(B6*SQRT(F4))-1)** in cell **F6**.

- **Down Movement / Period** = -(Annual Standard Deviation) * Square Root (Time / Period) under the discrete annualization convention or = exp[-(Annual Standard Deviation) * Square Root (Time / Period)] -1 under the continuous annualization convention. Enter **=IF($B$11=1,-B6*SQRT(F4),EXP(-B6*SQRT(F4))-1)** in cell **F7**.

The up movement / period and down movement / period are calibrated to correspond to the stock's annual standard deviation. It is not necessary to calibrate them to the stock's expected return.[6]

8. **Extend The Periods and Time to 50 Periods.** Select the range **B14:C14**, grab the fill bar (hover the mouse over the lower-right corner of the selection

---

[6] At full-scale (50 periods), the binomial option price is very insensitive to the expected return of the stock. For example, suppose that you calibrated this Amazon.com case to an annual expected return of 10%. Just add **10%*F4** to the formulas for the up and down movements / period. So the up movement / period in cell **F6** would become **=IF($B$11=1,10%*F4+B6*SQRT(F4),EXP(10%*F4+B6*SQRT(F4))-1)** and the down movement / period in cell **F7** would become **=IF($B$11=1,10%*F4-B6*SQRT(F4),EXP(10%*F4-B6*SQRT(F4))-1)**. This changes the option price by less than 1/100th of one penny! In the (Black Scholes) limit as the number of (sub)periods goes to infinity, the option price becomes totally insensitive to the expected return of the stock. Because of this insensitivity, the conventions for calculating the up movement / period and down movement / period ignore the expected return of the stock.

- when it turns to a "+" sign, click the left mouse button), and fill in the range **D14:AZ14**. Select the cell **B15** and copy it to the range **C15:AZ15**.

9. **Extend The Stock Price Tree to 50 Periods.** Add some rows to make space between the Stock Price Tree and the Option Price Tree. Select the range **A26:A67** and click on **Insert Rows**. Then, copy cell **C17** to the 50-by-51 range **C17:AZ67**. A binomial tree will form in the triangular area from **C17** to **AZ17** to **AZ67**.

FIGURE 13.11 Excel Model of Binomial Option Pricing - Full-Scale Real Data - Call Option (Continued).

	A	B	C	D	E	F	AX	AY	AZ
1	BINOMIAL OPTION PRICING			Full-Scale Real Data					
2				Call	Continuous				
3	**Inputs**				**Outputs**				
4	Option Type: 1=Call, 0=Put	1			Time / Period	0.006			
5	Stock Price Now	$48.89			Riskfree Rate / Period	0.01%			
6	Standard Dev (Annual)	55.56%			Up Movement / Period	4.38%			
7	Riskfree Rate (Annual)	0.96%			Down Movement / Period	-4.19%			
8	Exercise Price	$50.00			Risk Neutral Probability	49.00%			
9	Time To Maturity (Years)	0.2972							
10	Number of Periods	50							
11	Annualization Convention: 1=Discrete, 0=Continuous	0							
12									
13		**Now**							**Maturity**
14	**Period**	**0**	**1**	**2**	**3**	**4**	**48**	**49**	**50**
15	**Time**	**0.000**	**0.006**	**0.012**	**0.018**	**0.024**	**0.285**	**0.291**	**0.297**
68									
69	**Call**	$5.49	$6.63	$7.95	$9.45	$11.15	$332.10	$348.82	$366.27
70			$4.39	$5.37	$6.51	$7.82	$300.73	$316.08	$332.09
71				$3.45	$4.27	$5.24	$271.93	$286.02	$300.72
72					$2.66	$3.34	$245.50	$258.43	$271.93
73						$2.01	$221.24	$233.11	$245.50
74							$198.97	$209.86	$221.23
75							$178.53	$188.53	$198.97
76							$159.77	$168.95	$178.52
77							$142.55	$150.97	$159.76
78							$126.74	$134.47	$142.54
79							$112.23	$119.32	$126.73
80							$98.91	$105.42	$112.22
81							$86.68	$92.66	$98.90
82							$75.46	$80.95	$86.68
83							$65.16	$70.20	$75.46
84							$55.71	$60.33	$65.15
85							$47.03	$51.27	$55.70
86							$39.06	$42.96	$47.02
87							$31.75	$35.32	$39.06
88							$25.04	$28.32	$31.74

10. **Extend The Option Payoffs At Maturity to 50 Periods.** Copy the old payoffs at maturity starting in cell **J69** and to the new payoffs at maturity range **AZ69:AZ119**.

11. **Extend The Option Price Tree to 50 Periods.** Copy cell **B69** to the range **B69:AY118**. A binomial tree will form in the triangular area from **B69** to **AZ69** to **AZ119**.

We see that the Full-Scale Real Data model predicts an European call price of $5.49. This is only two cents different that what the Black-Scholes model predicts given identical inputs! Now let's check the put.

FIGURE 13.12 Excel Model of Binomial Option Pricing - Full-Scale Real Data - Put Option.

	A	B	C	D	E	F	AX	AY	AZ
1	BINOMIAL OPTION PRICING			Full-Scale Real Data					
2				Put	Continuous				
3	**Inputs**				**Outputs**				
4	Option Type: 1=Call, 0=Put	0			Time / Period	0.006			
5	Stock Price Now	$48.89			Riskfree Rate / Period	0.01%			
6	Standard Dev (Annual)	55.56%			Up Movement / Period	4.38%			
7	Riskfree Rate (Annual)	0.96%			Down Movement / Period	-4.19%			
8	Exercise Price	$50.00			Risk Neutral Probability	49.00%			
9	Time To Maturity (Years)	0.2972							
10	Number of Periods	50							
11	Annualization Convention: 1=Discrete, 0=Continuous	0							
12									
13		**Now**							**Maturity**
14	**Period**	**0**	**1**	**2**	**3**	**4**	**48**	**49**	**50**
15	**Time**	**0.000**	**0.006**	**0.012**	**0.018**	**0.024**	**0.285**	**0.291**	**0.297**
16									
17	**Stock**	$48.89	$51.03	$53.26	$55.59	$58.03	$382.09	$398.82	$416.27
18			$46.84	$48.89	$51.03	$53.26	$350.72	$366.07	$382.09
19				$44.88	$46.84	$48.89	$321.93	$336.02	$350.72
20					$42.99	$44.88	$295.50	$308.43	$321.93
21						$41.19	$271.23	$283.11	$295.50
22							$248.97	$259.86	$271.23
23							$228.52	$238.53	$248.97
24							$209.76	$218.94	$228.52
25							$192.54	$200.97	$209.76
26							$176.73	$184.47	$192.54
27							$162.22	$169.32	$176.73
28							$148.90	$155.42	$162.22
29							$136.68	$142.66	$148.90
30							$125.46	$130.95	$136.68
31							$115.15	$120.19	$125.46
32							$105.70	$110.33	$115.15
33							$97.02	$101.27	$105.70
34							$89.06	$92.95	$97.02
35							$81.74	$85.32	$89.06
36							$75.03	$78.32	$81.74

12. **Put Option.** Enter **0** in cell **B4**.

FIGURE 13.13 Excel Model of Binomial Option Pricing - Full-Scale Real Data - Put Option (Continued).

	A	B	C	D	E	F	AX	AY	AZ
1	BINOMIAL OPTION PRICING			Full-Scale Real Data					
2				Put	Continuous				
3	**Inputs**				**Outputs**				
4	Option Type: 1=Call, 0=Put	0			Time / Period	0.006			
5	Stock Price Now	$48.89			Riskfree Rate / Period	0.01%			
6	Standard Dev (Annual)	55.56%			Up Movement / Period	4.38%			
7	Riskfree Rate (Annual)	0.96%			Down Movement / Period	-4.19%			
8	Exercise Price	$50.00			Risk Neutral Probability	49.00%			
9	Time To Maturity (Years)	0.2972							
10	Number of Periods	50							
11	Annualization Convention: 1=Discrete, 0=Continuous	0							
12									
13		**Now**							**Maturity**
14	**Period**	**0**	**1**	**2**	**3**	**4**	**48**	**49**	**50**
15	**Time**	**0.000**	**0.006**	**0.012**	**0.018**	**0.024**	**0.285**	**0.291**	**0.297**
68									
69	**Put**	$6.46	$5.46	$4.55	$3.72	$2.99	$0.00	$0.00	$0.00
70			$7.41	$6.34	$5.34	$4.43	$0.00	$0.00	$0.00
71				$8.44	$7.30	$6.22	$0.00	$0.00	$0.00
72					$9.54	$8.33	$0.00	$0.00	$0.00
73						$10.69	$0.00	$0.00	$0.00
74							$0.00	$0.00	$0.00
75							$0.00	$0.00	$0.00
76							$0.00	$0.00	$0.00
77							$0.00	$0.00	$0.00
78							$0.00	$0.00	$0.00
79							$0.00	$0.00	$0.00
80							$0.00	$0.00	$0.00
81							$0.00	$0.00	$0.00
82							$0.00	$0.00	$0.00
83							$0.00	$0.00	$0.00
84							$0.00	$0.00	$0.00
85							$0.00	$0.00	$0.00
86							$0.00	$0.00	$0.00
87							$0.00	$0.00	$0.00
88							$0.00	$0.00	$0.00

We see that the Full-Scale Real Data model predicts an European put price of $6.46. This is only two cents different that what the Black-Scholes model predicts given identical inputs! The accuracy of the binomial model can be increased to any desired degree by increasing the number of periods. Whereas the Black Scholes model (and its natural extensions) is limited to a narrow range of derivatives, the Binomial Option Pricing model can be extended to price *any* derivative security (any type, any underlying asset(s), any underlying cash flows, and any derivative payoffs).

Problems

Skill-Building Problems.

1. The current stock price of a company is \$37.50, the potential up movement / period of the stock price is 22.0%, the potential down movement / period of the stock price is -13.00%, the risk-free rate is 4.0% per period, the exercise price of an one-period, European call option on the stock is \$39.00, the exercise price of an one-period, European put option on the stock is \$39.00, the time to maturity for both options is 0.58 years, and the number of periods for both options is 1. Determine the current prices of the call and put.

2. The current stock price of a company is \$23.75, the potential up movement / period of the stock price is 27.0%, the potential down movement / period of the stock price is -9.00%, the risk-free rate is 5.0% per period, the exercise price of an European call option on the stock is \$22.00, the exercise price of an European put option on the stock is \$22.00, the time to maturity for both options is 0.39 years, and the number of periods for both options is 8. Determine the current prices of the call and put.

3. The current stock price of a company is \$43.25, the potential up movement / period of the stock price is 19.0%, the potential down movement / period of the stock price is -14.00%, the risk-free rate is 4.0% per period, the exercise price of an European call option on the stock is \$45.00, the exercise price of an European put option on the stock is \$45.00, the time to maturity for both options is 0.83 years, and the number of periods for both options is 8. Determine the current prices of the call and put.

4. Collect Cisco Systems' historical stock prices from Yahoo Finance! From the financial media, collect the current stock price of Cisco Systems, the exercise price of an European call option on Cisco Systems, the exercise price of an European put option on Cisco Systems, the time to maturity for both options, and the yield on a risk-free Treasury Bill maturing as close as possible to the maturity date of the options. Determine:

   a. What is the annual standard deviation of Cisco Systems stock?

   b. What are the current prices of the call and put under the *continuous* annualization convention?

   c. What are the current prices of the call and put under the *discrete* annualization convention?

Skill-Extending Problems.

5. Extend the **Binomial Option Pricing – Risk Neutral** model to incorporate a \$2.00 / share dividend that will be paid out in period 5. In other words, all of the period 5 stock prices will be reduced by \$2.00. Determine the current prices of the call and put.

6. Extend the **Binomial Option Pricing – Risk Neutral** model to analyze Digital Options. The only thing which needs to be changed is the option's payoff at maturity.

a. For a Digital Call, the Payoff At Maturity = \$1.00 When Stock Price At Maturity > Exercise Price Or \$0.00 Otherwise.

b. For a Digital Put, the Payoff At Maturity = \$1.00 When Stock Price At Maturity < Exercise Price Or \$0.00 Otherwise.

7. Extend the **Binomial Option Pricing – Full-Scale Real Data** model to determine how fast the binomial option price converges to the price in the **Black Scholes Option Pricing – Basics** model. Reduce the Full-Scale model to a 10 period model and to a 20 period model. Increase the 50 period model to a 100 period model. Then for the same inputs, compare call and put prices of the 10 period, 20 period, 50 period, 100 period, and Black-Scholes models.

8. Extend the **Binomial Option Pricing – Full-Scale Real Data** model to determine how fast the binomial option price with averaging of adjacent odd and even numbers of periods converges to the price in the **Black Scholes Option Pricing – Basics** model. As you increase the number of periods in the binomial model, it oscillates between overshooting and undershooting the true price. A simple technique to increase price efficiency is to average adjacent odd and even numbers of periods. For example, average the 10 period call price and the 11 period call price. Reduce the Full-Scale model to a 10 period, 11 period, 20 period, and 21 period model. Increase the 50 period model to a 51 period, 100 period, and 101 period model. Then for the same inputs, compare call and put prices of the average of the 10 and 11 period models, 20 and 21 period models, 50 and 51 period models, 100 and 101 period models, and Black-Scholes model.

Live In-class Problems.

9. Given the partial Single Period file **BinosinZ.xls**, do steps **4 Option Payoffs at Maturity, 5 Create a Replicating Portfolio,** and **6 Calculate the Option Price Now**.

10. Given the partial Multi-Period file **BinomulZ.xls**, do step **7 The Option Price Tree**.

11. Given the partial Risk Neutral file **BinoneuZ.xls**, do step **2 Risk Neutral Probability** and **3 The Option Price Tree**.

12. Given the partial Full-Scale Real Data file **BinofulZ.xls**, do step **7 Calculate the New Outputs**.

Chapter 14 Black Scholes Option Pricing

14.1 Basics

Problem. In the afternoon of September 29, 2003, the stock price of Amazon.com was $48.89, the continuous annual standard deviation was 55.56%, the yield on a risk-free Treasury Bill maturing on January 15, 2004 was 0.96%, the exercise price of an January 50 call on Amazon.com was $50.00, the exercise price of an January 50 put on Amazon.com was $50.00, and the time to maturity for both January 16, 2004 maturity options was 0.2972 years. What are the current prices of the call and put?

FIGURE 14.1 Excel Model of Black Scholes Option Pricing - Basics.

	A	B	C	D	E	F
1	BLACK SCHOLES OPTION PRICING				Basics	
2						
3	**Inputs**					
4	Stock Price Now (S_0)	$48.89				
5	Standard Dev - Annual (σ)	55.56%				
6	Riskfree Rate- Annual (r)	0.96%				
7	Exercise Price (X)	$50.00				
8	Time To Maturity - Years (T)	0.2972				
9						
10	**Outputs**					
11	d1	0.087				
12	d2	-0.216				
13	N(d1)	0.535				
14	N(d2)	0.414				
15	Call Price (C_0)	$5.47				
16						
17	-d1	-0.087				
18	-d2	0.216				
19	N(-d1)	0.465				
20	N(-d2)	0.586				
21	Put Price (P_0)	$6.44				

How To Build This Excel Model

1. **Inputs.** Enter the inputs described above into the range **B4:B8**.

2. **d1 and d2 Formulas.** The d_1 formula is $\left(\ln\left(S_0/X\right)+\left(r+\sigma^2/2\right)\cdot T\right)/\left(\sigma\cdot\sqrt{T}\right)$. In cell **B11**, enter

   =(LN(B4/B7)+(B6+B5^2/2)*B8)/(B5*SQRT(B8))

   The d_2 formula is $d_1-\sigma\sqrt{T}$. In cell **B12**, enter

=B11-B5*SQRT(B8)

3. **Cumulative Normal Formulas.** Enter $N(d_1)$ using the cumulative normal function **NORMSDIST** in cell **B13**

   =NORMSDIST(B11)

   Copy the cell **B13** to cell **B14** or enter $N(d_2)$ using the cumulative normal function **NORMSDIST** in cell **B14**

   =NORMSDIST(B12)

4. **European Call Price Formula.** The Black-Scholes call formula is $C_0 = S_0 N(d_1) - Xe^{-rT} N(d_2)$. In cell **B15**, enter

   =B4*B13-B7*EXP(-B6*B8)*B14

   We see that the Black-Scholes model predicts a call price of $5.47. This is only two cents different that what the Binominal Option Pricing - Full-Scale Real Data model predicts given identical inputs! Now let's do the put.

5. **-d1 and -d2 Formulas.** For the labels, enter **'-d1** in **A17** and **'-d2 A18**. The **'** tells Excel that it is a label, not a formula. For the two put formula terms, they are just opposite in sign from their call formula counterparts. Enter =-**B11** in **B17** and =-**B12** in **B18**.

6. **Cumulative Normal Formulas.** Enter $N(-d_1)$ using the cumulative normal function **NORMSDIST** in cell **B19**

   =NORMSDIST(B17)

   Copy the cell **B19** to cell **B20** or enter $N(-d_2)$ using the cumulative normal function **NORMSDIST** in cell **B20**

   =NORMSDIST(B18)

7. **European Put Price Formula.** The Black-Scholes put formula is $P_0 = -S_0 N(-d_1) + Xe^{-rT} N(-d_2)$. In cell **B21**, enter

   =-B4*B19+B7*EXP(-B6*B8)*B20

We see that the Black-Scholes model predicts a put price of $6.44. This is only two cents different that what the Binominal Option Pricing - Full-Scale Real Data model predicts given identical inputs! The advantage of the Black Scholes model (and its natural extensions) is that it is quick and easy to calculate, but the disadvantage is that it is limited to a narrow range of derivatives.

14.2 Dynamic Chart

If you increased the standard deviation of the stock, what would happen to the price of the call option? If you increased the time to maturity, what would happen to the price of the call? You can answer these questions and more by creating a *Dynamic Chart* using "spinners." Spinners are up-arrow / down-arrow buttons that allow you to easily change the inputs to the model with the click of a mouse. Then Excel recalculates the model and instantly redraws the model outputs on the graph.

FIGURE 14.2 Excel Model of Black Scholes Option Pricing - Dynamic Chart - Call Option.

	A	B	C	D	E	F	G	H	I	J
1	BLACK SCHOLES OPTION PRICING					Dynamic Chart			Call	
2										
3	**Inputs**									
4	Option Type: 1=Call, 0=Put	1		1						
5	Standard Dev - Annual (σ)	60%		6						
6	Riskfree Rate- Annual (r)	1.0%		1						
7	Exercise Price (X)	$50.00		50						
8	Time To Maturity - Yrs (T)	0.30		3						
9										
10										
11										
12	**Dynamic Chart Outputs**									
13	Stock Price Now (S_0)	$0.01	$10.00	$20.00	$30.00	$40.00	$50.00	$60.00	$70.00	$80.00
14	Option Price	$0.00	$0.00	$0.01	$0.34	$2.20	$6.61	$13.36	$21.67	$30.85
15	Intrinsic Value									
16										
17	d1	-25.657	-4.707	-2.605	-1.375	-0.503	0.174	0.727	1.194	1.599
18	d2	-25.987	-5.037	-2.935	-1.705	-0.832	-0.156	0.397	0.865	1.270
19	N(d1)	0.000	0.000	0.005	0.085	0.308	0.569	0.766	0.884	0.945
20	N(d2)	0.000	0.000	0.002	0.044	0.203	0.438	0.654	0.806	0.898
21	Call Price (C_0)	$0.00	$0.00	$0.01	$0.34	$2.20	$6.61	$13.36	$21.67	$30.85
22										
23	-d1	25.657	4.707	2.605	1.375	0.503	-0.174	-0.727	-1.194	-1.599
24	-d2	25.987	5.037	2.935	1.705	0.832	0.156	-0.397	-0.865	-1.270
25	N(-d1)	1.000	1.000	0.995	0.915	0.692	0.431	0.234	0.116	0.055
26	N(-d2)	1.000	1.000	0.998	0.956	0.797	0.562	0.346	0.194	0.102
27	Put Price (P_0)	$49.84	$39.85	$29.86	$20.19	$12.05	$6.46	$3.21	$1.52	$0.70

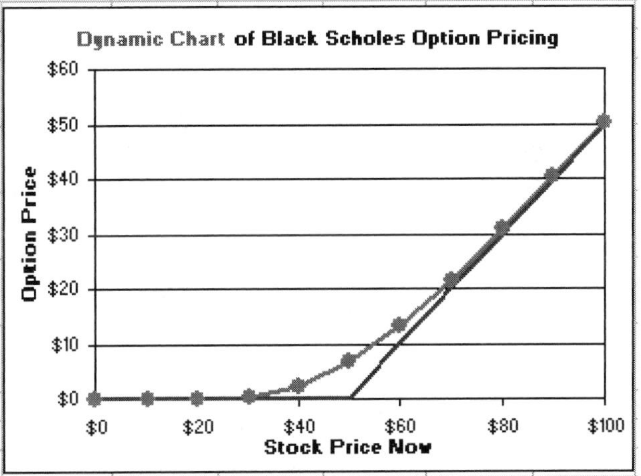

How To Build This Excel Model.

1. **Start with the Basics Excel Model, Rearrange the Rows, and Add A Switch.** Open the Excel model that you created for Black Scholes Option Pricing – Basics and immediately save the file under a new name using the **File Save As** command. Add six rows by selecting the range **A11:A16**, clicking on **Insert**, **Rows**. Select the range **A4:B4** and drag the range (hover

the cursor over the lower highlighted line, click on the left mouse button, and hold it down while you move it) to cell A13. Enter **1** in cell B4. This will serve as a switch between a call option and a put option. To highlight which type of option is being graphed, enter **=IF($B$4=1,"Call","Put")** in cell I1.

2. **Increase Row Height for the Spinners.** Select the range A4:A8. Then click on **Format Row Height** from the main menu. Enter a height of **30** and click on **OK**.

3. **Display the Forms Toolbar.** Select **View Toolbars Forms** from the main menu.

4. **Create the Spinners.** Look for the up-arrow / down-arrow button on the **Forms** toolbar (which will display the word "**Spinner**" if you hover the cursor over it) and click on it. Then draw the box for a spinner from the upper left corner of cell C4 down to the lower right corner of the cell. Then a spinner appears in the cell C4. Right click on the spinner (press the right mouse button while the cursor is above the spinner) and a small menu pops up. Click on **Copy**. Then select the cell C5 and click on **Paste**. This creates an identical spinner in the cell C5. Repeat the process three times more. Select cell C6 and click on **Paste**. Select cell C7 and click on **Paste**. Select cell C8 and click on **Paste**. You now have five spinners down column C.

5. **Create The Cell Links.** Right click on the first spinner in the cell C4 and a small menu pops up. Click on **Format Control** and a dialog box pops up. Click on the **Control** tab, then enter the cell link **D4** in the **Cell link** edit box and click on **OK**. Repeat this procedure for the other four spinners. Link the spinner in cell C5 to cell **D5**. Link the spinner in cell C6 to cell **D6**. Link the spinner in cell C7 to cell **D7**. Link the spinner in cell C8 to cell **D8**. Test your spinners by clicking on the up-arrows and down-arrows of the spinners to see how they change the values in the linked cells.

6. **Create Scaled Inputs.** The values in the linked cells are always integers, but they can be scaled appropriately to the problem at hand. Restrict the value in cell B4 to be either 1 or 0 by entering **=IF(D4>1,1,D4)**. In cell B5, enter **=D5/10+0.001**. In cell B6, enter **=D6/100**. In cell B7, enter **=D7**. In cell B8, enter **=D8/10+0.001**. The additional terms **+0.001** in cells B5 and B8, prevent the scaled value from going to zero when the linked cell goes to zero. When the standard deviation or a time to maturity literally became zero, then the Black Scholes call and put formulas blow-up.

7. **Create Stock Price Inputs.** In the range B13:L13, enter the values **0.01**, **10**, **20**, **30**, ..., **100**. In cell M13, enter **0.01**. In cell N13, enter **=B7**. In cell O13, enter **=L13**.

8. **Convert The Input Cell References To Absolute References.** In convert the input cell references contained in the formulas in cells B17, B18, B21, and B27 to absolute references. That is, put $s in front of any references to the *input cells* in the range B4:B8. When you are done, the formula in cell B17 will look like **=(LN(B13/$B$7)+($B$6+$B$5^2/2)*$B$8)/($B$5*SQRT($B$8))**. Cell

B18 will look like **=B17-$B$5*SQRT($B$8)**. Cell **B21** will look like **=B13*B19-$B$7*EXP(-$B$6*$B$8)*B20**. Cell **B27** will look like **=-B13*B25+$B$7*EXP(-$B$6*$B$8)*B26**.

9. **Copy The Formulas.** Select the formulas in the range **B17:B27** and copy them to the range **C17:O27**.

10. **Option Price.** Reference the Call Price or the Put Price depending on which type of option is selected in cell **B4**. Enter **=IF($B$4=1,B21,B27)** in cell **B14** and copy the cell to the range **C14:L14**.

11. **Add The Intrinsic Value.** If the option was maturing now, rather than later, its payoff would be:

    - For a call, **Max (Stock Price Now - Exercise Price, 0)**.
    - For a put, **Max (Exercise Price - Stock Price Now, 0)**.

    This is the so-called "Intrinsic Value" of the option. In cell **M15**, enter the formula

    =IF(B4=1,MAX(M13-$B$7,0),MAX($B$7-M13,0))

    and copy this cell to the range **N15:O15**.

12. **Graph the Option Price and Intrinsic Value.** Select the range **B13:O15**. Next choose **Insert Chart** from the main menu. Select an **XY(Scatter)** chart type and make other selections to complete the Chart Wizard.

FIGURE 14.3 Excel Model of Black Scholes Option Pricing - Dynamic Chart - Put Option.

	A	B	C	D	E	F	G	H	I	J
1	BLACK SCHOLES OPTION PRICING					Dynamic Chart			Put	
2										
3	**Inputs**									
4	Option Type: 1=Call, 0=Put	0		0						
5	Standard Dev - Annual (σ)	60%		6						
6	Riskfree Rate- Annual (r)	1.0%		1						
7	Exercise Price (X)	$50.00		50						
8	Time To Maturity - Yrs (T)	0.30		3						
9										
10										
11										
12	**Dynamic Chart Outputs**									
13	Stock Price Now (S_0)	$0.01	$10.00	$20.00	$30.00	$40.00	$50.00	$60.00	$70.00	$80.00
14	Option Price	$49.84	$39.85	$29.86	$20.19	$12.05	$6.46	$3.21	$1.52	$0.70
15	Intrinsic Value									
16										
17	d1	-25.657	-4.707	-2.605	-1.375	-0.503	0.174	0.727	1.194	1.599
18	d2	-25.987	-5.037	-2.935	-1.705	-0.832	-0.156	0.397	0.865	1.270
19	N(d1)	0.000	0.000	0.005	0.085	0.308	0.569	0.766	0.884	0.945
20	N(d2)	0.000	0.000	0.002	0.044	0.203	0.438	0.654	0.806	0.898
21	Call Price (C_0)	$0.00	$0.00	$0.01	$0.34	$2.20	$6.61	$13.36	$21.67	$30.85
22										
23	-d1	25.657	4.707	2.605	1.375	0.503	-0.174	-0.727	-1.194	-1.599
24	-d2	25.987	5.037	2.935	1.705	0.832	0.156	-0.397	-0.865	-1.270
25	N(-d1)	1.000	1.000	0.995	0.915	0.692	0.431	0.234	0.116	0.055
26	N(-d2)	1.000	1.000	0.998	0.956	0.797	0.562	0.346	0.194	0.102
27	Put Price (P_0)	$49.84	$39.85	$29.86	$20.19	$12.05	$6.46	$3.21	$1.52	$0.70

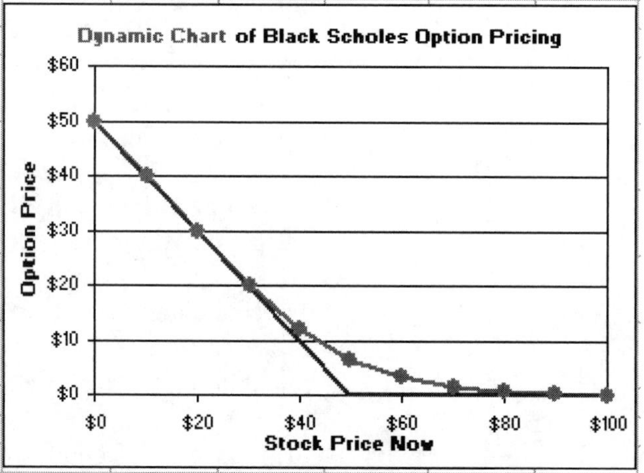

Your *Dynamic Chart* allows you to change Black-Scholes inputs and instantly see the impact on a graph of the option price and intrinsic value. This allows you to perform instant experiments on the Black-Scholes option pricing model. Below is a list of experiments that you might want to perform:

- What happens when the standard deviation is increased?
- What happens when the time to maturity is increased?
- What happens when the exercise price is increased?
- What happens when the riskfree rate is increased?
- What happens when the standard deviation is really close to zero?
- What happens when the time to maturity is really close to zero?

Notice that the Black-Scholes option price is usually greater than the payoff you would obtain if the option was maturing today (the "intrinsic value"). This extra value is called the "Time Value" of the option. Given your result in the last experiment above, can you explain *why* the extra value is called the "Time Value"?

14.3 Continuous Dividend

Problem. Amazon.com doesn't pay a dividend, but suppose that it did. Specifically, suppose that Amazon.com paid dividends in tiny amounts on a continuous basis throughout the year at a 3.00% / year rate. What would be the new price of the call and put?

Solution Strategy. Modify the Basics Excel model to incorporate the continuous dividend version of the Black Scholes model.

FIGURE 14.4 Excel Model of Black Scholes Option Pricing - Continuous Dividend.

	A	B	C	D	E	F	G	H
1	BLACK SCHOLES OPTION PRICING				Continuous Dividend			
2								
3	**Inputs**							
4	Stock Price Now (S_0)	$48.89						
5	Standard Dev - Annual (σ)	55.56%						
6	Riskfree Rate- Annual (r)	0.96%						
7	Exercise Price (X)	$50.00						
8	Time To Maturity - Years (T)	0.2972						
9	Dividend yield (d)	3.00%						
10								
11	**Outputs**							
12	d1	0.057						
13	d2	-0.246						
14	N(d1)	0.523						
15	N(d2)	0.403						
16	Call Price (C_0)	$5.24						
17								
18	-d1	-0.057						
19	-d2	0.246						
20	N(-d1)	0.477						
21	N(-d2)	0.597						
22	Put Price (P_0)	$6.64						

How To Build This Excel Model

1. **Start with the Basics Excel Model, Add A Row, and Enter The Dividend Yield.** Open the Excel model that you created for Black Scholes Option Pricing – Basics and immediately save the Excel model under a new name using the **File Save As** command. Add a row by selecting the cell **A9** and clicking on **Insert Rows**. Enter the dividend yield in cell **A9**.

2. **Modify the d1 Formula.** In the continuous dividend version, the d_1 formula is modified by subtracting the continuous dividend yield d in the numerator. The new d_1 formula is $\left(\ln\left(S_0 / X\right)+\left(r-d+\sigma^2 / 2\right)\cdot T\right)/\left(\sigma\cdot\sqrt{T}\right)$. In cell **B12**, enter

   =(LN(B4/B7)+(B6-B9+B5^2/2)*B8)/(B5*SQRT(B8))

3. **Modify the Call Price Formula.** The modified call formula is $C_0 = S_0 e^{-dT} N\left(d_1\right) - Xe^{-rT} N\left(d_2\right)$, where d is the continuous dividend yield. In cell **B16**, enter

   =B4*EXP(-B9*B8)*B14-B7*EXP(-B6*B8)*B15

   We see that the Black-Scholes Option Pricing - Continuous Dividend model predicts a call price of $5.24. This is a drop of 23 cents from the no dividend version. Now let's do the put.

4. **Modify the Put Price Formula.** The modified put formula is $P_0 = -S_0 e^{-dT} N\left(-d_1\right) + Xe^{-rT} N\left(-d_2\right)$. In cell **B22**, enter

   =-B4*EXP(-B9*B8)*B20+B7*EXP(-B6*B8)*B21

We see that the Black-Scholes model predicts a put price of $6.64. This is a rise of 20 cents from the no dividend version.

14.4 Implied Volatility

Problem. In the afternoon of September 29, 2003, SPX, a security based on the S&P 500 index, traded at 1,000.05. European call and put options on SPX with the exercise prices show below traded for the following prices:

Exercise price	975	995	1,005	1,025	1,1050
Call price	$71.00	$56.00	$51.00	$43.00	$32.00
Put price	$45.50	$56.00	$60.00	$70.00	$83.20

These call options mature on March 19, 2004. The S&P 500 portfolio pays a continuous dividend yield of 2.18% per year and the annual yield on a Treasury Bill which matures on March 18th is 1.01% per year. What is the implied volatility of each of these calls and puts? What pattern do these implied volatilities follow across exercise prices and between calls vs. puts?

Solution Strategy. Calculate the difference between the observed option price and the option price predicted by the continuous dividend yield version of the Black-Scholes model using a dummy value for the stock volatility. Have the Excel Solver tool adjust the stock volatility by trial and error until the difference between the observed price and the model price is equal to zero (within a very small error tolerance).

FIGURE 14.5 Excel Model of Black Scholes Option Pricing - Implied Volatility.

	A	B	C	D	E	F	G	H	I	J	K
1	BLACK SCHOLES OPTION PRICING					Implied Volatility					
2											
3	**Inputs**										
4	Option Type: 1=Call, 0=Put	1	1	1	1	1	0	0	0	0	0
5	Stock Price Now (S_0)	$1,000	$1,000	$1,000	$1,000	$1,000	$1,000	$1,000	$1,000	$1,000	$1,000
6	Riskfree Rate- Annual (r)	1.01%	1.01%	1.01%	1.01%	1.01%	1.01%	1.01%	1.01%	1.01%	1.01%
7	Exercise Price (X)	$975	$995	$1,005	$1,025	$1,050	$975	$995	$1,005	$1,025	$1,050
8	Time To Maturity - Yrs (T)	0.4722	0.4722	0.4722	0.4722	0.4722	0.4722	0.4722	0.4722	0.4722	0.4722
9	Dividend yield (d)	2.18%	2.18%	2.18%	2.18%	2.18%	2.18%	2.18%	2.18%	2.18%	2.18%
10	Observed Option Price	$71.00	$56.00	$51.00	$43.00	$32.00	$45.50	$56.00	$60.00	$70.00	$83.20
11											
12	**Outputs**										
13	d1	0.205	0.068	-0.003	-0.141	-0.330	0.212	0.067	-0.007	-0.159	-0.369
14	d2	0.050	-0.074	-0.145	-0.283	-0.466	0.072	-0.074	-0.145	-0.293	-0.495
15	N(d1)	0.581	0.527	0.499	0.444	0.371	0.584	0.527	0.497	0.437	0.356
16	N(d2)	0.520	0.470	0.442	0.388	0.321	0.529	0.471	0.442	0.385	0.310
17	Model Call Price (C_0)	$71.00	$56.00	$51.00	$43.00	$32.00	$64.95	$55.54	$49.59	$39.69	$28.00
18											
19	-d1	-0.205	-0.068	0.003	0.141	0.330	-0.212	-0.067	0.007	0.159	0.369
20	-d2	-0.050	0.074	0.145	0.283	0.466	-0.072	0.074	0.145	0.293	0.495
21	N(-d1)	0.419	0.473	0.501	0.556	0.629	0.416	0.473	0.503	0.563	0.644
22	N(-d2)	0.480	0.530	0.558	0.612	0.679	0.471	0.529	0.558	0.615	0.690
23	Model Put Price (P_0)	$51.55	$56.46	$61.41	$73.31	$87.20	$45.50	$56.00	$60.00	$70.00	$83.20
24											
25	**Solver**										
26	Differ (observed - model)	3E-09	-4E-09	-2E-08	1E-08	-9E-07	2E-08	3E-07	1E-09	1E-07	-3E-07
27	Implied Volatility from Calls	22.65%	20.73%	20.57%	20.66%	19.84%					
28	Implied Volatility from Puts						20.37%	20.57%	20.05%	19.43%	18.27%

How To Build This Excel Model.

1. **Start with the Continuous Dividend Excel Model, Rearrange The Rows, and Add A Switch.** Open the Excel model that you created for Black Scholes Option Pricing – Continuous Dividend and immediately save the file under a new name using the **File Save As** command. Add a row by selecting the cell **A4** and clicking on **Insert Rows**. Select the range **A6:B6** and drag the range (hover the cursor over the lower highlighted line, click on the left mouse button, and hold it down while you move it) to cell **A27**. Select the range **A7:B10** and drag the range to cell **A6**. Enter **1** in cell **B4**. This will serve as a switch between a call option and a put option.

2. **Enter the Call Inputs.** Enter the Call inputs in the range **B4:B9** and enter the observed Call option prices in cell **B10**.

3. **Difference (Observed – Model).** The Difference (Observed - Model) is:

   - Observed Option Price - Model Call Price for a Call Option

- Observed Option Price - Model Put Price for a Put Option.

Enter **=IF(B4=1,B10-B17,B10-B23)** in cell **B26**.

4. **Copy the Entire Column over Nine More Columns**. Select the range **B4:B27** and copy it to the range **C4:K27**.

5. **Enter the Options Inputs**. In the range **B4:F27**, enter the inputs for the five call options. In the range **G4:K27**, enter the inputs for the five put options. Select the put volatilities in the range **G27:K27** and drag the range down to cell **G28**.

6. **Call Up Excel Solver.** From Excel's main menu, click on **Tools** and then Solver. If you don't see **Solver** on the **Tools** Menu, then click on **Tools Add-Ins**, check the **Solver Add-In** box, and click on **OK**.)

7. **Set-up Solver.** In the Solver dialog box, enter cell **B26** as the Set Target Cell. In the Equal to row, click on the option button for Value of and enter **0** in the adjacent box. Enter cell **B27** as the By Changing Cell. See the figure below.

FIGURE 14.6 Solver dialog box.

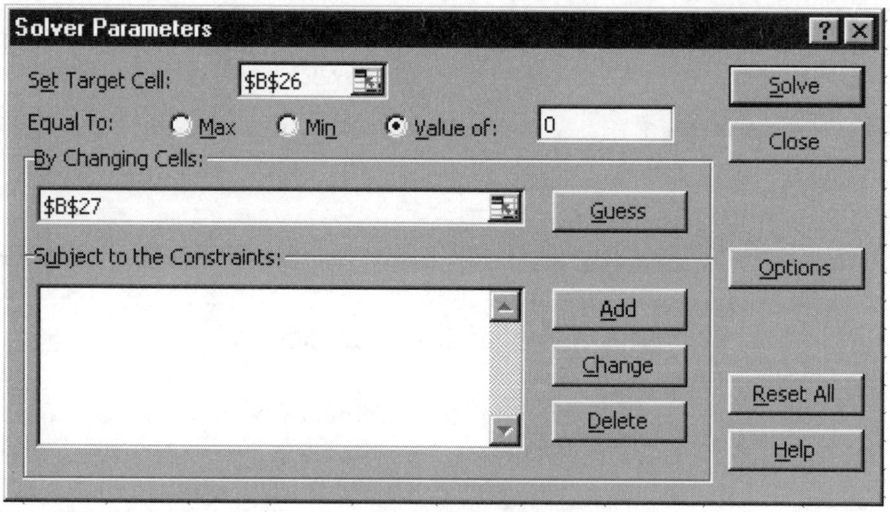

8. **Run Solver.** Click on the Solve button.

By trial and error, the Solver adjusts the value of the Implied Volatility in cell **B27** until the Difference (Observed – Model) in cell **B26** equals zero (within a very small error tolerance). This results in an implied volatility of 22.65%. Your results may differ by a slight amount (usually only in the second decimal) depending on Solver's error tolerance.

9. **Repeat.** Repeat steps **7** and **8** to solve the problems in columns **D, E, ..., K.**

10. Graph the Implied Volatilities Across Exercise Prices and Option Types. Highlight the range **B7:K7**, then hold down the Control button and (while still holding it down) select the range **B27:K28**. Next choose **Insert Chart** from the main menu. Select an **XY(Scatter)** chart type and make other selections to complete the Chart Wizard.

FIGURE 14.7 Graph of the "Scowl" Pattern of Implied Volatilities.

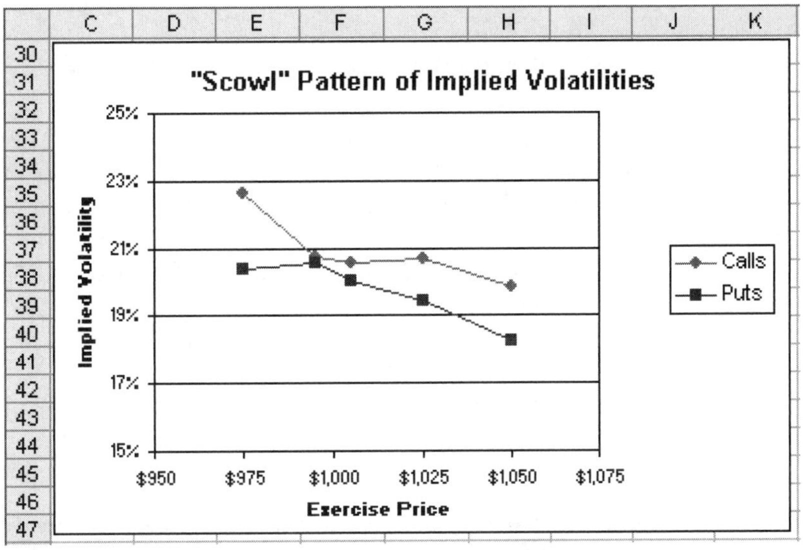

If the market's beliefs about the distribution of returns of the S&P 500 Index matched the theoretical distribution of returns assumed by the Black-Scholes model, then all of the implied volatilities would be the same. From the graph we see this is not the case. The implied volatility pattern declines sharply with the exercise price and puts have lower implied volatilities than calls. In the '70s and '80s, the typical implied volatility pattern was a U-shaped, "Smile" pattern. Since the '90s, it is more typical to see a downward-sloping, "Scowl" pattern.

Problems

Skill-Building Problems.

1. The current stock price of a company is $54.50, the continuous annual standard deviation was 53.00%, the exercise price of an European call on the stock is $58.00, the exercise price of an European put on the stock is $58.00, the time to maturity for both options is 0.43 years, and the yield on a risk-free Treasury Bill maturing on the same date at the options is 6.72%. Determine the current prices of the call and put.

2. Perform instant experiments on whether changing various inputs causes an increase or decrease in the Call Price and in the Put Price and by how much.

   a. What happens when the standard deviation is increased?

b. What happens when the time to maturity is increased?

c. What happens when the exercise price is increased?

d. What happens when the riskfree rate is increased?

e. What happens when the dividend yield is increased?

f. What happens when the standard deviation is really close to zero?

g. What happens when the time to maturity is really close to zero?

3. The current stock price of a company is $39.25, the continuous annual standard deviation was 47.00%, the exercise price of an European call on the stock is $36.00, the exercise price of an European put on the stock is $36.00, the time to maturity for both options is 0.82 years, the yield on a risk-free Treasury Bill maturing on the same date at the options is 4.23%, and the continuous dividend paid throughout the year at the rate of 2.40% / year rate. Determine the current prices of the call and put.

4. The S&P 500 index closes at 2000. European call and put options on the S&P 500 index with the exercise prices show below trade for the following prices:

Exercise price	1,950	1,975	2,000	2,025	2,050
Call price	$88	$66	$47	$33	$21
Put price	$25	$26	$32	$44	$58

All options mature in 88 days. The S&P 500 portfolio pays a continuous dividend yield of 1.56% per year and the annual yield on a Treasury Bill which matures on the same day as the options is 4.63% per year. Determine what is the implied volatility of each of these calls and puts. What pattern do these implied volatilities follow across exercise prices and between calls vs. puts?

Live In-class Problems.

5. Given the partial Basics file **BsoptbaZ.xls**, complete step **2 d1 and d2 Formulas, 3 Cumulative Normal Formulas,** and **4 European Call Price Formula**.

6. Given the partial Continuous Dividend file **BsoptdiZ.xls**, do steps **2 Modify the d1 Formula, 3 Modify the Call Price Formula,** and **4 Modify the Put Price Formula**.

7. Given the partial Dynamic Chart file **BsoptdyZ.xls**, do steps **10 Option Price** and **11 Add the Intrinsic Value**.

8. Given the partial Implied Volatility file **BsoptimZ.xls**, do steps **6 Call Up Excel Solver, 7 Set-up Solver, 8 Run Solver,** and **9 Repeat**.

Chapter 15 Spot-Futures Parity (Cost of Carry)

15.1 Basics

Problem. Suppose we recorded the monthly spot price of the S&P 500 index and corresponding futures price over a seven month period for a stock index futures contract maturing in month 7. Here are the prices in index points:

Month	1	2	3	4	5	6	7
Spot price	1117.36	1126.37	1136.73	1146.86	1155.14	1165.69	1178.23
Futures price	1144.38	1149.94	1155.05	1162.00	1167.24	1170.23	1178.23

Suppose that the riskfree rate is 0.42% per month. Analyze what happened over time to the basis and to the price difference between the model futures price implied by Spot-Futures Parity versus the actual futures price.

Solution Strategy. First calculate the basis. Then substitute the spot price into the Spot-Futures Parity to determine the model futures price. Then calculate the price difference between the model futures price and the actual futures price.

FIGURE 15.1 Excel Model of Spot-Future Parity (Cost of Carry) - Basics.

	A	B	C	D	E	F	G	H
1	SPOT-FUTURES PARITY (COST OF CARRY)					Basics		
2								
3	**Inputs**							**Maturity**
4	Calendar Time (months)	1	2	3	4	5	6	7
5	Observed Spot Price	1,417.8	1,436.3	1,426.6	1,456.8	1,455.5	1,460.2	1,476.6
6	Observed Futures Price	1,452.7	1,467.9	1,451.4	1,472.8	1,466.7	1,467.1	1,476.6
7	Risk-free rate / month	0.42%	0.42%	0.42%	0.42%	0.42%	0.42%	0.42%
8								
9	**Outputs**							
10	Basis (Futures - Spot)	34.9	31.6	24.8	16.0	11.2	6.9	0.0
11	Time to Maturity (months)	6	5	4	3	2	1	0
12	Model Futures Price	1,453.9	1,466.7	1,450.7	1,475.2	1,467.8	1,466.3	1,476.6
13	Price Difference (model-observed)	1.2	(1.2)	(0.7)	2.4	1.1	(0.8)	0.0

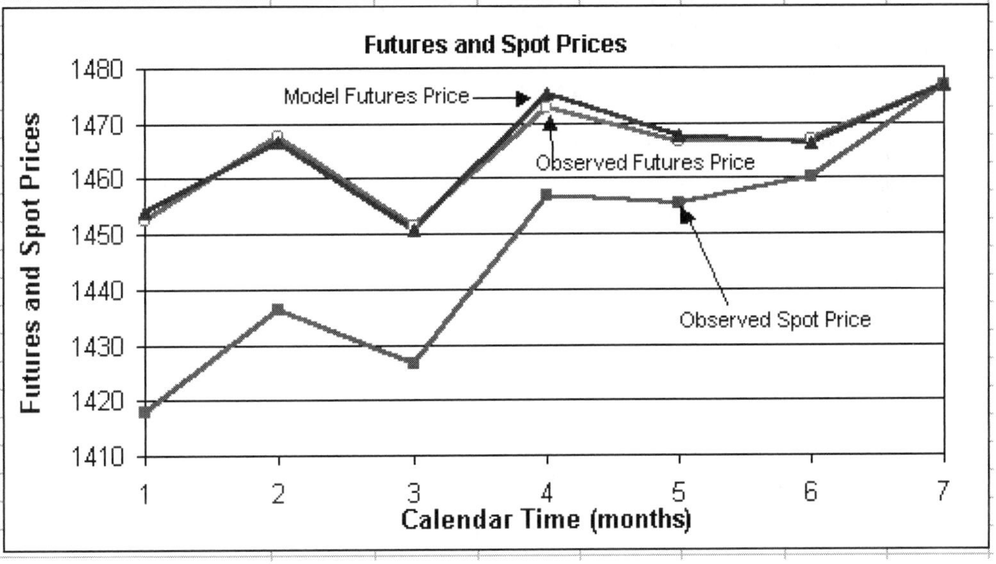

How To Build This Excel Model.

1. **Inputs.** Enter the inputs into the range **B4:H7**.

2. **Basis (Futures - Spot).** The formula for the Basis = Futures Price - Spot Price. Enter **=B6-B5** in cell **B10** and copy the cell to the range **C10:H10**.

3. **Time To Maturity (months).** In month *t*, the formula for Time To Maturity(t) = Maturity Date – Current Date(t). Enter **=$H$4-B4** in cell **B11** and copy the cell to the range **C11:H11**. The $s lock in the maturity date.

4. **Model Futures Price.** The Spot-Futures Parity formula predicts the Futures Price = Spot Price * (1 + Riskfree Rate) ^(Time to Maturity). Enter **=B5*(1+B7)^B11** in cell **B12** and copy the cell to the range **C12:H12**.

5. **Price Difference (Model - Observed).** The price difference = model futures price - actual futures price. Enter **=B12-B6** in cell **B13** and copy the cell to the range **C13:H13**.

6. **Graph the Futures and Spot Prices Over Time.** Highlight the range **B4:H6**, then hold down the **Control** button and (while still holding it down) select the range **B12:H12**. Next choose **Insert Chart** from the main menu. Select an **XY(Scatter)** chart type and make other selections to complete the Chart Wizard.

Notice that the basis is a substantial positive value and steadily declines over time before finally reaching zero when the futures contract matures. By contrast, the price difference is very small value and fluctuates between positive and negative values before going to zero when the futures contract matures.

15.2 Index Arbitrage

Given that there is a (nonzero) price difference between the two markets, is it possible to make an arbitrage profit? Suppose that the round trip transaction cost for doing an index arbitrage trade is 1.60 index points. Analyze the monthly data to determine if was possible to have made an arbitrage profit.

FIGURE 15.2 Excel Model of Spot-Future Parity (Cost of Carry) - Index Arbitrage.

	A	B	C	D	E	F	G	H
1	SPOT-FUTURES PARITY (COST OF CARRY)					Index Arbitrage		
2								
3	**Inputs**							**Maturity**
4	Calendar Time (months)	1	2	3	4	5	6	7
5	Observed Spot Price	1,417.8	1,436.3	1,426.6	1,456.8	1,455.5	1,460.2	1,476.6
6	Observed Futures Price	1,452.7	1,467.9	1,451.4	1,472.8	1,466.7	1,467.1	1,476.6
7	Risk-free rate / month	0.42%	0.42%	0.42%	0.42%	0.42%	0.42%	0.42%
8								
9	**Outputs**							
10	Basis (Futures - Spot)	34.9	31.6	24.8	16.0	11.2	6.9	0.0
11	Time to Maturity (months)	6	5	4	3	2	1	0
12	Model Futures Price	1,453.9	1,466.7	1,450.7	1,475.2	1,467.8	1,466.3	1,476.6
13	Price Difference (model-observed)	1.2	(1.2)	(0.7)	2.4	1.1	(0.8)	0.0
14	Transaction Costs (upper bound)	1.6	1.6	1.6	1.6	1.6	1.6	1.6
15	Transaction Costs (lower bound)	(1.6)	(1.6)	(1.6)	(1.6)	(1.6)	(1.6)	(1.6)

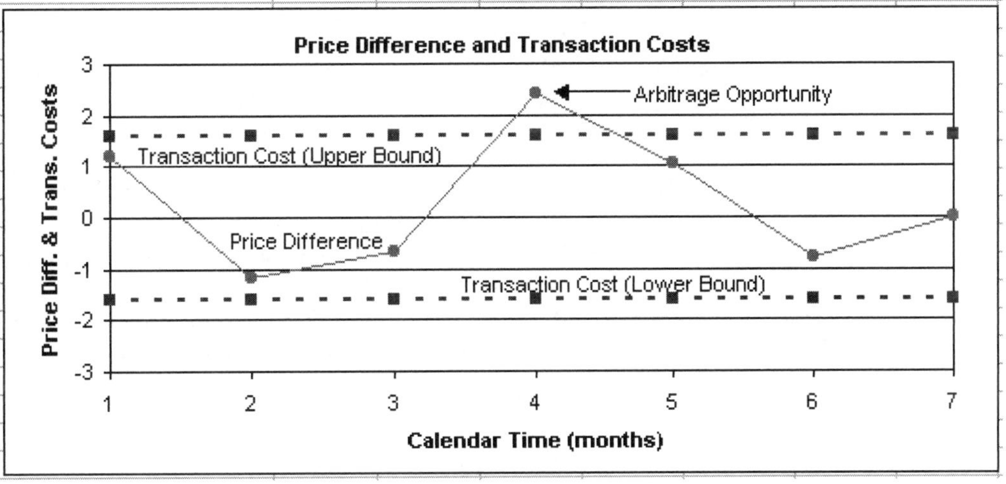

How To Build This Excel Model.

1. **Start with the Basics Excel Model.** Open the Excel model that you created for Spot-Futures Parity (Cost of Carry) - Basics and immediately save the file under a new name using the **File Save As** command. Delete the Futures and Spot Prices graph by clicking on it and pressing the **Delete** button.

2. **Transaction Cost Bounds.** Transaction costs create an upper bound and a lower bound on the price difference, within which it is not possible to make an arbitrage profit. Specify the upper bound by entering **1.60** in cell **B14** and the lower bound by entering **–1.60** in cell **B15**. Copy the range **B14:B15** to the range **C14:H15**.

3. **Graph the Price Difference and Transaction Costs.** Highlight the range **B4:H4**, then hold down the **Control** button and (while still holding it down) select the range **B13:H15**. Next choose **Insert Chart** from the main menu.

Select an **XY(Scatter)** chart type and make other selections to complete the Chart Wizard.

Most of the time the price difference was inside the transaction cost boundaries, so there wasn't an arbitrage opportunity. However in month 4, the price difference went outside the boundaries by rising above the upper bound. Thus, an arbitrage profit could made in month 4 by selling in the index portfolio in the spot market, using the proceeds to lend money at the riskfree rate, and going long in the futures market.

Problems

Skill-Building Problems.

1. Suppose we recorded the monthly spot price of the S&P 500 index and corresponding futures price over a seven month period for a stock index futures contract maturing in month 7. Here are the prices in index points:

Month	1	2	3	4	5	6	7
Spot price	1539.21	1552.95	1587.44	1603.48	1659.12	1653.47	1693.59
Futures price	1590.33	1593.68	1619.93	1630.37	1679.38	1661.81	1693.59

Suppose that the riskfree rate is 0.53% per month. Analyze what happened over time to the basis and to the price difference between the model futures price implied by Spot-Futures Parity versus the actual futures price.

2. The round trip transaction cost for doing an index arbitrage trade is 1.60 index points. Analyze the monthly data above to determine if was possible to have made an arbitrage profit.

Live In-class Problems.

3. Given the partial Basics file **SfparbaZ.xls**, complete steps **2 Basis (Futures – Spot), 4 Model Futures Price,** and **5 Price Difference (Model – Observed)**.

4. Given the partial Index Arbitrage file **SfparinZ.xls**, complete step **2 Transaction Cost Bounds**.

SINGLE PC LICENSE AGREEMENT AND LIMITED WARRANTY

READ THIS LICENSE CAREFULLY BEFORE OPENING THIS PACKAGE. BY OPENING THIS PACKAGE, YOU ARE AGREEING TO THE TERMS AND CONDITIONS OF THIS LICENSE. IF YOU DO NOT AGREE, DO NOT OPEN THE PACKAGE. PROMPTLY RETURN THE UNOPENED PACKAGE AND ALL ACCOMPANYING ITEMS TO THE PLACE YOU OBTAINED THEM FOR A FULL REFUND OF ANY SUMS YOU HAVE PAID FOR THE SOFTWARE. ***THESE TERMS APPLY TO ALL LICENSED SOFTWARE ON THE DISK EXCEPT THAT THE TERMS FOR USE OF ANY SHAREWARE OR FREEWARE ON THE DISKETTES ARE AS SET FORTH IN THE ELECTRONIC LICENSE LOCATED ON THE CD-ROM:***

1. GRANT OF LICENSE and OWNERSHIP: The enclosed computer programs and data ("Software") are licensed, not sold, to you by Pearson Education, Inc. publishing as Prentice-Hall, Inc. ("We" or the "Company") and in consideration of your purchase or adoption of the accompanying Company textbooks and/or other materials, and your agreement to these terms. We reserve any rights not granted to you. You own only the disk(s) but we and/or our licensors own the Software itself. This license allows you to use and display your copy of the Software on a single computer (i.e., with a single CPU) at a single location for academic use only, so long as you comply with the terms of this Agreement. You may make one copy for back up, or transfer your copy to another CPU, provided that the Software is usable on only one computer.

2. RESTRICTIONS: You may not transfer or distribute the Software or documentation to anyone else. Except for backup, you may not copy the documentation or the Software. You may not network the Software or otherwise use it on more than one computer or computer terminal at the same time. You may not reverse engineer, disassemble, decompile, modify, adapt, translate, or create derivative works based on the Software or the Documentation. You may be held legally responsible for any copying or copyright infringement that is caused by your failure to abide by the terms of these restrictions.

3. TERMINATION: This license is effective until terminated. This license will terminate automatically without notice from the Company if you fail to comply with any provisions or limitations of this license. Upon termination, you shall destroy the Documentation and all copies of the Software. All provisions of this Agreement as to limitation and disclaimer of warranties, limitation of liability, remedies or damages, and our ownership rights shall survive termination.

4. **LIMITED WARRANTY AND DISCLAIMER OF WARRANTY:** Company warrants that for a period of 60 days from the date you purchase this SOFTWARE (or purchase or adopt the accompanying textbook), the Software, when properly installed and used in accordance with the Documentation, will operate in substantial conformity with the description of the Software set forth in the Documentation, and that for a period of 30 days the disk(s) on which the Software is delivered shall be free from defects in materials and workmanship under normal use. The Company does not warrant that the Software will meet your requirements or that the operation of the Software will be uninterrupted or error-free. Your only remedy and the

Company's only obligation under these limited warranties is, at the Company's option, return of the disk for a refund of any amounts paid for it by you or replacement of the disk. THIS LIMITED WARRANTY IS THE ONLY WARRANTY PROVIDED BY THE COMPANY AND ITS LICENSORS, AND THE COMPANY AND ITS LICENSORS DISCLAIM ALL OTHER WARRANTIES, EXPRESS OR IMPLIED, INCLUDING WITHOUT LIMITATION, THE IMPLIED WARRANTIES OF MERCHANTABILITY AND FITNESS FOR A PARTICULAR PURPOSE. THE COMPANY DOES NOT WARRANT, GUARANTEE OR MAKE ANY REPRESENTATION REGARDING THE ACCURACY, RELIABILITY, CURRENTNESS, USE, OR RESULTS OF USE, OF THE SOFTWARE.

5. LIMITATION OF REMEDIES AND DAMAGES: IN NO EVENT, SHALL THE COMPANY OR ITS EMPLOYEES, AGENTS, LICENSORS, OR CONTRACTORS BE LIABLE FOR ANY INCIDENTAL, INDIRECT, SPECIAL, OR CONSEQUENTIAL DAMAGES ARISING OUT OF OR IN CONNECTION WITH THIS LICENSE OR THE SOFTWARE, INCLUDING FOR LOSS OF USE, LOSS OF DATA, LOSS OF INCOME OR PROFIT, OR OTHER LOSSES, SUSTAINED AS A RESULT OF INJURY TO ANY PERSON, OR LOSS OF OR DAMAGE TO PROPERTY, OR CLAIMS OF THIRD PARTIES, EVEN IF THE COMPANY OR AN AUTHORIZED REPRESENTATIVE OF THE COMPANY HAS BEEN ADVISED OF THE POSSIBILITY OF SUCH DAMAGES. IN NO EVENT SHALL THE LIABILITY OF THE COMPANY FOR DAMAGES WITH RESPECT TO THE SOFTWARE EXCEED THE AMOUNTS ACTUALLY PAID BY YOU, IF ANY, FOR THE SOFTWARE OR THE ACCOMPANYING TEXTBOOK. BECAUSE SOME JURISDICTIONS DO NOT ALLOW THE LIMITATION OF LIABILITY IN CERTAIN CIRCUMSTANCES, THE ABOVE LIMITATIONS MAY NOT ALWAYS APPLY TO YOU.

6. GENERAL: THIS AGREEMENT SHALL BE CONSTRUED IN ACCORDANCE WITH THE LAWS OF THE UNITED STATES OF AMERICA AND THE STATE OF NEW YORK, APPLICABLE TO CONTRACTS MADE IN NEW YORK, AND SHALL BENEFIT THE COMPANY, ITS AFFILIATES AND ASSIGNEES. HIS AGREEMENT IS THE COMPLETE AND EXCLUSIVE STATEMENT OF THE AGREEMENT BETWEEN YOU AND THE COMPANY AND SUPERSEDES ALL PROPOSALS OR PRIOR AGREEMENTS, ORAL, OR WRITTEN, AND ANY OTHER COMMUNICATIONS BETWEEN YOU AND THE COMPANY OR ANY REPRESENTATIVE OF THE COMPANY RELATING TO THE SUBJECT MATTER OF THIS AGREEMENT. If you are a U.S. Government user, this Software is licensed with "restricted rights" as set forth in subparagraphs (a)-(d) of the Commercial Computer-Restricted Rights clause at FAR 52.227-19 or in subparagraphs (c)(1)(ii) of the Rights in Technical Data and Computer Software clause at DFARS 252.227-7013, and similar clauses, as applicable.

Should you have any questions concerning this agreement or if you wish to contact the Company for any reason, please contact in writing: Director of New Media, Higher Education Division, Prentice Hall, Inc., Upper Saddle River, NJ 07458